D0849663

ETHICAL FORMATION

ETHICAL
FORMATION

Sabina Lovibond

HARVARD UNIVERSITY PRESS

Cambridge, Massachusetts

London, England · 2002

Library of Congress Cataloging-in-Publication Data

Lovibond, Sabina.
Ethical formation / Sabina Lovibond.
p. cm.
Includes bibliographical references and index.
ISBN 0-674-00650-X
1. Ethics.   2. Moral development.   I. Title.

BJ1012 .L677 2002
171′.2—dc21   2001039452

To my mother, Marie Lovibond
and to the memory of my father, George Lovibond
1914–1990

Contents

Preface

This book aims to bring together certain philosophical undertakings in which I have taken an interest over the past ten years and more. One of these is a particular approach to moral philosophy that comes down to us from the classical rationalist tradition, and which gives rise to terms such as "moral realism" (or "cognitivism") and "virtue ethics"; the other is a line of thought that owes more to (Continental) European philosophy and that can be described for the moment as consisting in a "*critique* of reason." For me personally, each of these areas of philosophy has had a natural claim to attention: the first as part of the local culture I acquired as a student, and later as a teacher, of the subject; the second as an adjunct to the attempt to see life politically and to gain some theoretical insight into one's own experience—ambitions which, for many people who (like me) came into philosophy in the 1970s, have given a special importance to the kind of intellectual work associated with oppositional tendencies such as feminism, Marxism, the internal critique of Marxism, and the question of a possible successor to it. But it takes time to see each of the relevant bodies of literature—that of analytical "moral realism" and that of postmodern skepticism about "reason" generally—in relation to a common tradition of enquiry into practical rationality. What I have to offer is the record of an attempt to do this; I have not been conscious, in writing the book, of any keen desire to make converts or to promote a particular "theory," but I hope it will strike those who know the relevant debates as a plausible mapping of the relevant bit of contemporary philosophical space. (I hope, too, that no one will be unduly distressed by the promiscuous contact that I inflict from time to time on Anglo-American and French source materials: I have chosen to assume that the implicitly common concerns on which I try

ix

to make these sources speak are more interesting than the well-known stylistic and methodological differences between their parent traditions.)

My discussion falls into three main parts. The first—entitled "Form"—aims to construct, or reconstruct from readily available sources, a maximally convincing version of the view that there is such a thing as ethical knowledge and that this knowledge can be thought of as grounded in the possession of a good character: in other words, it sets out a form of ethical cognitivism (or as I shall also call it, a "practical reason" approach to ethics) that is inspired in part by recent writing on the virtues. I believe the content of this, essentially affirmative, phase of my argument will be to some extent familiar, and have therefore allowed myself to develop it fairly rapidly and impressionistically, while at the same time seeking to explain the position in a way that will be accessible to newcomers. It is concerned, first, with the classical notion of moral virtue as a form, or system of interconnected forms, which can come to be imposed on human character;[1] and second, with what I take to be the successor to this idea within a modern (and fully naturalistic)[2] ethical cognitivism—that is, with the idea of moral intelligence as consisting in a grasp of certain concepts or rules, and so in a different *kind* of "form"—the kind that consists in patterns of social or linguistic usage, transmitted by upbringing from one generation to another.

The second part—entitled "Teleology"—continues to explore the consequences of seeing ethical upbringing as a natural process. But this form of words will hardly do as it stands, since the idea of upbringing as a "natural process"—thus abstractly stated—can be regarded as one that is already built into the ethics of Plato and Aristotle, who consider it to be a dictate of "nature" that each thing should *perfectly realize itself* as an instance of the kind of thing it is. A better way of speaking would take into account that while there is a line of descent connecting these philosophers with present-

1. "Form" is contrasted here with "matter" or "content." For example, if a lump of clay is shaped into the model of a human figure, then the model is made up of the same matter as the original lump but differs from it in respect of its form. Analogously, a writer may be told that the content of his or her work is good but that the form in which it is presented is confusing. We shall see later (Chapter 3) that it is possible to think of the psychological tendencies of human beings as constituting the raw material for various formative processes.

2. I mean by a "naturalistic" view not one that seeks to reduce the normative to the nonnormative, but one that represents the phenomena it studies as part of nature and as capable of being understood without recourse to the supernatural.

day varieties of ethical naturalism like the one to be developed here, they are also distanced from us by their adherence to a teleological conception of the "natural" that is no longer plausible today. So let me say instead that I shall explore the consequences of seeing upbringing as a process organized by values and interests emanating from the specifically *human* part of "nature," where there is no presumption that these values and interests are especially dear to "God," or that the natural world must be ordered in such a way as to secure their ultimate fulfillment.

Bearing in mind the social, and in particular the linguistic, "turn" given in Part I to the idea of ethical form, I concentrate especially in Part II on upbringing as the development of a certain relationship between individual human persons or "subjects" and the expressive forms available, within their communities, as vehicles of moral thought and sensibility. In describing this relationship, I give prominence to the idea of "seriously meaning" the sorts of things one learns to say, or the sorts of signs or gestures one learns to use, as tokens of one's own moral awareness—"seriously meaning" them, that is, in contrast to using them in a spirit of mere imitation or opportunism (though as I shall explain in due course, I do not mean to suggest that this element in our relation to the "sign system" of ethics can be eliminated in any absolute way). In connection with "seriously meaning," I develop a conception of *authorship* (of one's own utterances, gestures, and the like) according to which the status of author (or originator) of such items is something to which, in practice, one may approximate more or less closely: by implication, then, an *ideal* conception of authorship. This conception, or so I shall suggest, should be congenial to a fully naturalized version of the practical reason approach—a version that portrays moral rationality as grounded in the process of socialization. It is also of interest, I shall argue, as a possible clue to the appeal of the extreme Socratic thesis—not entirely unregarded even in the context of contemporary "virtue ethics," but too counterintuitive to be widely believable—that "no one does wrong voluntarily," or that all wrongdoing is in some sense due to ignorance. Finally in Part II, I introduce some skeptical considerations in respect of which my classical sources seem to me to converge with a certain strain of "postmodern" or "posthumanist" thinking about the ethical: considerations that seem to call for a self-consciously modest and undogmatic deployment of the idealism proper to the practical reason view, and to demand a correspondingly modest understanding of what is involved in "having a morality" or in "being a good (or decent) person."

The book's third part (entitled "Counter-Teleology") is concerned with the different moral and political scene that comes into view once we move away from a "rampantly" Platonist view of the acquisition of moral rationality—away from thinking of this as a process of attunement to reasons that owe nothing to the existence of any actual social formation—and instead come to understand it as one of *initiation into a culture,* that is, a historically existing form of life. Within this altered scene, such forms of life play the same kind of role that falls in Hegelian ethics to the "concrete universal": the actual moral order as it presents itself to a certain community; the sum total of practices maintained in a stable—or stable enough—condition by the particular (morally conscientious) acts of individual members of that community.

However, the last part of the discussion involves a change of standpoint with respect to this "concrete universal," or to moral rationality as something already constituted in advance of its exercise by this or that individual. We shall begin (in Part I) by thinking, as it were, entirely from *within* morality—by identifying ourselves with the claims exerted on any potentially "recalcitrant" element by an established form of ethical life; but by the time we reach Part III we shall be envisaging the possibility of a contrasting identification, one that would place us *on the side of* the "recalcitrant" and in opposition to those forces that work to bring particular subjects into line with a "universal" form or with a rule-governed social practice. I shall describe two alternative ways in which this oppositional attitude may account for itself: one already allowed for within a naturalized ethical cogitivism, according to which it expresses a demand—arising from critical reflection—for the modification of existing morality, so as to bring the latter into closer conformity with the ideals implicit in it; another, *not* already allowed for, which springs from a disposition to resist the claims of the universal as such. By the "universal as such" I mean not merely this or that "way of life" in all its concrete (and morally problematic) detail, but the very principle embodied in ethical upbringing: the demand addressed to particular persons, in their natural separateness or *difference,* to do or be the *same* as others—the same as those who have already undergone the process of upbringing, and who therefore already represent, in their choices and actions, what their community calls "moral rationality." It is this second mode of opposition to an established morality that will draw us into the discursive field of the postmodern critique of reason, whose unifying theme, insofar as it has one, seems to be a questioning of the ideology of *universalism.* "Questioning" here denotes a range of possibilities extending from the straightforwardly hostile, on one hand, to more nuanced attitudes of skepticism about the traditional value hierarchy in which (universal) form enjoys a status superior to that of the (particular) matter it organizes. My overall aim in Part III is to determine what—if anything—each of the two genres of oppositional thinking that I distinguish may have to learn from the other, and to elicit the distinctive insight that each provides into the negative side of our relation to the "moral universal."

It will be obvious to anyone reading this book that my most important philosophical debt, at any rate in regard to the "practical reason" view of ethics, is to the work of John McDowell. That being the case, I would like to stress that I am just one reader of McDowell among others and do not consider myself to be a privileged interpreter of his writings. Whether or not I am on something like the right track in my account of those writings, however, he bears no responsibility for any further use that I have made of them.

Most of the material was tried out in a graduate class at Oxford in Michaelmas Term 1998. Earlier versions of Chapter 5 were also delivered at a meeting of the Scots Philosophical Club in Glasgow in December 1997, at the University of Sussex in February 1998, and at the conference of the British Society for Ethical Theory at Durham in July 1999. I am very grateful to all those who offered comment and criticism on these occasions. I would also like to thank my colleagues at Worcester College, Oxford, for granting me two terms' sabbatical leave in the academic year 1997–1998, and the University of Oxford for the award of a "special lecturership" (the equivalent in teaching remission of a further sabbatical term) in 1995–1996; it was during these two periods of leave that a first draft of much of the book was set down. Finally, my warm thanks are due to several people who have helped me to develop the text itself and to correct some of its faults. John Tasioulas, Stephen Williams, and two anonymous referees for Harvard University Press all subjected the penultimate draft to detailed and insightful criticism, which I have done my best to bring to bear on the final revision. David Bemelmans made many improvements to the manuscript at the copy-editing stage, and Thomas Nørgaard provided valuable help with the index. My editor, Lindsay Waters, encouraged me in this project from the start and has waited patiently for me to finish it.

Acknowledgements

This book develops certain themes from my previously published work. The following articles in particular should be mentioned: "True and False Pleasures," in *Proceedings of the Aristotelian Society* 90, pt. 3 (1989/90), pp. 213–230; "Feminism and Pragmatism: A Reply to Richard Rorty," in *New Left Review* 193 (May–June 1992), pp. 56–74; "An Ancient Theory of Gender: Plato and the Pythagorean Table," in Léonie Archer, Susan Fischler, and Maria Wyke, eds., *Women in Ancient Societies: An Illusion of the Night* (Basingstoke: Macmillan, 1994), pp. 88–101; "The End of Morality?" in Kathleen Lennon and Margaret Whitford, eds., *Knowing the Difference: Feminist Perspectives in Epistemology* (London: Routledge, 1994), pp. 63–78; "Feminism and the 'Crisis of Rationality'," in *New Left Review* 207 (September–October 1994), pp. 72–86; "Ethical Upbringing: From Connivance to Cognition," in Sabina Lovibond and S. G. Williams, eds., *Essays for David Wiggins: Identity, Truth and Value* (Oxford: Blackwell, 1996), pp. 76–94; "Meaning What We Say: Feminist Ethics and the Critique of Humanism," in *New Left Review* 220 (November–December 1996), pp. 98–115; "The Feminist Stake in Greek Rationalism," in Jennifer Hornsby and Miranda Fricker, eds., *The Cambridge Companion to Feminism in Philosophy* (Cambridge: Cambridge University Press, 2000).

ETHICAL FORMATION

PART

I

Form

ONE

The Practical Reason View
of Ethics

1

Consider the class of moral judgements,[1] as exemplified by thoughts about whether or not a particular course of action would be wrong. Some philosophers have held that such judgements are inherently problematic, since they possess two features that appear to be mutually incompatible: *objectivity*, because as moral thinkers we have a sense of being accountable to standards of correctness which, if our thinking is of poor quality, we may fail to meet; and *practicality*, because of the special relationship between moral judgement and action—a relationship that can be summed up by saying that in the absence of coercion, failure to act in the way called for by your professed moral opinions tends, logically, to discredit the sincerity of those opinions.[2] We can call this an "internal" relationship, meaning that the condition of being motivated to act is (somehow) contained, or implicit, in that of sincerely believing the relevant action to be called for.[3]

---

1. *Pace* Bernard Williams (*Ethics and the Limits of Philosophy* [London: Fontana Press, 1985]), this discussion will not make use of any technical philosophical distinction between the "moral" and the "ethical." Stylistically, though, the word "ethical" seems better suited to contexts where what is in question is someone's overall state of receptivity to value (as in the "ethical formation" of the title), rather than just their state of receptivity to the kind of value that we call "moral" or "ethical" in respect of its distinctive content. (For some suggestions about this content, see Chapter 2, §2.)

2. See R. M. Hare, *Freedom and Reason* (Oxford: Oxford University Press, 1963), p. 79.

3. Confusingly, the recognition of an "internal" connection—in the sense intended here—between moral judgement and action (or motivation) must be distinguished from the view that all practical reasons are "internal" in the different sense associated with an influential discussion by Bernard Williams: that is, internal to the subjective "motivational set" of a

Why should these features be thought to be incompatible? Michael Smith explains:

> The objectivity of moral judgement suggests that there are moral facts, determined by circumstances, and that our moral judgements express our beliefs about what these facts are. This enables us to makes good sense of moral argument, and the like, but leaves it entirely mysterious how or why having a moral view is supposed to have special links with what we are motivated to do. And the practicality of moral judgement suggests just the opposite, that our moral judgements express our desires. While this enables us to make good sense of the link between having a moral view and being motivated, it leaves it entirely mysterious what a moral argument is supposed to be an argument about.[4]

Each characteristic, in other words, answers to something in our experience. But it is unclear how moral judgement can possess both, because the very idea of objectivity can seem to conflict with that of an internal relation between judgement and action. If Hume was right to protest against the attempted derivation of "ought" from "is,"[5] then we had better respect the thought on which his protest was based—namely, that awareness of how things stand in a reality independent of the thinking subject is compatible, indifferently, with *any* motivational attitude towards the reality apprehended (including a simple lack of interest). It is against this background that the idea of reality itself as containing (unconditionally) action-guiding features has been condemned by J. L. Mackie as unacceptably "queer"; that is, as calling for an ontology and epistemology whose relation to the domain of natural fact cannot be intelligibly explained.[6]

---

particular agent. For clarification of the terminology in this area, see Garrett Cullity and Berys Gaut, eds., *Ethics and Practical Reason* (Oxford: Clarendon Press, 1997), Introduction.

4. Michael Smith, "Realism," in Peter Singer, ed., *A Companion to Ethics* (Oxford: Blackwell, 1991), p. 402. In a subsequent review of various possible "internalist" claims, Smith describes one of these—the thesis that "If an agent judges that it is right for her to φ in circumstances *C*, then either she is motivated to φ in *C* or she is practically irrational"—as the "practicality requirement on moral judgement" (*The Moral Problem* [Oxford: Blackwell, 1994], pp. 61–62).

5. See David Hume, *A Treatise of Human Nature*, ed. L. A. Selby-Bigge, rev. P. H. Nidditch (Oxford: Clarendon Press, 1978), p. 469.

6. J. L. Mackie, *Ethics: Inventing Right and Wrong* (Harmondsworth: Penguin, 1977), pp. 38–42. The qualification "unconditionally" is needed here because the difficulties that

The general idea of an intellectual "queerness" or "strangeness" surrounding morality is not new. Kant, in particular, places emphasis on it in the *Critique of Practical Reason*. He says it is "strange" that the moral law should be experienced as a source of demands whose force is independent of our inclinations.[7] Our respect for this law is a "singular feeling, which cannot be compared with any pathological feeling"[8]—a respect for something "entirely different from life."[9] Yet this "mysterious and wonderful"[10] attribute is the central datum for moral philosophy; its reality and efficacy are what the moral philosopher has to keep in view, however unsatisfactorily from the standpoint of empirical psychology.

Now there does currently exist a body of thought—admittedly at some philosophical distance from the work of Mackie and Smith—that is deeply indebted to Kant for its manner of doing justice to the "strangeness" of the ethical. This body of thought is defined by a "rebellion against the priority of psychology"[11] in understanding ethical motivation. For present purposes, to give priority to psychology is to follow Hume in holding that what moves us to action of any kind is always a desire or "pro-attitude," directed in one way or another by relevant factual beliefs (including, centrally, beliefs about causal relations); it is to assume that my having a reason to do something must ultimately consist in, or rest on, an empirical (psychological) fact about me. To rebel against the priority of psychology is to hold that, on the contrary, the study of ethical motivation should take the form of an enquiry into the structure of a certain species of rationality.

In keeping with the positive value attributed to "rational" thought and action, antipsychologistic thinkers approach the phenomenon of ethically motivated behaviour not from a point of view that is neutral on the ques-

concern Mackie do not arise, for example, in connection with the act of alerting someone to facts to which their own contingent evaluative attitudes happen to give significance (see A. J. Ayer, *Language, Truth and Logic* [Harmondsworth: Penguin, 1971], pp. 146–147), or with the attempt to restore coherence to a "fractured sensibility" (see Simon Blackburn, *Spreading the Word: Groundings in the Philosophy of Language* [Oxford: Clarendon Press, 1984], p. 195).

7. Immanuel Kant, *Critique of Practical Reason*, trans. L. W. Beck (Indianapolis: Bobbs-Merrill, 1956), p. 31.

8. Ibid., p. 79.

9. Ibid., p. 91.

10. Ibid., p. 84, note.

11. See Thomas Nagel, *The Possibility of Altruism* (Princeton: Princeton University Press, 1970), p. 11.

tion of how we *ought* to be motivated, but from one with certain inbuilt evaluative commitments. For this kind of thinker, understanding (or explaining) why a certain act was performed—if indeed we are dealing with something singled out as an *act,* an expression of intelligent life rather than just a reflex movement—is a matter of identifying the value the agent saw in it. (One may recall here the Thomist view that we pursue only what we can represent to ourselves "under the aspect of good.")[12] And while such explanations obviously need to allow for the potentially divergent evaluative attitudes of agent and observer—for the fact that in practice we don't all value the same things—they could not get started otherwise than on the assumption that both parties inhabit a common "space" of value: a world in which the reasons why something is valued by one person are in principle, even if not immediately, accessible to another.[13]

To understand an action, then, will be to see it as one that a *rational* person might—however hastily or one-sidedly—have thought worth doing; and insofar as, from the observer's standpoint, we find it possible to refrain from criticisms like "hasty" or "one-sided," our account of why the agent acted as she[14] did will tend increasingly towards the status of a *vindicatory* explanation[15]—a view of the act in question as an inherently unpuzzling, because rationally defensible, bit of behaviour.[16] The limiting

12. See Mark Platts, *Moral Realities: An Essay in Philosophical Psychology* (London: Routledge, 1991), pp. 21, 27–29. The thesis of G. E. M. Anscombe in *Intention* (Oxford: Basil Blackwell, 1963, p. 9) that intentional actions are "[those] to which a certain sense of the question 'Why?' is given application" belongs to the same intellectual tradition, which, as we shall see, has its source in the ethical rationalism of Plato and Aristotle.

13. This is a point that will be familiar to anyone who knows the literature of Davidsonian "radical interpretation." See in particular David Wiggins, "Truth, Invention, and the Meaning of Life," §7, in *Needs, Values, Truth: Essays in the Philosophy of Value* (Oxford: Clarendon Press, 1998).

14. In my *Realism and Imagination in Ethics* (Oxford: Basil Blackwell, 1983), I rejected the inclusive usage of the feminine pronoun with some fighting talk about "futile reformist turns of phrase" (p. 4, note 4). Whether or not this was a sound policy in the early 1980s, I would not volunteer to make out a case for it today. I must confess to still finding the inclusive feminine faintly grotesque, but I fully accept that the (unvarying) masculine is no longer tolerable, except in some special contexts such as the exposition of premodern authors.

15. For the term "vindicatory," see Wiggins, *Needs, Values, Truth,* p. 356 and elsewhere.

16. The view outlined in the text diverges from that of Smith (*The Moral Problem,* pp. 95–96) in treating as merely relative the contrast between what he calls "motivating" and "normative" reasons, and in rejecting the idea that these are "quite different concepts of a reason

case of this "friendly" attitude—the attitude of forbearing to suppose any lapse of judgement on the part of the agent—will be that in which an act is characterized as the very act we would have expected to be forthcoming, in the given circumstances, from someone disposed in a general way to do the right thing. For example, we might portray a particular conscientious act as simply an expression of the agent's awareness that that act is morally required of her in the given circumstances, and hence that *there is* a compelling reason of a certain kind (namely, a moral reason) for her to do it. Obviously this mode of understanding is available only on the condition that it makes sense to talk about moral reasons that exist, not just for this or that person, but impersonally or "objectively"; and this will be so just in case it is correct to see ethics as conforming to the general principle that insofar as we are rational, our acts can be understood and explained as expressions of our sensitivity to the various sorts of reason that there are— that is, to the various "dictates of reason" which "are there anyway, whether or not one's eyes are opened to them."[17]

2

If we do accept such talk as intelligible, it will be natural to say that the reasons for behaving in a particular way in this or that situation may weigh differently (that is, more or less forcefully) with different people. Not everyone is equally sensitive to considerations of profit and loss, or of safety, or on the other hand of loyalty or fairness or truthfulness; not everyone is equally prone to the sort of tendencies (greed, laziness, timidity, and so on) that make for occasional, or indeed chronic, neglectfulness of such considerations. Once again, though, we should note that neither of these kinds of variation is value neutral. It is, of course, *better* to measure up to the normal human standard of sensitivity to objective features of one's surround-

for action," coordinated respectively with "two different ways in which we can see an agent in her role as Rational Animal" (ibid., p. 140).

17. John McDowell, *Mind and World* (Cambridge: Harvard University Press, 1994), p. 91. For the idea of "the reasons that there are," see also Thomas Nagel, *The View from Nowhere* (Oxford: Oxford University Press, 1986), p. 148; Christine M. Korsgaard, "Skepticism about Practical Reason," in her *Creating the Kingdom of Ends* (Cambridge: Cambridge University Press, 1996), pp. 311–334, esp. pp. 323–325; Philippa Foot, "Does Moral Subjectivism Rest on a Mistake?" *Oxford Journal of Legal Studies,* 15 (1995), pp. 1–14, esp. p. 10.

ings than to fall short of that standard, and it is better to possess strong defences against the typical interfering factors than to be at their mercy. Such evaluative distinctions suggest the further thought that there is such a thing as a *best possible* condition of the individual deliberator with respect to the appreciation of objective reasons, and this is why, as Christine Korsgaard has written, "some ethical theories centred on the idea of practical reason are best thought of as establishing ideals of character. A person with a good character will be, on such a view, . . . one whose motivational structure is organized for rational receptivity, so that reasons motivate in accord with their proper force and necessity."[18]

The character ideal introduced in this passage rests on an unusually abstract conception of "character," since the assumption behind it is that we should aim to become people with a proper sensitivity to the force of reasons in general, theoretical as well as practical—a sensitivity that will also come into play, for example, when someone recognizes the intellectual coerciveness of an argument or of a mathematical proof. However, if we speak of a "rationalist character ideal" in this inclusive sense, we can think of the ideal as being among other things—or from one point of view—an ethical one; or we can think of the relevant point of view as itself determining a particular rationalist character ideal of a more local kind. This local instance of the rationalist character ideal is the object we undertake to explicate if we adopt a *"practical reason" approach to ethics:*[19] an approach in which the ethical theorist is pictured not as a mere onlooker, but also, and primarily, as an ethical subject, actively engaged in the mode of thought on which (as a theorist) she reflects, and finding her incentive to theory precisely in the desire to think more competently or intelligently about ethical matters. One variant of the practical reason approach which has been moving into the ascendant in recent years is "virtue ethics," whose central

18. Korsgaard, "Skepticism about Practical Reason," p. 324. Note that in speaking of a "best possible" condition of receptivity to reasons one must hope, with Aristotle, to be understood in a way that respects the differences between subject matters. For example, if we are trying to place an object as close as possible to a wall without actually touching it, there is presumably no *belief* of the form "It should go here" that is the best possible one to hold. But this does not mean that there is, in practice, no such thing as *the best one can do* about the problem.

19. For this terminology, see Korsgaard, *Creating the Kingdom of Ends*, Introduction; also Foot, "Does Moral Subjectivism Rest on a Mistake?"

question is: what must a moral agent be like in order to display this kind of competence or intelligence in living? Or: what does it take to qualify as a person who can be relied on, so far as humanly possible, to do the (objectively) right thing?

Mackie correctly names Plato as the first known philosopher in the European tradition to put forward an explicit doctrine of objective moral demands: "In Plato's theory the Forms, and in particular the Form of the Good, are eternal, extra-mental, realities. They are a very central structural element in the fabric of the world. But it is held also that just knowing them or "seeing" them will not merely tell men what to do but will ensure that they do it, overruling any contrary inclinations."[20] He does not fill in the psychological background which, in Plato's scheme of things, explains how a feature of "extra-mental reality" can be inherently action-guiding for those who are aware of it. This, however, is where we encounter a second main source of inspiration (along with the Kantian influence mentioned in §1) for the practical reason approach. For to my mind the most striking development in ethical theory since the 1970s has been an attempt to supply the very thing that Mackie omitted: I mean, to reactivate the Platonic–Aristotelian ethical tradition and to provide an updated account of its leading idea—namely, that moral virtue is the outcome of a successful process of *formation*.[21]

Admittedly, this development has not manifested itself as a conscious programme in all the writers who could be regarded as having contributed to it. As we turn from one text to another we find different themes within the tradition receiving emphasis. Sometimes, as in Iris Murdoch and Mark Platts, an uncompromising moral realism has been defended, taking Plato as the main authority and concentrating on such ontological and epistemological themes as the "sovereignty" of objective good and the inadequacy or "tawdriness" of the cognitive powers we bring to bear on it.[22] More often, attention has been focussed on Aristotle's account of the acquisition of moral rationality as a process with both an affective and a

20. Mackie, *Ethics*, p. 23.

21. For further detail see Chapter 3, §3.

22. Iris Murdoch, *The Sovereignty of Good* (London: Routledge and Kegan Paul, 1970); Mark Platts, *Ways of Meaning: An Introduction to a Philosophy of Language* (London: Routledge and Kegan Paul, 1979), chap. 10 (p. 252 for the phrase "tawdry, inadequate epistemic creatures struggling with an indefinitely complex world"); Platts, *Moral Realities*.

cognitive aspect: representatives of this tendency include John McDowell, Alasdair MacIntyre, Martha Nussbaum, and David Wiggins.[23] And the ideas made available by this second group can be seen as informing the work of still others, such as Susan Hurley and Jonathan Dancy, who refer to the ethics of Aristotle in more or less friendly terms but who would be unlikely to see themselves as engaged in the revival of a unitary "Platonic–Aristotelian" approach[24] (indeed, Hurley's usage enables her to "assume that in ethics, at least, Platonism is not a live option").[25] However, despite the difficulty of reconstructing a common body of doctrine that connects all the names I have cited, I believe they are held together by certain historical affiliations which, once understood, may allow us to register a long-term change of mood—perhaps even the emergence of a new phase of "normal science"—in moral philosophy.

I have already mentioned the contrasting policies of allowing, and of refusing to allow, ethical theory to be governed by the concerns of psychology; and it was in pursuing the theme of "antipsychologism" that I noted the availability of the practical reason approach, and of virtue ethics as an instance of it. The idea of an affinity between virtue ethics and the rejection of psychologism may be initially surprising in that a virtue is, after all, a psychological trait—a *state of character* whose possessors can, as such, be expected to display certain consistent patterns of feeling and choice. A connection can be established, however, if we recall the Aristotelian ancestry

23. See especially John McDowell, "Virtue and Reason," *Monist*, 62 (1979), pp. 331–350; "The Role of *Eudaimonia* in Aristotle's Ethics," in Amélie Rorty, ed., *Essays on Aristotle's Ethics* (Berkeley: University of California Press, 1980), pp. 359–376; "Eudaimonism and Realism in Aristotle's Ethics," in Robert Heinaman, ed., *Aristotle and Moral Realism* (London: UCL Press, 1995), pp. 201–218; Alasdair MacIntyre, *After Virtue: A Study in Moral Theory* (London: Duckworth, 1981); Martha C. Nussbaum, *Love's Knowledge: Essays on Philosophy and Literature* (Oxford: Oxford University Press, 1990), chap. 2; David Wiggins, *Needs, Values, Truth*, Essays III, V–VII. A more extended development of the neo-Aristotelian position is to be found in Rosalind Hursthouse, *On Virtue Ethics* (Oxford: Oxford University Press, 1999).

24. For the thesis of intellectual continuity between Plato and Aristotle as philosophers who studied reality through the medium of language—of *logoi* or *eidê*—see Hans-Georg Gadamer, *The Idea of the Good in Platonic-Aristotelian Philosophy*, trans. P. Christopher Smith (New Haven: Yale University Press, 1986), esp. Preface.

25. Jonathan Dancy, *Moral Reasons* (Oxford: Blackwell, 1993); S. L. Hurley, *Natural Reasons: Personality and Polity* (Oxford: Oxford University Press, 1989) (pp. 14–15 for her working definition of "Platonism"). I do not mean to suggest that Hurley's definition is eccentric: compare for example Allan Gibbard, *Wise Choices, Apt Feelings: A Theory of Normative Judgment* (Oxford: Clarendon Press, 1990), p. 154.

of the concept of (moral) virtue, which traditionally consists—under one aspect—in a capacity for *thinking correctly* about how to respond to particular situations as they arise.[26] (This is the capacity summed up in the concept of *phronêsis*, "practical wisdom"—in Aristotle's terms an "intellectual," not a "moral" virtue, but one that has to be understood by abstracting the common cognitive element from a range of different virtues that *are* genuinely moral: virtues consisting in the reliable disposition to deal in an appropriate, felicitous, or at least not contemptible way with the various sorts of circumstance attendant on human life.) The subject matter of this kind of correctness is not itself psychological:[27] it relates, first, to the evaluatively significant features of situations, and second, to the identification and weighing of any reasons for action that these features may generate. (I expand on this in Chapter 2, §2.)

The class of "evaluatively significant" phenomena is not, of course, exhausted by the ethically significant, and this is why a "practical reason" account of ethics will see practical rationality as having both an ethical and a nonethical component; it will see the latter as supporting, in particular, the various kinds of self-interested behaviour that we expect of a rational person and of which the absence would give grounds for criticism (taking reasonable care to preserve one's health,[28] not to lose one's means of subsis-

26. See Aristotle, *Nicomachean Ethics*, 1106b36–1107a2: "Virtue, then, is a state of character concerned with choice, lying in a mean, i.e. the mean relative to us, *this being determined by a rational principle, and by that principle by which the man of practical wisdom would determine it*" (trans. David Ross, *The Nicomachean Ethics of Aristotle* [London: Oxford University Press, 1954], p. 39; emphasis added).

27. Compare Gottlob Frege, *The Foundations of Arithmetic*, trans. J. L. Austin (Oxford: Basil Blackwell, 1980), p. 37: "Arithmetic is no more psychology than, say, astronomy is. Astronomy is concerned, not with ideas of the planets, but with the planets themselves, and by the same token the objects of arithmetic are not ideas either." ("Idea" here means a private, psychological phenomenon.) Frege's point is echoed by Nagel, *The View from Nowhere*, pp. 150–151: "We cannot replace practical reasoning by the psychology of our practical reasoning capacity, any more than we can replace mathematical reasoning by the psychology of our mathematical capacity. The pursuit of objective practical principles is not to be conceived of as a psychological exploration of our moral sense, but as an employment of it."

28. Mentioned by Aristotle as a matter in which one can incur blame (*Nicomachean Ethics*, 1114a21–25), and cited by Dancy in a passage criticizing the view that moral imperatives differ from others—as Kant held—in being categorical: he says we should note the possibility that prudential imperatives may be so too, "or some of them may be anyway, for instance 'You should look after your health.' Some may insist that this is a moral imperative, but there

tence or alienate one's friends, and so forth). So someone whose overall sensitivity to practical reasons is as it should be will credit prudential considerations, as much as others, with their proper weight. "The root notion [linking the different parts of practical rationality]," in the words of Philippa Foot,[29] "is that of the goodness of human beings in respect of their actions," and specifically in respect of the will or choice represented by those actions; so this "goodness" will contain the same internal diversity as the range of situations in which human beings can be called on to make evaluatively significant choices. Still, one component of practical rationality which must (logically, on the present view) be adequately realized in any normal (nondefective) member of the human species, given the kind of species that is, will be the disposition to respond as one should to the requirements of morality, even where this is contrary to what would otherwise count as one's interests. Because human beings are social creatures, their upbringing has to equip them with a due sense not just of physical but of "moral danger,"[30] and the absence or inadequate development of this sense is a deviation from the psychological norm determined by the form of life of the species.

Virtue ethics, then, can be seen as aiming at the elucidation of the rationalist character ideal as it relates to practical rationality, and within practical rationality, to the proper appreciation of those (potentially action-guiding) values that lie beyond the range of ordinary self-interest.[31] Accordingly, one theoretical device that it can employ is the figure of the vir-

is at least room for the idea that it is a categorical prudential imperative" (*Moral Reasons,* p. 44).

29. Foot, "Moral Subjectivism," p. 7.

30. Barbara Herman, *The Practice of Moral Judgment* (Cambridge: Harvard University Press, 1993), p. 78. Note, however, that in agreeing that the dangers to be encountered in a human life include moral ones, I do not take myself to be pronouncing in favour of the view that moral factors will always be *paramount* in the deliberations of a rational person; whatever the merits of this view, it is not one to which we commit ourselves simply by invoking the idea of a proper overall sensitivity to practical reasons.

31. This characterization is quite crude and provisional; for example, it does not yet register any distinction between ethical and aesthetic value. Intuitively, we may feel that there is something to be said for silence on this point, since the action-guiding power of the aesthetic is becoming ever more visible in the postindustrial world—in Britain for example, where significant numbers of people are now prepared to sacrifice time and comfort in order to bear witness against the building of new roads. For present purposes, anyway, we can simply mark off instrumental from noninstrumental value and postpone any subdivision of the latter category.

tuous (or "practically wise") *person*, who represents a condition of ideal sensitivity to the claims exerted by different sorts of value. This figure has suggested a possible response to the "strangeness" of moral motivation, or to the problem of how moral judgements can combine the properties of objectivity and practicality.

In setting out that response we can begin with the idea, familiar by now from a celebrated paper by John McDowell,[32] that the virtuous person has a *distinctive way of seeing* situations, persons, courses of action, or anything else that we regard as a logically appropriate object of moral evaluation. This way of seeing is *objective* in that those who become party to it are thereby alerted to genuine features of the world. And it is *practical* in that, for the virtuous, to draw attention to such a feature of a situation (or other suitable object) may be to give a nonelliptical explanation of why something has to be done—an explanation that does not need to be filled out by appealing to any independent desire of the agent.[33] Ethical considerations appeal to the virtuous not through the mediation of their own contingent interests, but (at least sometimes) in the same sort of way in which a rationally coercive argument calls upon any reasonable person to draw its conclusion: the interest such people take in maintaining the patterns of conduct characteristic of the virtues is *motivated* by their grasp of the (not merely instrumental) value of those patterns of conduct.[34]

Because the virtuous person represents an ideal, the centrality of this figure within virtue ethics endows the latter with a characteristic already mentioned as typical of antipsychologistic thinking about practical reason, namely, that of partisanship. Virtue ethics refuses to adopt a neutral stance

---

32. John McDowell, "Are Moral Requirements Hypothetical Imperatives?" *Proceedings of the Aristotelian Society*, supp. vol. 52 (1978), pp. 13–29. See also his "Virtue and Reason," and compare Korsgaard, *Creating the Kingdom of Ends*, p. 180 (but with the caveat entered in note 48 below). I am concerned in this book only with the characteristic of cognitive ideality attaching to McDowell's (1978) virtuous person—not with those further, problematic elements in his account that place the virtuous person "out on a limb" by representing her as uniquely capable of purely cognitive motivation, and that apparently make her the unique locus of the process whereby one practical reason "silences" another (see Dancy, *Moral Reasons*, chap. 3, §§3–4). For some further thoughts on the ideal advanced by the paper in question, and on its possible basis in experience, see Chapter 5.

33. That is, "independent" of the agent's (expected) moral appreciation of the relevant circumstances.

34. See Nagel, *The Possibility of Altruism*, pp. 29–30; McDowell, "Are Moral Requirements Hypothetical Imperatives?" §3.

as between the virtuous person's "way of seeing" human situations and that of any random person: it holds that while some constituents of the world of value (for example, those relating to the avoidance of immediate pain) declare themselves more or less impartially to everyone, others do so only to those with suitably informed powers of judgement. So if two people see a given situation in a different moral light (one perhaps thinking that it demands some kind of action on her part, while the other acknowledges no such demand), it will sometimes be true to say that one of them understands or appreciates the situation better than the other. Virtue ethics, in other words, offers a character ideal not just in the edifying sense (an example we should strive to imitate) but also in an epistemological one: it follows Aristotle in holding out a standard of correct judgement.[35]

3

However, at this stage in the argument, the idea of "correct judgement" is one to which we are merely helping ourselves in a dogmatic fashion. For we have not yet negotiated the obstacle posed by the neo-Humean outlook mentioned earlier: that is, we have not yet said anything to persuade the uncommitted that the idiom of epistemology, with its implication of a sorting or ordering of belief states in point of conformity to truth, has any genuine bearing on the ethical.

35. Daniel Statman, in a helpful recent survey, proposes to distinguish between moderate and extreme versions of virtue ethics according to whether they represent juridical or "deontic" concepts (those of right, duty, and so on) as entitled to a place of their own alongside "aretaic" ones in our ethical thinking; as worthy of retention, but on the understanding that they are reducible to aretaic concepts, or in other words that person appraisals are more basic than act appraisals; or (the most extreme view) as an objectively superfluous or pernicious group of concepts which we should seek to *replace* with those of a range of specific virtues. Statman, ed., *Virtue Ethics: A Critical Reader* (Edinburgh: Edinburgh University Press, 1997), Introduction, pp. 8–9. In these terms, the "virtue ethics" envisaged here will be supremely moderate, since it will owe its label not to any eliminative designs on the deontic but to its regard for the ultimate dependence of *any* social practice—not excluding the practice of using concepts like "right" and "duty"—on the availability of suitable resources of *tacit knowledge*, and hence on something like the inner *hexis* or disposition in which an Aristotelian moral virtue consists (see Chapters 2 and 3). For reasons not to take too seriously the categories of "deontology," "consequentialism," and "virtue ethics" as devices for mapping the terrain of moral philosophy, see also Christine M. Korsgaard, "From Duty and for the Sake of the Noble: Kant and Aristotle on Morally Good Action," in Stephen Engstrom and Jennifer Whiting, eds., *Aristotle, Kant and the Stoics: Rethinking Happiness and Duty* (Cambridge: Cambridge University Press, 1996), pp. 203–236, at pp. 232–234.

In confronting this ("noncognitivist") obstacle afresh, we may wish to make the experiment of suspending judgement about a principle that enjoys a good deal of authority within the analytical tradition—namely, the assumption that a descriptive discipline such as sociology can have nothing to contribute to the normative discipline of ethics. It is hard, after all, to dismiss the idea that some theoretical interest might attach to the existence of impersonal standards of correctness within a given region of discourse—to the (sociological) fact that some participants in the discourse are credited with the authority to *pronounce* the usage of others correct or otherwise. Any philosophy that hopes to understand normativity, or the existence of rule-governed practices, as a natural phenomenon can reasonably be expected to give some weight to this fact. And texts that bear out that expectation are not far to seek. Thus Wittgenstein finds it worthwhile to include in his review of the "physiognomy" of our linguistic practice a reminder that "[d]isputes do not break out (among mathematicians, say) over the question whether a rule has been obeyed or not";[36] while Michael Dummett cites with approval the view that in order to evaluate the doctrine of Platonism in mathematics we should ask "not whether there are mathematical objects, but whether mathematical statements are objective,"[37] a question that calls for reflection on the practice of mathematical reasoning.

An analogous procedure is open to us in regard to "evaluative objects," or in a more familiar phrase, objective values. As a remedy for the state of mental paralysis induced by trying to specify what such "queer" entities would have to be like, we can switch to the alternative question: is it the case that what we *say* about evaluative subject matters such as ethics and aesthetics displays the characteristics associated, phenomenologically, with "objective" or truth-seeking discourse? For example, if I commit myself to a particular moral judgement, does this mean that I regard the judgement as one that "will under favourable circumstances command conver-

36. Ludwig Wittgenstein, *Philosophical Investigations*, trans. G. E. M. Anscombe (Oxford: Basil Blackwell, 1967), §240. The idea here is that in the normal course of communication it will not be controversial whether a particular linguistic move—the use of a word, the continuation of a numerical series—is or is not in accord with the rules. Competent speakers (those speakers whom we all agree in *calling* competent) simply will not disagree about such questions: if anyone has doubts, we will regard that very fact as calling their competence into question. Mathematics happens to be a particularly natural choice of subject matter to illustrate this point.

37. Michael Dummett, *Frege: Philosophy of Language* (London: Duckworth, 1973), p. xxi.

gence"[38]—that is, one in which other persons with their own indefinitely various points of view on the world could be non-coercively led to concur? If the answer seems to be yes (as I suggested, following Michael Smith, in §1), then this—so far as it goes—will tell in favour of the acceptance of ethics as a domain in which there can be knowledge, truth, and error.

Suppose, then, that we reflect on the experience of moral discussion, and that this reflection leaves us—as it has done many philosophers— more impressed by those structural features that seem to mark ethics as a truth-seeking enterprise than by any that point the other way. (Perhaps we shall find ourselves dwelling on phenomena such as the exchange of "evidence," the struggle to reach a just appreciation of all ethical aspects of a case, and the readiness—sometimes—to persist in our own views even when we cannot make them convincing to others, rather than on the breakdown of reasoned argument or on the feeling that all we can do with our evaluative attitudes is to "compare notes.")[39] And suppose we are struck by a characteristic which some ethical concepts, at least, seem to have in common with other kinds of concept whose suitability to figure in factual statements is not in question—namely, that there is such a thing as the *right way* to project them into new contexts not explicitly covered by linguistic training, and that this "right way" will not necessarily coincide with what seems right to *me*.[40] (Every human action is, from one point of view, unique, since history never exactly repeats itself; but this does not prevent competent observers from reaching substantial agreement on the moral quality of many individual actions.) Granted this outcome, we ought to be at least provisionally sympathetic to the idea of the virtuous

38. For this and other "marks" of the concept of truth, and for discussion of how far moral judgements exhibit them, see Wiggins, *Needs, Values, Truth,* Essay IV; quotation from p. 147. I return in Chapter 2, §3 to the role in moral philosophy of the description of linguistic practices.

39. For some pessimistic considerations on moral epistemology, see F. P. Ramsey, *Philosophical Papers,* ed. D. H. Mellor (Cambridge: Cambridge University Press, 1990), Epilogue; Ayer, *Language, Truth and Logic,* chap. 6; or (from a contrasting philosophical standpoint) Alasdair MacIntyre, *After Virtue,* chaps. 1–2.

40. This line of thought derives its best support from the case of substantive, or descriptively "thick," ethical concepts such as "brave," "kind," "honest," or—Philippa Foot's well-known negative example—"rude" (see her *Virtues and Vices* [Oxford: Basil Blackwell, 1978], chap. 7; see also G. E. M. Anscombe, *Collected Philosophical Papers,* vol. 3 [Oxford: Basil Blackwell, 1981], pp. 32–33; McDowell, "Virtue and Reason"; Platts, *Ways of Meaning,* p. 246; Williams, *Ethics and the Limits of Philosophy,* p. 140).

person as someone characterized by a certain state of receptivity—a state that enables ethical (and other practical) reasons to motivate her "in accord with their proper force and necessity." But to establish such sympathy on the basis of an optimistic phenomenology of moral discourse is not yet to dispose of the Humean tradition against which the practical reason approach is in revolt. For example, the hope that we sometimes entertain of resolving evaluative disagreement by converting the opposition from (what we see as) a narrowly selfish to a more public-spirited or "universal" point of view is entirely at home within that tradition also.⁴¹ The difference is that in its empiricist setting, this hope is attended by the caveat that "intersubjectivity is not objectivity"⁴²—merely the product of a common socialization which leads the members of a given community to "gild or stain" their experience with the same array of subjective attitudes;⁴³ and by a conviction that while the belief in objective moral requirements may well be a "strange" feature of human consciousness, the task of a theory of ethics is to "*remove* the mystery from the subject"⁴⁴ by describing it in terms that will make it accessible to the natural and social sciences.

A philosopher who takes this view is likely to object to the approach outlined so far that all it offers us is an account of a certain character type for which it is *as if* there are objective moral requirements, or perceptions that are inherently action-guiding; and that to say of someone that they have that sort of character just means that they happen to care enough about the relevant values to be reliably moved to action by thoughts expressed in terms of them. That there are, or may be, such people contradicts no claim advanced by the ethical noncognitivist. But as for the suggestion that they are epistemically *exemplary*, the noncognitivist may object that this reveals the practical reason approach as simply a version of idealism about ethics, since what it boils down to is the thought that if only

41. See David Hume, *Enquiry Concerning the Principles of Morals*, ed. L. A. Selby-Bigge, rev. P. H. Nidditch (Oxford: Clarendon Press, 1975), §9, esp. pp. 272–273.

42. Mackie, *Ethics*, p. 22.

43. Hume, *Enquiry Concerning the Principles of Morals*, p. 294: "[Reason] discovers objects as they really stand in nature, without addition or diminution: [taste] has a productive faculty, and gilding or staining all natural objects with the colours, borrowed from internal sentiment, raises in a manner a new creation." Compare Hume, *Treatise*, pp. 468–469; Mackie, *Ethics*, pp. 42–46; Blackburn, *Spreading the Word*, chap. 6.

44. Simon Blackburn, "The Flight to Reality," in Rosalind Hursthouse, Gavin Lawrence, and Warren Quinn, eds., *Virtues and Reasons: Philippa Foot and Moral Theory* (Oxford: Oxford University Press, 1995), pp. 35–56; quotation from p. 56; emphasis added.

we can locate the right sort of thinking subject to serve as a point of reference, then *the fact that that subject thinks that p makes it the case that p.* Idealism as a general epistemological position is, of course, exposed to the objection that regardless of how well confirmed a belief or theory may be by internal criteria (in this case, the endorsement of the supposedly exemplary judge), it may for all we know still be false; and to retreat to the thesis that in ethics, in contrast to some other subject matters, "true" just *means* "accepted by the best judges" (or "warrantably assertible") would be to grant to noncognitivism everything it was looking for.

4

We might seek to avoid such a concession by pointing out that there are more things in heaven and earth, or in "objective reality," than the proverbial array of medium-sized dry goods—and more properties and relations too.[45] But this easy-going attitude, if it is to be of use to the practical reason view in rebutting the charge of dogmatism, stands in need of philosophical support. For as long as we concede the "queer" character of anything not covered by a neo-Humean conception of the natural,[46] we implicitly endorse that conception as the one that will make sense, insofar as sense can be made at all, of the contested items. Mackie, for example, pictures his opponent seeking to provide objective values with ontological "companions in guilt"[47]—companions such as number, substance, modal notions, and causation. But he suggests that most of these can be satisfactorily accounted for in empiricist terms and says that if any resist such treatment, then they too should be included among the targets of his argument (and, presumably, eliminated from our ontological scheme).

In order to prevail over this eliminative impulse, it is not enough to ar-

---

45. Compare Paul Horwich, *Truth* (Oxford: Basil Blackwell, 1990), p. 38: "'is true' is a perfectly good English predicate—and (leaving aside nominalistic concerns about the very notion of 'property') one might well take this to be a conclusive criterion of standing for a property of *some* sort."

46. For this conception, see for example G. E. Moore, *Principia Ethica* (Cambridge: Cambridge University Press, 1903), p. 40: "By 'nature' . . . I do mean and have meant that which is the subject-matter of the natural sciences and also of psychology. It may be said to include all that has existed, does exist, or will exist in time." It is probably fair to regard this as a characterization of what McDowell, as we shall see later, calls "nature as the realm of law."

47. Mackie, *Ethics*, p. 39.

gue that the alleged ontological "guilt" is widespread—we need to go further and show that it is *groundless* or *illusory*. And one possible step in that
direction is to establish a position from which we can say the following: for
any putatively truth-directed region of discourse, if we are not disposed on
grounds of general intellectual integrity and good sense to think that that
discourse is claptrap (as, for instance, most people reading this are likely to
think about astrology), then our respect for it as a potential mode of access
to truth is *something to which philosophy must adapt itself*—not something
that should be required to adapt itself to the conclusions of philosophy.[48]

The inspiration for this move comes from the later philosophy of
Wittgenstein—in particular, from Wittgenstein's disavowal of "metaphysics," or of any substantive philosophical doctrine.[49] Particularly interesting
for our purposes is the view developed by McDowell in *Mind and World*.
This book offers an account of the mind–world encounter which aims,
precisely, to avoid the pitfalls of the two substantive treatments of this
theme available within our philosophical tradition—empiricism and idealism. McDowell argues that the way to emancipate ourselves from these
traditional doctrines, between which he sees conventional philosophical
thought as doomed to oscillate, is by giving due weight to a bit of linguistic
phenomenology: that is, to the truism that "When one thinks truly, what
one thinks *is* what is the case." Thought, he continues, "can be distanced
from the world by being false, but there is no distance from the world implicit in the very idea of thought."[50] Just as judgement reaches all the way
out to reality,[51] so mental life (or "experience") is itself a matter of "openness to the layout"[52] of the reality captured in (successful) acts of judgement.

McDowell infers from his truistic thesis (that to think truly is to *think*

48. Since I introduced the "practical reason approach" partly by reference to the work of
Christine Korsgaard, I should mention here that this way of proceeding has little in common
with that of Korsgaard herself, who writes: "What brings 'objectivity' to the realm of values
is not that certain things *have* objective value, but rather that there are constraints on rational choice" (*Creating the Kingdom of Ends*, p. x). Kant will continue to make his presence felt
in this book, but in general, the positive side of my discussion will be more strongly influenced by neo-Aristotelian than by neo-Kantian sources.

49. See especially *Philosophical Investigations* §§109–133.

50. McDowell, *Mind and World*, p. 27.

51. Compare Wittgenstein, *Philosophical Investigations* §95.

52. McDowell, *Mind and World*, p. 26.

what is the case) that for language-using animals, the content of experience is essentially such as to lend itself to conceptual articulation.[53] My current experience, for example, is (among other things) of *the fact that* this room contains certain objects, is lit in a certain way, and so forth; but if I am not hallucinating, then these very facts—which require for the specification of their content the same conceptual resources as the corresponding experiential judgements on my part—can be counted as "aspects of the perceptible world" which are currently being disclosed to me.[54] Conversely, the same truism suggests a view of conceptuality itself, or of the "sphere of the conceptual," as "unbounded": although the judgements that embody our particular efforts in the direction of truth and knowledge proceed from the exercise of "*passive* natural powers"[55] of responsiveness to the world around us, this passivity is a matter of rational dependence not on "something *outside* the conceptual realm,"[56] but—once again—on the very facts that our (true) judgements record. Just as failure to acknowledge the moment of passivity in experience leads to an idealist position in which thought is denied the "external friction"[57] needed to provide it with empirical content, so empiricism succumbs to the contrasting error of attempting, hopelessly, to ground thought in a "bare [extraconceptual] presence,"[58] an error for which Wittgenstein's critique of the idea of a private language is available as therapy.[59]

This reasoning is governed by a generalized form of the principle we found at work in the practical reason approach to ethics, when we said that according to that approach the theorist understands herself not just as an

---

53. Is this way of speaking discredited by the uncontroversial fact that we often find it hard to put our thoughts and feelings into words? For the moment, we can simply say: no, because although it would no doubt make sense to describe the mental items involved in such cases as merely potential (that is, not yet fully actual) vehicles of significance, this would be for a different (and nonmetaphysical) reason. (But the phenomenon of resistance to articulation will surface again in Part III.)

54. McDowell, *Mind and World,* p. 26.

55. Ibid., p. 89; emphasis added.

56. Ibid., p. 16; emphasis added.

57. Ibid., p. 11.

58. Ibid., p. 19. McDowell also refers to this "bare presence" as the "Given," preferring to speak of a "dualism of scheme and Given" rather than of Donald Davidson's "dualism of scheme and content" (ibid., p. 4).

59. The doctrine of the "unboundedness of the conceptual" is derived, more remotely, from Hegel.

onlooker but always also as a participant in the mental operations she seeks to describe. Instead of trying to picture the encounter between mind and world "sideways on"[60]—that is, from a position external to any scheme of values and concerns actually generated by this encounter—McDowell's model invites us, so to speak, to *acquiesce* in the measure of intelligence conferred on us by the experience of living a certain kind of embodied life. Instead of trying to abstract from the fact that, through our participation in human society, we have acquired a "rationally organized network" of capacities for the adjustment of thought to reality,[61] the proposal is that we consent to think from within the "space of reasons"[62] with which we are acquainted, that is, from within the horizon set in place by our actual state of understanding of "what is a reason for what."[63] And since this state of understanding embraces every variety of rational dependence or implication that our upbringing has taught us to recognize, acceding to the proposal will lead us to regard the phenomenon of sensitivity to moral requirements—assuming that such requirements are, indeed, a feature of the "space of reasons" actually known to us—as no more (though no less) "strange" than the emergence of a natural species whose form of life demands such an upbringing.

Adopting McDowell's own terminology, we can characterize this attitude of forswearing "constructive," or "sideways on," philosophy as one of *quietism*.[64] The label is a potentially confusing one, in that—depending on the user—it may carry either positive or negative connotations. Crispin

60. McDowell, *Mind and World*, p. 34; see also p. 95, where McDowell speaks of "constructive" philosophy in much the same negative sense. And compare Jürgen Habermas's complaint that "[Richard] Rorty absolutizes the perspective of the observer" and leaves us not really engaged in the critical appraisal of opinions and arguments, but "merely look[ing] over our own shoulders as historians and ethnographers." Habermas, "Questions and Counterquestions," in Richard Bernstein, ed., *Habermas and Modernity* (Cambridge: Polity Press, 1985), pp. 192–216; quotations from pp. 195, 194.

61. McDowell, *Mind and World*, p. 29. McDowell comments: "That is what a repertoire of empirical concepts is."

62. Ibid., p. 5.

63. Ibid., p. 126.

64. For this idea, see *Mind and World*, Lecture V, §3; see also John McDowell, "Meaning and Intentionality in Wittgenstein's Later Philosophy," *Midwest Studies in Philosophy*, 17 (1992), pp. 40–52. (It should be borne in mind that "constructive" in the context of *Mind and World* is not, as in standard usage, the opposite of "destructive" or "critical" but is a pejorative term meaning something like "foundationalist.")

Wright, for example, employs the term "quietism" in his *Truth and Objectivity*—again in a Wittgensteinian context—to mean "the view that significant metaphysical debate is impossible";[65] but this view is one from which he wishes to distance himself, insisting retrospectively that the ("minimalist") account of truth defended in his book "[does] *not* imply Quietism and [is], to the contrary, at the service of resistance to it."[66] "Quietism," for Wright, involves a reprehensible refusal to persevere with legitimate debates between realism and antirealism in relation to this or that specific region of discourse—debates which, he hints, can even be interpreted as exercises in applying Wittgenstein's advice to attend to the multiple communicative functions of language rather than to the formal (grammatical) homogeneity of much of its "surface."[67] By contrast, McDowell's way of introducing the term is intended to secure its claim to a nonpejorative usage. To be a "quietist," in his idiom, is not to shy away from any properly philosophical task, but to call attention to a sense of "metaphysics" in which metaphysical debate is indeed impossible (though this fact tends to be hidden from us because we succumb to the delusion, or fantasy, of being able to occupy an intellectual vantage point that is in fact inaccessible).[68] I shall find it convenient in this book to use the term "quietism" in the second of the two ways just mentioned: to denote, not a failure to pursue worthwhile questions about the comparative "physiognomy" of different linguistic practices, but a (correct) policy of accepting that the investigation of such practices must be carried out from a position of immanence within them; a policy of giving up that fantasized external standpoint from which we could supposedly pass judgement on whether this or that entire region of discourse succeeds in making contact with the "real world."

It will be remembered that my motive in invoking the quietist attitude (in this sense of "quietist") was to establish what I take to be the most favourable philosophical setting for the development of a practical reason approach to ethics. The idea of a topic-neutral "experience" consisting in

65. Crispin Wright, *Truth and Objectivity* (Cambridge: Harvard University Press, 1992), p. 202.

66. Crispin Wright, "Comrades against Quietism: Reply to Simon Blackburn on *Truth and Objectivity*," *Mind*, 107 (1998), pp. 183–203; quotation from p. 185.

67. Ibid., p. 196.

68. On the role of "fantasy" here, see Cora Diamond, *The Realistic Spirit: Wittgenstein, Philosophy and the Mind* (Cambridge: MIT Press, 1991), pp. 49–51.

openness to the layout of an equally topic-neutral "reality" appears well qualified to form part of this favourable setting. Equipped with such a conception, we can of course agree that there is one reading of the claim that "intersubjectivity is not objectivity" according to which it expresses something incontrovertible (since to say that a proposition is generally agreed to be true is not to say that it *is* true). But we can also note that without benefit of those cultural processes that initiate successive generations into the "space of reasons," none of us would be party to the "store of historically accumulated wisdom"[69] by virtue of which the sensory awareness of our environment can become the knowledge of a world.[70]

To make this kind of point, however, is not yet to employ quietist considerations in anything more than a defensive role in the exposition of the practical reason approach—that role being to dispel the idea that the indebtedness of moral consciousness to upbringing makes it inadmissible *a priori* to speak of *objective* moral values or requirements. So what can we say about the positive merits of the position arrived at by applying these considerations to ethics? How plausible is it to represent the virtuous person's distinctive conception of situations as consisting in "openness to the layout" of a distinctively moral reality?

69. McDowell, *Mind and World,* p. 126.

70. This formulation exploits McDowell's philosophically loaded usage of "environment" and "world" (ibid., Lecture VI). Knowledge of a "world," according to this usage, is something nonhuman animals do not have—even though they may know the way to this or that place, the smell of other friendly or hostile animals, and much else that is of practical importance to them.

CHAPTER

TWO

Practical Wisdom Scrutinized

_____1_____

We saw in Chapter 1 that the idea of an objective, unconditional practical demand—the sort of demand that seems to be recognized by ordinary moral consciousness—has met with a cool reception in modern philosophy. There may be a tradition of more or less artless talk about our individual "sensitivity" (or otherwise) to the presence of moral reasons (for example, about the existence of people whom such reasons motivate "in accord with their proper force and necessity": Chapter 1, §2), but it has been widely believed that any intellectually serious treatment of this kind of talk must seek to make sense of it from a standpoint that can be occupied without yet drawing on the resources of the very sensitivity that is in question. According to the alternative view introduced in Chapter 1, §4, by contrast, this reductive ambition is misguided. Experience should, rather, be understood as consisting in "openness to the layout" of reality—a reality comprising just those facts of which we express awareness when we claim truly to know, for example, *that the door of this room is shut* or that *it would be tactless to mention* x *to* N. So far, I have been concerned to bring out the way in which this alternative view (derived from John McDowell) might disarm opposition to a certain kind of "practical reason" approach to ethics—an approach centred on the idea of a person who is properly responsive to the reasons that there are for acting in a particular way. But I have not yet considered how it might help to bring out any positive attributes of moral experience or consciousness, and that is the task to which I now turn.

In developing his position in *Mind and World,* McDowell draws upon the Kantian idea of experience as issuing from a union of "receptivity" and "spontaneity."[1] With this idea in place, he argues that what gives rise to the "structure of awareness and object"—and hence to the *objectivity* of the things presented to awareness—is a certain combination of passive and active psychological principles. Thus experience involves *submission* to the impact of events or conditions in the world around us; but these events or conditions, as they impinge on us, bring into play a "rationally organized network of capacities for *active* adjustment of one's thinking to the deliverances of experience."[2]

What more can one say—in a naturalistic idiom, as opposed to one taken over from Kantian transcendental idealism—about the way in which these active and passive elements come together? Perhaps something like the following. Human beings are a species to whom it is natural—at the level of "first," or biological, nature—to undergo initiation into a culture; this initiation may or may not have an official, legally regulated aspect, but in any case depends upon learning to talk and to take part in a variety of social *activities,* as envisaged by Wittgenstein under the heading of "language-games."[3] Over time, our participation in these activities—while creating a succession of new contexts for thought and decision—gives rise to a "second," or acquired, nature.[4] This second nature is manifested in behaviour which, though learned, is largely unreflective (like the speaking of a first language); and which, if we do make it into an object of reflection, usually produces in us a sense of inevitability.[5] From one point of view, the

1. "Receptivity" is the capacity of a subject to receive impressions or to be affected by objects; "spontaneity" is the subject's power to know an object through the representations supplied by sensibility. See Howard Caygill, *A Kant Dictionary* (Oxford: Blackwell, 1995), pp. 350, 375.

2. John McDowell, *Mind and World* (Cambridge: Harvard University Press, 1994), p. 29; emphasis added.

3. See Ludwig Wittgenstein, *Philosophical Investigations,* trans. G. E. M. Anscombe (Oxford: Basil Blackwell, 1967), §7: "I shall also call the whole, consisting of language and the actions into which it is woven, the 'language-game.'"

4. McDowell, *Mind and World,* p. 84. Speaking colloquially, someone might say that it was "second nature" to them to act in the way dictated by some inveterate, though arbitrary, personal habit, like that of making tea rather than coffee for breakfast. The "second nature" at issue in the text, however, is not a matter of *mere* habit (that is, of behaviour that could just as well have developed quite differently), but comprises those dispositions which we had to acquire as a condition of entry into a particular social world or "form of life." (I am not suggesting that it is clear where one of these categories ends and the other begins—only that there is a distinction to be drawn here.)

5. For an illustration of the relevant kind of bonding of linguistic and cognitive inevitability, see Wittgenstein, *Philosophical Investigations* §381: "How do I know that this colour is red? It would be an answer to say: 'I have learnt English.'"

dispositions that constitute our second nature are passive, for they are dispositions to be affected in a certain way: ideally, to register the "proper
force and necessity" of reasons for judgement (or for action). However, it is
a feature of human socialization—of the sum of "activities" in the simple
(non-Kantian) sense into which we (humans) have been initiated—that
one is led not just to receive and process sensory input from one's environment, but to recognize the state of the world as imposing rational constraints on one's thinking. And the dawning of this recognition is what
converts us into bearers of (something conceptually affiliated to) Kantian
"spontaneity"—that is, it enlists us as participants in the "*active* adjustment" of thought to world.

2

Let us now try, on this basis, to give a more concrete account of the virtuous agent's "awareness" that a particular act is morally required of her in
some given situation—her awareness that there is a compelling (moral)
reason for her to perform that act. An obvious move is to represent this
awareness as having a moral proposition for its content. Our agent will
then be portrayed as thinking, "I ought to (or: "I must") ϕ";[6] the suggestion is that if she is right, this thought will express awareness of an obligation under which she actually stands. (Or: under which a morally sensitive
person, placed in those circumstances, would take herself to stand.) We can
also build into our representation of her thought a reference to the reasons
which she takes to force this judgement on her: "I must ϕ, because . . ."—
the sentence to be completed by some value-laden observation which, in
the agent's view, leaves her no alternative in the given situation but to ϕ.
Among the simplest examples would be "I must ϕ because I promised to."

It's equally obvious, however, that an agent who is open to this kind of
morally compulsive observation can be assumed also to entertain, from
time to time, a variety of other evaluative thoughts which do not in themselves lead her to conclude that she *must* do anything in particular; they
form, as it were, the milieu from which a sense of moral necessitation may
(or may not) emerge. (Thus the observation "He looks miserable" may or
may not lead a morally competent person to conclude that they *must* do

---

6. I am passing over the question of the actual logical relationship between "ought" and
"must."

something to cheer him up. Only in the light of further information could we judge whether the latter thought would even be a reasonable one—most of us make no attempt to cheer up miserable-looking strangers on public conveyances, for example.) This general receptivity to value and disvalue will not express itself in a continuous flow of practical directives, but the quality of our deliberation will nevertheless vary according to the depth and accuracy of our evaluative awareness. So the ideal deliberator will be one whose moral thinking registers truly or correctly both the evaluatively significant features of her surroundings and the practical demands, such as they may be, which those features exert.[7]

The inventory of distinct species of value—and hence of phenomena with a potential bearing on rational action—is, of course, contested and historically changeable. But the idea of moral consciousness as comprising an evaluative element on one hand and, on the other, a practical element seems sufficiently abstract to be indifferent to such changes. In fact, this looks like something we might be able to accept as a legacy from the Aristotelian account of moral reason that I touched on briefly in Chapter 1. For (i) the appreciation by an agent of particular features of her situation that have *evaluative significance* of the kind relevant to ethics—for example, that person N is shy and sensitive or that every newborn baby in Ethiopia has a notional indebtedness of $\$n$—recalls the cognitive capacity attributed by Aristotle to the possessor of a "moral virtue" (or "virtue of character"): that is, it illustrates the sort of point we expect to be noticed or registered by someone who shows goodness of character in a particular respect, and who can be relied on in the relevant kind of deliberative context to see what needs doing.[8] On the other hand, (ii) the ability to *apply* such awareness to the formation of a rationally defensible view about what should be done "all things considered" recalls the Aristotelian virtue of *phronêsis* or "practical wisdom"—that comprehensive grasp of what matters in life which, by its presence, makes (or reflects) the difference between a patchy approximation to good character and a genuine realization of it.[9]

7. For the contrast between "practical" and "evaluative" components of moral thinking, see David Wiggins, *Needs, Values, Truth: Essays in the Philosophy of Value* (Oxford: Clarendon Press, 1998), pp. 95–96.

8. Compare Aristotle, *Nicomachean Ethics* 1106b18–35, 1109b20–23.

9. Ibid., 1144b30–1145a2. The thought is that without practical wisdom, even the moral qualities a person might actually claim to possess will constitute something less than genuine instances of the virtues they adumbrate. Richard Sorabji ("Aristotle on the Role of Intel-

These Aristotelian ideas have recently found a role in criticizing the consequentialist ambition to reduce practical rationality to the maximization of some single value, and in developing a pluralist alternative to consequentialism. The starting point here is Aristotle's quasi-definitional statement that the function of *phronêsis* is to "deliberate with a view to the good life as a whole" (as opposed to aiming at specific goods such as health).[10] Aristotle subsequently implies that it does this by bringing together, on one hand, a *general insight* into what is of value or worth pursuing and, on the other, insight into the *concrete possibility* of realizing value in particular situations. People who have the quality of *phronêsis* will therefore excel in the construction of "practical syllogisms," which we can think of as verbal representations of the thought expressed in an episode of purposive action.[11] They will have a good eye for the evaluatively significant particular, and so will be among the active supporters of that structure of concern which makes such a particular "significant" (that is, potentially action-guiding) in the first place. (For example, it is by *noticing* rather than overlooking the fact that someone nearby "looks miserable" that one can be led to do something practical in response to general moral

lect in Virtue," in A. O. Rorty, ed., *Essays on Aristotle's Ethics* [Berkeley: University of California Press, 1980], p. 207) explains: "Why should all the virtues go together? And why should we need a conception of the good life in general in order to be virtuous? Why should it not suffice to have a conception of each of the separate virtues? The answer is that the virtues are not separate, for courage is not a matter of facing any danger for any reason but of facing the right danger for the right reason . . . what is right here depends partly on the claims of the other virtues, such as justice, and also on what kind of life we should be aiming at . . . So we cannot know what courage requires of us now without knowing what the good life in general requires."

10. Aristotle, *Nicomachean Ethics* 1140a25–28.

11. See ibid., 1141b8–22, 1146b35–1147a10. On the basis of these and other passages we can think of an Aristotelian practical syllogism as comprising (1) a major premiss "relating to the good," and expressed in a universal statement; (2) a minor premiss "relating to the possible," and expressed in a particular statement; (3) a conclusion that is the verbal equivalent of an action. For example, "Other things being equal, one shouldn't hurt people's feelings; the remark I am about to make would be hurtful; so I won't make it." (For further detail, see M. C. Nussbaum, *Aristotle's De Motu Animalium* [Princeton: Princeton University Press, 1978], Essay 4.) We need not suppose that action whose rational aspect can be so verbalized must actually be accompanied by any inward speech; indeed, a person of good character may be one who typically does the right thing *without* deliberation (compare Aristotle, *Nicomachean Ethics* 1117a17–22), and hence without the subjective sense of acting for reasons.

claims like those of benevolence or compassion—a point which reflects the thought that however good our principles, they will not make us act well unless we are alive to the detail that endows them with relevance to this or that episode of lived experience.) But they will also be capable of a certain critical distance from the materials presented in this way. For in order to move from a mere list of value considerations to a rationally defensible practical decision, an agent needs to be able to hold all these considerations before her mind and act in a way appropriate to their relative importance;[12] and this means that another indispensable constituent of practical wisdom will be good judgement about the relative practical urgency or "saliency" attaching, from moment to moment, to different ethical considerations.[13] Whether or not we are inclined to believe that a "correct" (or even a satisfactory) ordering of value considerations can always be achieved in practice, we must agree, if we are prepared to entertain this picture at all, that the practically wise (or virtuous) agent will at any rate produce an ordering that cannot be improved upon; and that by putting this ordering into effect, she will emerge from the given deliberative situation with as much credit as that situation allows.

The other Aristotelian theme that we must notice in contemporary discussions of practical reason is that of the *uncodifiability* of what the virtuous person knows. What this amounts to is that someone who has been successfully initiated into a culture cannot make explicit all that she has thereby learned about the ethical—either about what counts as an instance of some concept figuring in the common ethical vocabulary, or about how to assess the relative "saliency" of different value considerations bearing on a particular case. McDowell again: "If one attempted to reduce one's

12. Wiggins can appeal here to the integrative function of Aristotelian practical reason: in his paraphrase of *De Anima* 434a5–10 (*Needs, Values, Truth*, p. 258), "A rational animal is one with the power to arbitrate between diverse appearances of what is good and integrate the findings into a unitary practical conception." More literally, such an animal would be "able to make one image out of many."

13. Thus according to Wiggins, "The person of real practical wisdom is the one who brings to bear upon a situation the greatest number of genuinely pertinent concerns and genuinely relevant considerations commensurate with the importance of the deliberative context. The best practical syllogism is that whose minor premise arises out of such a one's perceptions, concerns and appreciations. It records what strikes the person as the *in the situation most salient feature of the context in which he has to act*. This activates a corresponding major premise that spells out the general import of the concern that makes this feature the salient feature in the situation" (*Needs, Values, Truth*, p. 233).

conception of what virtue requires to a set of rules, then, however subtle and thoughtful one was in drawing up the code, cases would inevitably turn up in which a mechanical application of the rules would strike one as wrong—and not necessarily because one had changed one's mind; rather, one's mind on the matter was not susceptible of capture in any universal formula."[14]

Of course, it would be unconvincing to claim that ethical knowledge is *no more* capable of being captured in words than the kind of practical know-how involved in, say, swimming or riding a bicycle; there is plenty of scope in ethics for the development of a verbal "register . . . of our agreements and disagreements about what to do,"[15] as Aristotle recognizes when he says that law—and hence legal justice—is inherently universal.[16] Yet evaluative, and consequently ethical, discourse does seem to display with a special clarity the dependence of our powers of rational communication on a "likemindedness" not of our own making—one that goes beyond any mere collective adherence to a common code of rules. It serves as a reminder that the process from which human intelligence emerges—the construction of a "second" nature on the basis of the first—does not amount to an absolute supersession of "nature" by the "culture" with which it is standardly contrasted: rather, "nature" continues to operate

14. John McDowell, "Virtue and Reason," *Monist,* 62 (1979), pp. 331–350; quotation from p. 336. For a rebuttal of the demand that moral philosophy should enable us to "codify" our knowledge, see also Rosalind Hursthouse, "Applying Virtue Ethics," in Rosalind Hursthouse, Gavin Lawrence and Warren Quinn, eds., *Virtues and Reasons: Philippa Foot and Moral Theory* (Oxford: Clarendon Press, 1995).

15. See Onora O'Neill, *Towards Justice and Virtue: A Constructive Account of Practical Reasoning* (Cambridge: Cambridge University Press, 1996), p. 84. The same point is well made by Samuel Scheffler in *Human Morality* (Oxford: Oxford University Press, 1992), p. 12, where he notes that "[t]he articulation and discussion of [moral] principles within a society provides a shared reference point for the formulation and adjudication of challenges to existing configurations of power and privilege, and to existing social institutions and practices more generally. Ideally, it provides a public standard of accountability to which everyone has access and from which nobody is exempt." I have no wish to dispute any of this.

16. *Nicomachean Ethics* 1137b11–24. The general point that emerges from this important passage—namely, that while (universal) rules may be indispensable to social order, they can be of use to us only by virtue of our ultimately *implicit* (rather than explicit) grasp of what would count as applying them correctly or intelligently in particular cases—sheds light on Aristotle's more famous doctrine that (general) truths of ethics hold only "for the most part" (ibid., 1094b21). The passage should serve as a warning against any facile classification of ethical theories in terms of "universalism versus particularism." See Chapter 3, §4.

within "culture" through those common (though involuntary) patterns of response which allow us to understand one another—when we do—by experiencing one another's signs and gestures as *immediately* meaningful.[17] A smile, for example—considered as part of the expressive repertoire of an adult human being—is deeply embedded in "culture" in regard to the control one can exercise over its style and timing, but the role of that particular facial gesture as a sign of friendly rather than hostile feelings is not merely conventional: the gesture itself, and the way we respond to it, seem to form part of the background against which communicative conventions can take shape.

Our latest borrowing from Aristotle, then, involves the idea of an exemplary state of character such that those in whom it is present can be credited with certain "uncodifiable" reserves of knowledge. Because this state (or disposition)[18] of character as pictured by Aristotle includes and integrates all of the various lower-order dispositions that we call "courage," "self-control," "liberality," and so forth, the cognitive ingredient in these lower-order dispositions will likewise be included and integrated in the cognitive state of his ideally rational agent or "virtuous person." And because the cognitive ingredient in the Aristotelian moral virtues consists in sensitivity to what is required, moment by moment, of someone for whom courage, self-control, liberality, and so forth have taken on the role of *values* to be promoted by his own actions,[19] our updated account can preserve the spirit of Aristotle's ethics by representing the virtuous person's

17. "Immediately" here means "without any intermediary interpretation." See Wittgenstein, *Philosophical Investigations* §201 ("There is a way of grasping a rule which is *not an interpretation*"); see also Gareth Evans and John McDowell, eds., *Truth and Meaning: Essays in Semantics* (Oxford: Clarendon Press, 1976), p. xxii. (And for an application to the problem of "other minds" skepticism of the idea of living bodies as legible surfaces, see Simon Glendinning, *On Being with Others: Heidegger, Derrida, Wittgenstein* [London: Routledge, 1998].)

18. In *The Virtues of Aristotle* (London: Routledge and Kegan Paul, 1986), D. S. Hutchinson notes that for Aristotle a "disposition" *(diathesis)* is simply "an arrangement of the parts of a complex thing" (p. 10). However, the psychical "arrangement" that constitutes an Aristotelian virtue also gives rise to a "disposition" in the modern philosophical sense, that is, to the propensity to behave in a particular way.

19. As part of his specification of the criteria for genuinely virtuous action, Aristotle says that the agent must understand the nature of his act—that is, know that it is just, temperate, or whatever—and must choose it, as such, for its own sake (*Nicomachean Ethics*, 1105a28–33). See further Chapter 4, §1.

uncodifiable knowledge as knowledge about values and about the reasons for action, such as these may be, arising from actual instances of value or disvalue in the world.

It would be natural to think of each of these two kinds of insight—the evaluative and the practical—as open to suggestion from the other: although the balance of emphasis in the story set out above has been tilted towards the passage from value appreciation to decision, it is presumably our capacity (or incapacity) for orientation within the *total* "space" of ethical reasons that will determine whether or not we can be relied on (like Wiggins's "person of practical wisdom" with his flair for supplying the minor premiss of a practical syllogism) to meet a situation with an appropriate selection of value concepts, and so to register its morally "salient" features. But wherever we enter the exchange between enduring moral concern and situational appreciation, practical reasoning will be seen to involve the deployment of forms of *knowledge* which, nevertheless, outrun anything we could "reduce to a set of (mechanically applicable) rules." If it is true that, as ethical cognitivists have argued, our value concepts are not projectible into new contexts except by way of the specifically evaluative "shape" they acquire for us through upbringing,[20] how much more forcibly must this apply to the concept of "the best thing to do in the circumstances"? And yet here too it is possible to become more skilful at finding one's way around.

Despite this uncodifiability, it looks as if the distinctive sphere of interest (or competence) of the virtuous person is at any rate picked out by a certain conceptual repertoire. "Thick" ethical concepts form a recognizable zone within the vocabulary of English and other natural languages.[21] The present attempt to place practical reason within the framework of a "re-

---

20. For this application of the concept of "shape," see Jonathan Dancy, *Moral Reasons* (Oxford: Blackwell, 1993); see also John McDowell, "Non-Cognitivism and Rule-Following," in Steven Holtzman and Christopher Leich, eds., *Wittgenstein: To Follow a Rule* (London: Routledge and Kegan Paul, 1981), pp. 155–156; David Wiggins, "A Neglected Position?" in John Haldane and Crispin Wright, eds., *Reality, Representation and Projection* (Oxford: Oxford University Press, 1993), §§4–6. Revisiting the same point in *Mind and World,* McDowell argues that "[t]o see exercises of spontaneity as natural, we do not need to integrate spontaneity-related concepts into the structure of the realm of law; we need to stress their role in *capturing patterns* in a way of living" (p. 78; emphasis added).

21. For the term "thick" in this sense, see Chapter 1, note 40. The claim about "other natural languages" is not intended as an empirical one, but rests on an application to ethics of the thought that insofar as we hope to communicate at all with speakers of another language, we must proceed on the assumption that some of their vocabulary will turn out to be

laxed naturalism"[22] respects this point, and builds on the ethical "natural-ism" of the 1950s in that it assumes ethics to have some determinate con-tent—a content traceable to the fact that certain things can befall human beings which are liable to benefit or harm them irrespective of any views of their own.[23] The ethical, let us say, pertains to what people learn to value through immersion in a community acquainted with ideas of right, duty, justice, solidarity, and common social or cultural interests extending be-yond the lifetime of the present generation; and the transmission of any qualities regarded by the relevant community as virtues of character would no doubt be one "interest" figuring under the last of these headings. Of course, to the extent that we acknowledge the presence of this social or cul-tural region within the "firmament of values,"[24] we must resign ourselves to a state of affairs in which there will not always be a definite answer to the question whether this or that consideration is an "ethical" (as opposed, say, to an "aesthetic" or an "educational") one.[25] But though this complication may create a penumbra around the edges of the domain of ethical value,

apt for the expression of concerns that we share—an *a priori* point deriving from the con-straints upon "radical interpretation."

22. See McDowell, *Mind and World,* p. 89.

23. See Philippa Foot, *Virtues and Vices* (Oxford: Basil Blackwell, 1978), p. 106 (from the paper "Moral Arguments," first published in 1958): "How exactly the concepts of harm, ad-vantage, benefit, importance, etc. are related to the different moral concepts, such as right-ness, obligation, goodness, duty and virtue is something that needs the most patient investi-gation, but that they are so related seems undeniable, and it follows that a man cannot make his own personal decision about the considerations which are to count as evidence in mor-als." Compare Foot, "Does Moral Subjectivism Rest on a Mistake?," in *Oxford Journal of Legal Studies,* 15 (1995), pp. 1–14: "It is obvious that there are objective, factual evaluations of such things as human sight, hearing, memory and concentration, based on the life-form of our own species. Why, then, does it seem so monstrous a suggestion that the evaluation of the human will should be determined by facts about the nature of human beings and the life of our own species?" (quotation from p. 14).

24. This phrase is taken from J. N. Findlay, *Axiological Ethics* (London: Macmillan, 1970), p. 13.

25. Think for example of concepts employed in the appraisal of persons—say, "servile"—which have a partly aesthetic flavour (the behaviour causes a quasi-physical *displeasure*), but may also be associated with a certain moral attitude (the behaviour offends against demo-cratic or egalitarian values). See also Chapter 1, note 31. As long as we remain faithful to a more or less intuitive conception of the content of "ethics," this kind of indeterminacy seems to favour the view of Bernard Williams that *moral* necessity is not the only kind of *practical* necessity: "A conclusion of practical necessity is the same sort of conclusion whether it is grounded in ethical reasons or not." Williams, *Ethics and the Limits of Philosophy* (London: Fontana Press, 1985), p. 188.

there is still a central area within which certain evaluative concepts (or in linguistic terms, predicates) will clearly fall. And the outcome of our re-working of the Aristotelian character ideal seems to be a conception of the practically wise, or virtuous, person as someone who shows competence (or who excels) in thinking about the subject matter corresponding to this particular group of predicates.

3

What I have just been trying to do is to assemble some observations about the form of our moral reasoning. In keeping with the approach set out in Chapter 1, this has been a phenomenological rather than a "sideways on" or foundationalist exercise. But how satisfactory is it as phenomenology—as a description of the moral "language game" and of the kind of thinking displayed in it?

Some misgivings are expressed in a recent essay by Cora Diamond. This is a piece which I have a special incentive to examine, since it contains a critique of themes from my *Realism and Imagination in Ethics*,[26] which was my first published attempt to think about the subject of the present discussion. Diamond is dissatisfied with what she sees as an excessive emphasis on moral *vocabulary* in the argument of that book, and by implication, in a "practical reason" view of ethics of the kind I have just been expounding. "The presence of moral thought," she writes, "may be reflected in language, not in the use of moral predicates, but in some of the ways we use language about all sorts of not specifically moral things, like death in war, for example, or pulling horses out of deep snow . . . Being about good and evil is a matter of use, not subject matter."[27] Thus we can imagine a community without any words in its language at all for moral *properties,* but still with a keen interest in ethics, which it transmits to the young through story-telling. Even if this community practises no other method of moral education, there seems to be no reason in principle why the stories should need to be driven home by explicit moralizing. Perhaps they have a function which

26. Sabina Lovibond, *Realism and Imagination in Ethics* (Oxford: Basil Blackwell, 1983).

27. Cora Diamond, "Wittgenstein, Mathematics and Ethics: Resisting the Attractions of Realism," in Hans Sluga and David Stern, eds., *The Cambridge Companion to Wittgenstein* (Cambridge: Cambridge University Press, 1996), pp. 226–260; quotation from p. 245. Diamond's examples in this passage are drawn from Virginia Woolf's *To the Lighthouse* and Laura Ingalls Wilder's *The Long Winter.*

makes such moralizing redundant: "If asked why they admire someone, [these people] tell a story about the person in reply."[28] Diamond's thought experiment points to the way in which our conception of the ethical can be impoverished by an undue emphasis on the business of spelling things out.

> The very idea of 'the moral vocabulary' is the idea of a particular group of nouns and adjectives; it expresses the hold on our minds, when we think philosophically about ethics, of bits of language having the form of *judgements* . . . If we want to see what moral thinking is, we need to be able to look away from the case of 'moral propositions', and to free ourselves from the idea that goes easily with exclusive focus on that case, of sentences as about moral subject matter through the presence in them of moral words.[29]

Although the practical reason view as I have developed it here has maintained that the content of moral rationality is uncodifiable, it still looks vulnerable to the criticism contained in the sentence just quoted. For it seems tacitly to endorse the idea of the moral thinker as essentially a problem solver: someone for whom the data of moral awareness exist primarily as a basis for answering questions or reaching decisions. (It pictures such a thinker—often, and revealingly, described as "the moral *agent*"—as needing above all to know such things as "What does honesty require of me here?," or "Given that to disclose my thoughts would be hurtful and to conceal them dishonest, which consideration carries more weight in this case?") The preoccupation of academic moral philosophy with judgement (as opposed, say, to contemplation) is hardly surprising in view of its links with overtly practical disciplines such as law, politics, and government, but this does not diminish the interest of Diamond's complaint, which recalls Wittgenstein's reported distaste for "all the chatter about ethics."[30]

According to the philosophy of Wittgenstein's early period, an account of ethics in terms of practical reason would be doomed either to lead to

28. Ibid.

29. Ibid., pp. 251–252.

30. See Ludwig Wittgenstein et al., "Wittgenstein's Lecture on Ethics," in *Philosophical Review*, 74 (1965), pp. 3–26. Wittgenstein reportedly said in a 1929 conversation: "I regard it as very important to put an end to all the chatter about ethics—whether there is knowledge in ethics, whether there are values, whether the Good can be defined, etc. In ethics one constantly tries to say something that does not concern and can never concern the essence of the matter" (p. 13).

"nonsense" (that is, to a way of speaking devoid of cognitive content); or, if it consisted simply in the *description* of a certain way of speaking, to remain trapped at the level of empirical fact—in which case it would fall under the principle that "*in* [the world] no value exists—and if it did exist, it would have no value."[31] This early position is probably fatal to the attempt to look at ethics from anything but a "religious point of view" (meaning one characterized by a certain subjective state of mind or "heart"—the state by whose changes the world is, so to speak, made to "wax and wane as a whole").[32] If on the other hand there is an activity of "describing language-games"[33] which can be directed towards the practices of capturing truth (or registering value) in our ordinary language, then "description," one might argue, will lose its connotations of unqualified positivism and will become available to the kind of enquiry that seeks to make those practices more transparent to the people engaged in them. In other words: if we conduct such an enquiry not from "sideways on," but as occupants of the space within which truth (or value) manifests itself, then we will find that we can no longer think of the end product of our efforts as a mere inventory of behavioural fact, but must see ourselves as simultaneously engaged in a project of *ideal* description—the description of what happens when participants in a language game get things *right* (by the standards applicable within the game). And one such project would be to study the structure of moral rationality by seeking to reconstruct the characteristic patterns of thought of the virtuous person.

Still, ideal description is answerable to the constraints on description in general.[34] In particular, it is open to criticism if it misrepresents an object by overemphasizing some partial aspect of it to the detriment of our grasp of the whole. Diamond's argument suggests that in order to escape this

31. Ludwig Wittgenstein, *Tractatus Logico-Philosophicus*, trans. D. F. Pears and B. F. McGuinness (London: Routledge and Kegan Paul, 1961), 6.41.

32. Ibid., 6.43. One of Wittgenstein's pupils, M. O'C. Drury, reports him as having said: "I am not a religious man but I cannot help seeing every problem from a religious point of view" (Rush Rhees, ed., *Recollections of Wittgenstein* [Oxford: Oxford University Press, 1984], p. 79).

33. See *Philosophical Investigations* §486.

34. When I speak here of "constraints on description," I am thinking of description orientated to truth or understanding, not to hedonistic or other aesthetic ends—though of course there is a place for these sorts of description too. (This contrast anticipates that between "serious" and "nonserious" utterance, which will receive more direct attention in Part II.)

kind of criticism within moral philosophy, we must offer a more realistic and inclusive account of how the virtuous or morally exemplary person comes to qualify as a bearer of "uncodifiable" knowledge. Instead of portraying this person's distinctive "way of seeing" in terms of an ability to perform correctly, though without formal criteria, the operations already mentioned—projecting value predicates into new contexts, rating alternative practical syllogisms for adequacy to a given deliberative situation—we should think of it, in the first place, as a matter of attunement to *significance*.[35]

By calling this state of attunement "*practical* wisdom," we can duly acknowledge it as the enabling condition of good action. But we also risk obscuring the point that its relevance is by no means limited to a certain more or less clearly demarcated class of circumstances in which we feel called upon to "do something." This point was noted above in §2, where I suggested that even if, for example, our openness to the thought that someone "looks miserable" is integrated with a general disposition to try to act in a way that will alleviate misery, such thoughts can sometimes occur to us in a way that spins quite free of any current plan of action. And it emerges still more clearly when we consider how much intellectual energy can be channeled into the evaluatively revealing representation of human phenomena, not with any practical end in view, but simply to discharge the tension of our involvement with a certain kind of "pointless knowable detail";[36] much modern fiction, with its emphasis on psychological process, seems designed to give a pleasurable imaginary exercise to the capacity for such involvement.[37]

It is easy enough, perhaps, to agree that this capacity represents something "uncodifiable" in our thinking. (The idea that we might attempt to formulate, from a standpoint external to ethics, criteria for the presence of *potential ethical significance* in a train of events looks if anything even more baffling than the corresponding proposal in regard to courage, honesty, or any of our other "thick" ethical properties.) But is it plausible to say that

35. The idea of evaluative "significance" takes on a prominent role in Diamond's critique of consequentialism as a framework for discussion of the moral status of animals. See Cora Diamond, *The Realistic Spirit: Wittgenstein, Philosophy and the Mind* (Cambridge: MIT Press, 1991), pp. 325, 351–352.

36. See McDowell, *Mind and World*, p. 119.

37. This theme is explored in Martha Nussbaum, *Love's Knowledge: Essays on Philosophy and Literature* (Oxford: Oxford University Press, 1990).

what is in question here is still an exercise of moral *rationality?* Can it be credibly maintained that when we hit upon an ethical application for a remark about some "not specifically moral thing" such as Woolf's (and Diamond's) "Twenty or thirty young men were blown up in France,"[38] or when we feel we understand an application of this sort by another speaker, we are moving within a "space of reasons"—a space within which our thinking is constrained "from outside thinking and judging"?[39] Or does this style of communication amount, after all, only to a putting-out of emotional feelers (like Ramsey's "comparing notes"),[40] and so exhibit a "relation between mind and world in which norms are obliterated"?[41]

In order to lay such doubts to rest, the practical reason approach needs to find a way of embracing the idea that moral thought—much of the time at any rate—is like irony or humour in being identifiable not by the occurrence of any special vocabulary, but only through a more holistic appreciation of the spirit of an utterance. Now since that approach conceives of the space of reasons as one mapped out for us by immersion in a culture and by initiation into an array of "language games," the task that lies before it at this point is to convince us of the existence of a form of thought in which the skilled participant, in thinking as she does, is responding to "the reasons that there are"; yet where this responsiveness does not seem to have any close linguistic counterpart in the shape of competence with "a particular group of nouns and adjectives."

38. "Wittgenstein, Mathematics and Ethics," p. 244.

39. McDowell, *Mind and World*, p. 28: "[I]f we are to give due acknowledgement to the independence of reality, what we need is a constraint from outside *thinking* and *judging*, our exercises of spontaneity. The constraint does not need to be from outside *thinkable contents*."

40. See Chapter 1, note 39. Ramsey writes: "Another thing we often do is to discuss what sort of people or behaviour we feel admiration for or ashamed of. E.g., when we discuss constancy of affection, it consists in *A* saying he would feel guilty if he weren't constant, *B* saying *he* wouldn't feel guilty in the least. But that, although a pleasant way of passing the time, is not discussing anything whatever but simply comparing notes." F. P. Ramsey, *Philosophical Papers*, ed. D. H. Mellor (Cambridge: Cambridge University Press, 1990), p. 247; the paper quoted dates from 1925.

41. See John McDowell, "Wittgenstein on Following a Rule," in *Synthese*, 58 (1984), pp. 325–363; quotation from p. 347. The question posed in the text is meant to recapitulate, with reference to Diamond's vision of a form of moral thinking relieved of the baggage of obviously "moral" nouns and adjectives, the familiar objection to ethical intuitionism that it can offer only the verbal trappings and not the substance of an epistemology for ethics. See my *Realism and Imagination in Ethics*, p. 12.

4

One possible parallel[42] for this idea emerges from the record of some 1938 lectures by Wittgenstein, published as the *Lectures and Conversations on Aesthetics, Psychology and Religious Belief*. In these lectures, Wittgenstein is reported as having said that "in real life, when aesthetic judgements are made, aesthetic adjectives such as 'beautiful,' 'fine,' etc. play hardly any role at all . . . The words you use are more akin to 'right' and 'correct' (as these words are used in ordinary speech) than to 'beautiful' and 'lovely.'"[43] In matters of aesthetic appreciation, the knowledge that separates "a person who knows what he is talking about and a person who doesn't"[44] is expressed not by interjections ("Oh! How marvellous!" and the like), but by a language of *satisfaction* and *dissatisfaction* with particular aesthetic effects. Sometimes the simple expression of, say, dissatisfaction may admit of some discursive backing (for example, in music: "Does this harmonize? No, the bass is not quite loud enough"). At others there may be nothing to say but (for example, at the tailor's, discussing the colour or cut of a suit): "too dark," "too loud," "too long" . . . "all right.")[45] Or again there are cases where a sense of "correctness" may not enter into our response at all, but instead we feel ourselves to be in the presence of something "tremendous" (a Beethoven symphony, a Gothic cathedral);[46] perhaps it is one of those works of art that make us "look up."[47]

The text just cited seems to reveal Wittgenstein's thought about value in movement around the fixed point of his contempt for "chatter." In his *Tractatus* period, this attitude had been rationalized by a conception of value as lying outside the "world" constituted by the totality of atomic

---

42. This parallel is noted by Mark Platts (*Ways of Meaning: An Introduction to a Philosophy of Language* [London: Routledge and Kegan Paul, 1979], p. 246).

43. Ludwig Wittgenstein, *Lectures and Conversations on Aesthetics, Psychology and Religious Belief*, ed. Cyril Barrett (Oxford: Basil Blackwell, 1970), p. 3, §8. (It must be remembered that this text was not written by Wittgenstein, but compiled from lecture notes made by his students.)

44. Ibid., p. 6, §17.

45. Ibid., p. 7, §§19, 23. Note that we are not meant to think of the kind of judgement discussed in this passage as "merely subjective." Wittgenstein does not belong to a culture in which decisions about clothing—even to quite a fine degree of detail—fall under the principle that "whatever is going to seem right to me is right."

46. Ibid., p. 8, §23.

47. Ibid., p. 12, §5.

facts, and therefore outside the scope of representation—a view that required no separate treatment of the cases of ethics and aesthetics.[48] Now, as he moves towards the naturalism of his later philosophy, he discovers—at any rate in relation to aesthetics—a different rationale in the phenomenon of what we might call "educated taste" (though as the tailoring example shows, the new considerations are by no means restricted to the traditional "fine arts").[49] At the heart of this different way of thinking we seem to see the paradigm of a conversation which *rests as lightly as possible on the surface* of the speakers' common understanding of effects to be achieved or avoided, and which proceeds by a series of moves calculated to call attention to just those points that may not be obvious (or indeed fully determinate, as with the question of what is "too loud" for suit material) on this common basis. The situation evoked is one in which an "artist" (or craftsman, or performer) faces, or can be seen to have faced, certain technical problems, and where the user or spectator may join the artist—either in a practical way, as at the tailor's, or imaginatively—in assessing the work produced as a better or worse response to those problems.

It is clear that Wittgenstein is aware of the idealization (in a bad sense now: the unrealism) that would be involved in a *theory* of aesthetic judgement as based on imaginative identification with the position of the producer. In practice, the extent to which this sort of talk is current with respect to a particular art form varies historically according to the kind of objects that attract aesthetic interest in a given society.[50] And in any case the *Lectures* belong to that phase of Wittgenstein's thought in which his aim is precisely not to present "theories" but to survey linguistic phenomena and "draw [our] attention to differences"[51]—in this case, to the differ-

48. Wittgenstein, *Tractatus* 6.421: "Ethics and aesthetics are one and the same."

49. Compare Fania Pascal in Rhees, ed., *Recollections of Wittgenstein*, p. 27: "Roy and I went to the Tivoli to see Fred Astaire and Ginger Rogers in *Top Hat*, and in the foyer we met Wittgenstein and Skinner; Wittgenstein spoke of their dancing with lively admiration, with enthusiasm, making detailed and quite serious comments on their technique."

50. See *Lectures and Conversations*, p. 7, §22, with note 2: "You can get a picture of what you may call a very high culture, e.g. German music in the last century and the century before, and what happens when this deteriorates." Again, "a great number of people are highly interested in the detail of a dining-room chair. And then there is a period when a dining-room chair is in the drawing-room and no one knows where this came from or that people had once given enormous thought in order to know how to design it." Later (p. 10, §§33–34) we find Wittgenstein attempting, not wholly convincingly, to represent the word "deterioration" in this context as descriptive rather than pejorative.

51. Ibid., p. 10, §32.

ent forms in which we actually encounter "aesthetic appreciation." Far from maintaining a metaphysical doctrine of the unity of ethics and aesthetics, he now insists on the internal diversity of "aesthetics" itself, construed as the array of phenomena relating to aesthetic judgement ("an immensely complicated family of cases").[52] So it would hardly be in the spirit of this text to assume a "parallel" between aesthetics and ethics on the *a priori* ground that two disciplines concerned with value must have a common intellectual structure. Yet the discussion on aesthetics does call to mind some neglected features of the phenomenology of moral language. One such feature, which may be especially resistant to direct consideration by philosophers, is the difficulty of producing realistic and interesting examples of "moral judgement" for philosophical purposes. Examples of morally significant *situations* suggest themselves readily enough— we know that there is more to this side of life than car-parking and cat-torturing—but when we turn to the discourse supposedly arising out of our imagined cases, we find ourselves faced by something for which Wittgenstein's treatment of aesthetics looks like a direct preparation: that is, we have to admit that while the imagined cases may be such as to prompt a highly sophisticated response in anyone affected by them, the verbal expression of this response may be as minimal as what passes between the tailor and his customer ("Too long," "All right").

This phenomenon can be observed in what I earlier identified (§2) as the intermediate zone between aesthetics and ethics. Two or more people decide, say, to send a message of condolence to another; they compose it carefully with a view to hitting just the right note (sympathetic, consoling, neither too brisk nor too solemn); the aim is to produce, within a certain literary genre, something which is also a gesture of concern and support and which is produced only because such a gesture is felt to be (morally, not aesthetically) required. The choice between alternative forms of words within the letter may give rise to little or no explicit discussion ("What about 'distressed'?" . . . "All right"), but the exchanges needed in order to reach agreement on these points presuppose a "whole environment" or "way of living."[53]

The same is arguably true of a good deal of conversation about ethics "proper," at any rate when such conversation is removed from its professional setting and directed towards personal ends such as clarifying

52. Ibid.
53. Ibid., pp. 7, §20; 11, §35.

one's attitude to something or facilitating a particular decision. For example, consider the following conversation schema: "Had you thought of just . . . ?"—"Oh, I couldn't possibly do that"—"No, I suppose not." The second speaker (B) offers no reason why the other's (A's) suggestion is unacceptable. Their common history of "immersion" in a moral culture makes that superfluous. Nevertheless, the exchange is not useless for purposes of moral guidance since it leads A to manifest a view of her own suggestion—that is, as just worth making but not worth defending in argument—which, if sincere, gives B a certain very precise insight into the way A takes that culture to impinge on the problem at hand. (Perhaps B could not have predicted that A would make the suggestion at all—or on the other hand that she would *not* go so far as to defend it.)

If we had to describe the nature of the "family resemblance" now emerging between aesthetic and ethical thinking, we might begin by saying that some conversations about ethics seem to share the quality of *intimacy* that is necessary for successful communication about such things as the cut of a suit or the performance of a string quartet. The term "intimacy" suggests itself because the activity just singled out for attention within each of these "language games"—the disclosure of a sense of (something akin to) correctness or incorrectness about a particular item of human expression—proceeds against the background of an essentially shared evaluative environment.

This intimate character is more clearly visible in another kind of conversation noticed by Wittgenstein, this time as evidence against the reduction of aesthetics to psychology: "There is a 'Why?' to aesthetic discomfort not a 'cause' to it. The expression of discomfort takes the form of a criticism and not 'My mind is not at rest' or something. It might take the form of looking at a picture and saying 'What's wrong with it?'"[54] The most striking idea that Wittgenstein arrives at about the resolution of this kind of discomfort is that if an interlocutor undertakes to explain it for us (or to relieve it by supplying the word we are looking for, or the thought at the back of our mind), then "the criterion for it being the one that was in your mind is that when I tell you, you agree . . . Explanation here is like an utterance supplied by another person—like teaching him to cry."[55]

---

54. Ibid., pp. 14–15, §19.

55. Ibid., p. 18, §37 and §40, note 5; compare with the last sentence *Philosophical Investigations* §244.

Here too we have a pattern that seems to be repeated in ethics. Questions such as "Why don't I like *N*?" (or "Why don't I feel OK about having killed that useless old woman?") resemble "What's wrong with this picture?," on one hand, in sounding like fragments of soliloquy, but they also share the property of being readable as invitations to someone else to supply the explanation that will be acceptable to us. To read them in this second way is to take them as signifying our openness to the possibility of adopting another person's thought as the more adequate expression of some inchoate thought of our own. Even if the case in which we formulate such a question with a view to answering it for ourselves is empirically more typical than that in which we make it public, the question itself creates a logical space which can in principle be filled by an *acceptable answer originating elsewhere*. And the fact that not just any answer will be acceptable suggests that we take the question to belong to a discourse which, however sparing in the use of distinctive "nouns and adjectives," is nevertheless governed by the norm of responsiveness to "the reasons that there are"—reasons which, since they are "there" to be appreciated, can be a matter for cooperative enquiry.[56]

The effect of Diamond's criticism, then, has been to make us substitute a more inclusive conception of the virtuous person's "uncodifiable" knowledge for the relatively crude, vocabulary-centred conception with which we began. This revised conception appeals—like its predecessor, but more ambitiously—to the idea of a *common evaluative culture* or way of life that would give some determinate content to the perceptions and intentions of the virtuous. In the next chapter I shall move on to consider a certain evolution, within the practical reason approach, in the way we are asked to understand the psychological basis of this determinacy. According to the classical (Platonic–Aristotelian) account, as we shall see, it depends on the realization in individuals of a distinctive psychological *form* or structure—on the fact that the "soul" of a just (or brave, or temperate . . .) person is arranged or disposed in a particular way, which naturally finds expression in the corresponding kind of behaviour. But a terminology in which in-

---

56. We need not try to specify, in abstraction from any actual form of moral life, what the answers to our sample questions ought to look like. In our own moral "language game," the question "Why don't I like *N*?" (or, "Other people like *N*—why don't I?") may well elicit some moral adjectives. In the community of Diamond's thought experiment, by contrast, it presumably calls for a story about *N* that will prompt the reply: "Yes, that's it." In this "language game," telling the story *constitutes* giving the reason.

ward (psychological) form is contrasted with its outward (behavioural) expression is no longer the obvious choice, in this context, for the practical reason view. Instead, the notion of form can be replaced by that of *order,* the kind of order that we try to impose on our own behaviour insofar as we take ourselves to be answerable to norms of correctness; and this change of perspective can open up our conception of the virtuous person to the influence of modern discussions about norm-governed *practices,*[57] thus helping us to a more complete acceptance of the phenomenon of morality as "part of our natural history."[58]

57. As an interim measure, the term "norm-governed" is used here (in preference to the more familiar "rule-governed") in order to avoid confusion with the idea of a "mechanically applicable rule" introduced in §2 above—that is, the idea of an algorithm or decision procedure that would remove the need to exercise one's own judgement in relation to particular cases. The thought sketched in §2 was that while "rules" in the informal sense of norms are often capable of more explicit interpretation, and so of transformation into something *more like* "rules" in the sense of algorithms, this process inevitably comes to an end somewhere.

58. See Wittgenstein, *Philosophical Investigations* §25.

THREE

Form, Formlessness, and Rule-Following

1

The position developed in Chapters 1 and 2 was based on a general account of experience which I described as "quietist"—a label suggested by certain secondary writings on the later philosophy of Wittgenstein. The interest of this account for ethics, or so I have suggested, is that if we bring moral judgement within its scope we can think of particular moral judgements—when they are true rather than false—not just as bringing us into harmony with a certain consensus of feeling or opinion, but as disclosing to us the "layout" of a certain domain of reality, namely, the moral domain.

This move, if successful, has consequences for our conception of the "virtuous person"—the ideal type who provides the point of reference for the "practical reason" view of ethics which I began to construct in Chapter 1. It allows us, in good conscience, to take the step to which empiricist ethical theory traditionally raises an objection—that is, the step from observing that (at least some) moral thought and discourse has the phenomenological features we associate with the pursuit of truth, to regarding such discourse as (indeed) a potential source of *knowledge*, where "knowledge" is (by definition) of how things are in the (real) world.

I then went on (in Chapter 2) to picture moral knowledge, in neo-Aristotelian fashion, as an uncodifiable "practical wisdom,"[1] consisting in the intelligent appreciation both of specific value features in concrete ("lived") situations (features that may be either positive or negative—though per-

---

1. As I explain in the text below, the word "uncodifiable" is to be read in the spirit of the concession made in Chapter 2, §2—namely, as not implying that it is impossible *even to get started* on the business of explicit generalization.

haps the negative features are apt to make a livelier claim on our attention), and also of the relative practical importance of the features present in any particular case. But I acknowledged, too, the force of an objection (Cora Diamond's) to any version of this picture that binds moral understanding too tightly to the use of a characteristic set of "nouns and adjectives" with "moral" content. In response to that objection, I proposed to give to the idea of the virtuous person's uncodifiable knowledge a maximally inclusive interpretation.[2] On this more inclusive view, such knowledge would be expressed not only in the kind of form represented, for example, by the major and minor premises of the practical syllogism—I mean by general principles about what is to be pursued or avoided, and

---

2. I have persisted, in the present discussion, in picturing ethics as one more domain within which a "mind" encounters a "world." In opposition to this picture, Diamond ("Wittgenstein, Mathematics and Ethics: Resisting the Attractions of Realism," in Hans Sluga and David G. Stern, eds., *The Cambridge Companion to Wittgenstein,* pp. 226–260, at p. 231) cites material from Wittgenstein's 1939 "Lectures on the Foundations of Mathematics" which specifically warns against the idea of mathematical propositions as describing a "mathematical reality." (Compare also Ludwig Wittgenstein, *Remarks on the Foundations of Mathematics,* ed. G. H. von Wright, R. Rhees, and G. E. M. Anscombe, trans. G. E. M. Anscombe (Oxford: Basil Blackwell, 1978), Part I, Appendix II, §§1–2, where we read that "the mathematician is not a discoverer: he is an inventor.") While these remarks are obviously integral to a train of thought aimed at establishing the natural, or constructed, character of the practice of mathematics, the price of treating them as the last word on usage in this area is a high one, namely—if we still wish to speak of mathematical *truth*—a severance, in relation to mathematics, of the internal connection between "truth" and "reality." It may be preferable, therefore—whether or not this view would have been accepted by Wittgenstein himself—to see his warning as representing a certain stage in a dialectic which it might subsequently, and on the basis of a more perfect "quietism," be possible to transcend. Having inoculated ourselves against the misleading spatial imagery of a "realm of numbers" ("Wittgenstein, Mathematics and Ethics," p. 236)—the Platonic *noêtos topos* of *Republic* 509d—and grasped that "[t]he realm with which we are concerned, when we work out mathematical propositions, is found by considering their application" ("Wittgenstein, Mathematics and Ethics," p. 236), might we not (on the resulting, more enlightened intellectual basis) be able to speak of mathematical "reality" in the same spirit of metaphysical innocence in which Diamond envisages that we might come to speak of mathematical propositions as being *about numbers* (ibid., pp. 235–236)? "Reality" is undoubtedly a candidate for the illusory role of "super-concept" (see Ludwig Wittgenstein, *Philosophical Investigations,* trans. G. E. M. Anscombe (Oxford: Basil Blackwell, 1967), §97, and compare ibid., §402); but Wittgenstein is also capable of putting it to a "humble" use, as at *On Certainty,* ed. G. E. M. Anscombe and G. H. von Wright, trans. Denis Paul and G. E. M. Anscombe (Oxford: Basil Blackwell, 1969), §66: "I make assertions about reality."

by particular observations about the incidence of value properties—but equally in that feeling for ethical "significance" which enables us to detect, or invent, ethical *uses* for bits of language not marked as ethical by any special vocabulary.

This adjustment does not make it any harder to agree, as I was ready to do in Chapter 2, that explicit rules or principles of conduct have a place in communal life: the fact that moral thinking extends beyond the confines of moral vocabulary does not show that *all* such thinking displays the kind of inexplicitness captured by the "Too loud . . . All right" model (Chapter 2, §4). What it does is to reveal the *magnitude of the role* which our practical reason view will have to assign to a common culture or "form of life" in sustaining the inexplicit element in moral understanding.

We might think here of Wittgenstein's much-discussed pupil–teacher scenario at *Philosophical Investigations* §185, where the problem is to understand how the teacher's intentions can "run ahead" of any actual series of examples and determine correct and incorrect ways of obeying the command "add 2" at *any* point in the series of natural numbers. Reverting to the subject of rules at the end of Part I of the *Investigations,* Wittgenstein writes:

> 692. Is it correct for someone to say: 'When I gave you this rule, I meant you to . . . in this case'? Even if he did not think of this case at all as he gave the rule? Of course it is correct. For 'to mean it' did not mean: to think of it. But now the problem is: how are we to judge whether someone meant such-and-such?—The fact that he has, for example, mastered a particular technique in arithmetic and algebra, and that he taught someone else the expansion of the series in the usual way, is such a criterion.

Applying this thought to the earlier scenario, we can say: what makes it the case that the teacher *means* his pupil to write "1002" and not "1004" after "1000" is not that he thought in advance about what should happen at that point, but that the exercise is one involving the use of signs with a determinate meaning.[3] It is because *there is* a technique of addition with a "usual way" of being taught that *there is* something which the teacher, as

---

3. "Determinate" here can be explained by reference to phenomena such as that of mathematicians' "not coming to blows" over the solution to "1000 + 2," which for this purpose are "bedrock"—that is, they should not be seen as consequences of some other, underlying kind of fact.

an exponent of this technique, means by the sign "+." The technique provides a context within which he can rightfully say, after the event, that the "1004" continuation was not what he intended.[4] (Of course, we have to abstract here from the teacher's possible defectiveness as a practitioner of arithmetic—a factor which, if sufficiently pronounced, will eventually cast doubt on the claim that he "meant" anything in particular. But the choice of an example as straightforward as that of "adding 2" makes this possibility a merely academic one.)

These considerations (about the grounding of determinate meanings or intentions in a common practice) would already need to be built into our account of practical wisdom even if we were to think of that quality in the limited way criticized by Diamond—that is, as consisting in mastery of a certain list of concepts. If that conception were adequate, we could formulate our Wittgensteinian thought by saying, for example: the moral educator need not have entertained, in advance, the thought that a particular situation would or would not count as "unfair"; but it might still be correct to say that she intends her pupils, if faced with just that situation, to see it as unfair. The correctness of this claim might be something that we could read off from the "technique," or practice, of using the word "unfair" in moral thinking. If on the other hand, as Diamond suggests, the property of "belonging to ethics" accrues to an utterance not from its vocabulary but from the application given to it, then this should lead us to a rather different view of what it is that corresponds, in ethics, to the arithmetical techniques invoked in Wittgenstein's "1004" case—that is, of what makes it correct to say that one person *intends* another to find certain features of a situation ethically "salient" or significant. It should lead us to picture the relevant discursive practice as a way of talking (and listening) through which one manifests a certain orientation towards life in general.

The point I want to stress here, and which I think is well displayed by the "Diamond amendment" to our practical reason view, is the comparatively superficial character of *explicit reason-giving* as an aid to finding our way around within a "space of reasons." As an illustration, take the scenario at

---

4. Compare *Philosophical Investigations* §289, "To use a word without justification does not mean to use it without right": so here with the teacher's declarations about what he did or did not mean the student to do. (He has no *justification* for saying he did not mean the student to write "1004," if a justification would have to consist in his having, at some particular moment, thought of the "1004" continuation and made a mental note that it was excluded.)

the bottom of p. 33 of *Philosophical Investigations* (not a numbered section): "Someone says to me: 'Show the children a game.' I teach them gaming with dice, and the other says 'I didn't mean that sort of game.' Must the exclusion of the game with dice have come before his mind when he gave me the order?" This is an ethical (or perhaps educational) application of the principle from §692 that "'to mean it' [does] not mean: to think of it." (The other adult *did* mean gaming with dice to be excluded, although he didn't think of it.)[5] An intelligent, or "practically wise," response to "Show the children a game" will interpret this request in the spirit in which it would be made by someone who knows the layout of the space of ethical reasons—that is, such a response will interpret it as being tacitly accompanied by any exclusions or qualifications that *there is reason* to make (taking into account the particular characteristics of the children, the surroundings, and so on). The implication is that there is no reason why we should not regard the production of an inexplicit response to perceived value or disvalue[6]—in common with the use of an overtly "moral" *proposition*—as standing in a rational, or norm-governed, relation to the world.

2

"Quietism" in philosophy, as described so far, has had both a negative and a positive side. Negatively, it has entailed a rejection of the attempt to view the mind–world encounter from "sideways on," and hence to make this encounter a topic for metaphysical theory.[7] Positively, it has entailed an ac-

---

5. Stephen Williams has reminded me that tacit exclusions can sometimes be problematic for reasons which, given a certain context of utterance, have nothing to do with any tendency to hinder effective communication: for example, "Everyone in Argentina plays polo."

6. See again Ludwig Wittgenstein, *Lectures and Conversations on Aesthetics, Psychology and Religious Belief*, ed. Cyril Barrett (Oxford: Basil Blackwell, 1970), p. 10, §32: "An immensely complicated family of cases [of aesthetic judgement] is left, with the highlight—the expression of admiration, a smile or a gesture, etc."

7. Note that it is a specifically metaphysical project that is rejected here, not the very possibility of thinking theoretically about the nature of our response to the world around us. To object to the latter would be to write off a wealth of intellectual undertakings ranging from, say, research into the physiology of perception to studies of the construction of the "gaze" in film theory—a move that would be wholly unmotivated, since none of these undertakings needs to picture the theorist as working from anywhere but within the relevant category of perceiving subjects. Compare Wittgenstein, *Philosophical Investigations* §121: "[Orthography] deals with the word 'orthography' among others without then being second-order."

ceptance of our actual location within a "space" which is in any case—that is, even without any input from metaphysics—such as to accommodate our legitimate interest in "how thought relates to reality," namely, the interest we display when we think critically about whether certain propositions are true.

Quietism in its particular application to ethics exhibits the same two aspects. On its negative side, it rejects the idea of ethics as aiming at a fully autonomous theoretical account of how rational moral judgement tracks the changing state of the world—an account which, if placed at the conscious disposal of individual agents, would be sufficient on its own (without the support of any power of intuitive "judgement") to tell them how to act from moment to moment. This rejection is summed up in the thesis that the knowledge possessed by the virtuous person is uncodifiable.

But to be a quietist about ethics is also to invoke the positive image of the *bearer* of this ideal, though uncodified, knowledge. In effect, it is to install this image in the place that might otherwise have been occupied by ethical theory. First it transpires that there is something we *cannot* do: in this case, to formulate explicitly the precise emotional and behavioural patterns we expect to see in someone conforming to the rationalist character ideal for ethics. (Again the point can be more carefully stated, bearing in mind the actual existence of explicit rules and principles: what we cannot do is to formulate these in such a way that their correct uptake owes nothing to any substratum of *tacit* likemindedness on the part of our audience.) But this reflection on our own incapacity is then displaced by the thought that what we have admitted we cannot make (fully) explicit are not after all "mere" ideals, but are presented to us through actual persons—individuals whose cognitive powers are no different in kind, but at most superior in quality, to our own. The uncodifiability of what is apparent to the morally exemplary person is offset, according to this different (and positive) line of thought, by the endless availability of real-life material from which the spirit of their thinking can be reconstructed (even if the work of reconstruction proceeds, as it often seems to in practice, partly under the impetus of negative *feelings* such as angry or critical reactions to perceived moral obtuseness). And this state of affairs—I mean the availability of right, or good-enough, answers to at least some moral questions—can draw us towards a conception of moral rationality that dispenses more or less completely with general principles and affirms instead, in the words of Jonathan Dancy, the "authority of the present case."[8] In fact, it almost seems designed to prepare us for a return to the opening phase of Nietzsche's "History of an Error," the "relatively sensible, simple, convincing" set-up in which certain people (in their own eyes—but not only there) just "*are* the truth."[9]

Classical rationalist ethics seems already to contain within itself the positive and negative moments just described. It responds to the boundlessness of its subject matter, and to the negative or pessimistic epistemological attitude which might flow from this, by an appeal to the notion of *form*. McDowell puts the point with reference to "form" as an object of intellectual aspiration, transcending the confusion of experience but qualified (if only we could grasp it) to help us overcome that confusion. He writes:

> It seems plausible that Plato's ethical Forms are, in part at least, a response to uncodifiability: if one cannot formulate what someone has come to know when he cottons on to a practice, say one of concept-application, it is natural to say that he has seen something . . . The remoteness of the Form of the Good [in Books VI and VII of Plato's *Republic*] is a metaphorical version of the thesis that value is not in the world, utterly distinct from the dreary literal version which has obsessed recent moral philosophy. The point of the metaphor is the colossal difficulty of attaining a capacity to cope clear-sightedly with the ethical reality which *is* part of our world.[10]

8. See Jonathan Dancy, *Moral Reasons* (Oxford: Blackwell, 1993), p. 65. The thing to which "authority" is attributed in this passage seems to be (whatever we are disposed to accept as) an *appraisal* of this or that "present case" that does justice to the particular configuration of evaluative features to be found in it, rather than applying a rule abstracted from some previous case in which some of the same features have occurred, but in different surroundings which (as Dancy would insist) may change their significance.

9. See Friedrich Nietzsche, *Twilight of the Idols and The Antichrist*, trans. R. J. Hollingdale (Harmondsworth: Penguin, 1968), p. 40. Nietzsche's "How the 'Real World' at Last Became a Myth: History of an Error" begins: "1. The real world, attainable to the wise, the pious, the virtuous man—he dwells in it, *he is it*. (Oldest form of the idea, relatively sensible, simple, convincing. Transcription of the proposition 'I, Plato, *am* the truth.')" For the moment, it will be enough just to take Nietzsche's hint that this claim is not guaranteed an earnest reception.

10. John McDowell, "Virtue and Reason," *Monist*, 62 (1979), pp. 331–350; quotation from

Suppose we read this passage against the background of Plato's middle-period conception of form as both *immanent* and *transcendent* with respect to the particulars that instantiate it—present in them insofar as they can be credited with a certain character, but never fully submitting to the "effort" of particulars to be what the form itself is.[11] We can then take McDowell's words as directing us, here at any rate, to that part of Plato's metaphorical scheme in which ethical form is represented as *transcending* the actual state of understanding of any human being. This emphasis promotes a sense of the "colossal difficulty" of ethical life, and may lead one to picture the way in which the mind would have to engage with ethical form in order to seek relief from this difficulty as involving something akin to a "religious conversion."[12] By contrast, an emphasis on the idea of ethical form as *immanent*—that is, actually realized—in the emotional and intellectual responses of human beings to their experience favours a conception of ethical life, not indeed as free from difficulty, but not as beyond our grasp either; certainly not as putting up such resistance to human intelligence that the latter could not set a standard of excellence in regard to it.

The availability, within a philosophy of ethical form, of these different choices of emphasis is what allows Aristotle to develop Plato's ethics in the direction of a more self-contained enquiry into the immanent form of the virtuous "soul"—the form actually present in it or realized by it.[13] For

p. 347. McDowell takes up the same theme in relation to Aristotle in his "Deliberation and Moral Development in Aristotle's Ethics" (in Stephen Engstrom and Jennifer Whiting, eds., *Aristotle, Kant and the Stoics: Rethinking Happiness and Duty* [Cambridge: Cambridge University Press, 1996], pp. 19–35), where he writes: "Talk of responsiveness to the specifics of situations, in the reading of Aristotle that I am urging, *functions instead of a certain kind of generality* that modern commentators tend to hanker after, in an account of how deliberation with a view to doing well might work" (quotation from p. 28; emphasis added). The Aristotelian (as distinct from the Platonist) influence on McDowell's account of moral rationality is, however, already in evidence in "Virtue and Reason," §§3–5.

11. For examples of the language of "effort" or "striving" in this connection, see Plato, *Phaedo* 74d, 75a. (The term "middle-period" in the text refers to the conventional chronology of Plato's writings, though Julia Annas has recently questioned whether this has any objective basis: see her *Platonic Ethics, Old and New* [Ithaca: Cornell University Press, 1999], chap. 1.)

12. McDowell, "Virtue and Reason," p. 347.

13. It is worth stressing that what is in question here is a difference of emphasis rather than an outright theoretical conflict. Hence we should not be dismayed by the suggestion that Aristotle's ethics sometimes displays a "Platonizing" tendency: see, for example, Chapter 5, note 22 and accompanying text.

Plato in the *Republic*, such an enquiry is precisely not "self-contained" because in order to cultivate in ourselves the character ideal of justice, we must model our souls not on any paradigm furnished by the existing, corrupt, state of communal life but on one located in the "heaven" of dialectical speculation.[14] So if we set on one side the moral demands already implicit in the activity of dialectic (which Plato clearly takes to be pretty well known to us, even in advance of bringing the philosophical project to completion), the question of what form the human soul should ideally exhibit becomes no less problematic than the nature of the "heavenly" paradigm itself, and hence ultimately no less so than the Form of the Good in all its "colossal difficulty."[15] Aristotle, on the other hand, believes that the purpose of studying politics—and by implication, ethics—is "not knowledge but action" (especially action in the public domain).[16] It is therefore appropriate for him to place at the centre of these disciplines the *visibly attainable* ideal of a mind so ordered that it can give correct (or, anyway, maximally acceptable) answers to questions arising in moral and political practice. The ideal in question can be described as "visibly" attainable because when Aristotle reminds us of the authority we attribute to those who possess practical wisdom (who appreciate the "ultimate and particular" features of situations, "have the eye of experience," "see aright," and so forth),[17] he does not envisage or leave room for the protest that we do not know who these people are: *that* there are such people is supposed to be a feature of everyone's social experience, and if so, then it must be possible to point to some of them.

3

As we saw earlier (Chapter 1, §2), J. L. Mackie cites Plato's theory of forms as the inspiration for all subsequent objectivist positions in European ethical theory. In fact, it is probably apparent by now that the development I have been tracing—the attempted reconstruction of an ethics of practical reason on the basis of considerations about the virtues—is more immedi-

14. Plato, *Republic* 592b.

15. That the problem glimpsed at this point is a real one will be suggested in Chapter 9, §4.

16. Aristotle, *Nicomachean Ethics* 1095a5–6. A few lines before (1094b10–11) we are told that ethics is a subdivision of politics (*politikē tis*—"a kind of enquiry relating to the *polis*").

17. Ibid., 1143a32–34; 1143b11–14.

ately indebted to Aristotle's predominantly immanent conception of ethical form than to the transcendent conception associated with Plato. Still, the main idea before us is that of moral upbringing as aiming at the establishment of a certain character structure: a structure such that the person in whom it is present will know (insofar as anyone ever does) how they should act "occasion by occasion,"[18] even if they cannot state any fully explicit, exceptionless principle from which, on a given occasion, the relevant bit of knowledge is deduced. And we may find that this idea is best understood as emerging from a unitary (Platonic–Aristotelian) tradition of thought organized by the contrast between "form" and its absence.

The intellectual value claimed for Platonic "form" lies in its ability to provide the mind with an object of thought which is itself definite (in that it is capable of precise definition) and which can therefore enter into the formulation of definite thoughts; these thoughts, unlike the flow of experience within which this or that intelligible character is presented in a "confused" manner through its instances,[19] are available for communication and (at least in principle) for definitive evaluation as true or false. However, the philosophical exploitation of a contrast between *form* and *formlessness* does not originate with Plato but has an older source in the mathematical thought of the Pythagorean school, of which Aristotle sees Plato as "in most repects a follower."[20] The curious "table of opposites," a list of ten pairs of opposed principles recognized (again according to Aristotle)[21] by certain members of this school, raises two main points of interest for our purposes: first, the principles that head the list are those of "limit" *(peras)* and the "unlimited" or indefinite *(apeiron);* and second, the table manifestly contains one "good" and one "bad" column, so that each term appearing in it carries a positive or a negative value.[22]

18. McDowell, "Virtue and Reason," p. 347.

19. See Plato, *Republic* 524c, and compare ibid., 473a (speech, *lexis*, has more of a grip on truth than action, *praxis*, does); also *Parmenides* 132bc (thought must be of some *one* real character common to the many particulars which instantiate that character).

20. See Aristotle, *Metaphysics* 987a30.

21. Ibid., 986a22–986b4.

22. The full table runs:

Limit	Unlimited
Odd	Even
One	Many
Right	Left

Within the evaluative context of the table, the *apeiron* signifies not just the numerically indeterminate but, more generally, that which lacks a definite character and is to that extent defective or imperfect. It thus provides Plato, and subsequently Aristotle, with a negative point of reference in the philosophy of value as well as in logic. Plato argues through Socrates in the *Philebus* that beauty results from the submission of disorganized matter to determinate form or order, or from a successful "blending of the unlimited with the limited,"[23] and in the *Gorgias* that it is "order" and "arrangement" (*kosmos* and *taxis*) that make each thing—including mind or "soul," *psuchê*—good of its kind;[24] Aristotle agrees that the main species of the beautiful are "order, symmetry and definiteness."[25] And since both philosophers incorporate into their own enquiries the traditional Greek question of how *to kalon* (the beautiful, fine, or noble) can be brought into being in human life, they find it natural to give the partly aesthetic categories of form and formlessness a psychological application. In relation to human beings they posit, on one hand, an indefinite or merely potentially form-bearing condition which precedes the advent of "character" (*êthos);* on the other, a perfectly formed or finished condition which moral (*êthikê*) upbringing has to realize; and finally a process which mediates between these two by working to impose the (ideal) form of human character on the raw

Male	Female
Resting	Moving
Straight	Curved
Light	Darkness
Good	Bad
Square	Oblong

W. D. Ross (*Aristotle's Metaphysics* [Oxford: Clarendon Press, 1924], vol. 1, p. 150) notes that not all of the ten pairs of principles were equally essential to the Pythagorean system, the first two pairs being the dominant ones; also that other pairs were sometimes included in the list. For the mathematical reasoning behind some of the less obvious inclusions, see F. M. Cornford, *Plato and Parmenides* (London: Routledge and Kegan Paul, 1939), Introduction, chap. 1.

23. Plato, *Philebus* 26b.

24. Plato, *Gorgias* 506d–507a. E. R. Dodds (*Plato: Gorgias* [Oxford: Clarendon Press, 1959], p. 333) comments that "[t]his . . . completes in a positive sense Socrates' refutation of the thesis that the Good is Pleasure . . . What is important is the recognition that the Good is an *organizing* principle which makes a living creature or an artefact capable of fulfilling its function."

25. Aristotle, *Metaphysics* 1078b1.

material presented in any particular individual.[26] This process can be described as one of *ethical formation.*

Plato and Aristotle are in broad agreement as to how individuals are sensitized to the demands of ethics.[27] Both explain this process by reference to the redirection of desire, and so of subjectively experienced practical concern. Plato says that *mousikê,* culture, must "terminate in desire for *to kalon,*"[28] and that acquiring an intuitive love (or hatred) for the right objects is a necessary preliminary to the exercise of reason-based evaluative judgement;[29] Aristotle treats the instinctual desire for pleasure as the key fact around which ethical upbringing must be organized, the aim being to get the learner to pursue pleasure (and perhaps more important, to avoid displeasure) in appropriate, culturally mediated ways.[30] And both think of the result aimed at as one in which the learner's evaluative responses (or, eventually, judgements) come to be determined by (a) *logos.* The word *"logos"* in its abstract, philosophical usage is standardly translated "reason," but seems also to retain some association with the mathematical concept of ratio or proportion. For Aristotle especially, virtuous action is action in proportion to the occasion:[31] thus the virtuous person's anger or fear will be in proportion to the objectively fearful or anger-provoking features of his situation; it will not be disfigured by anything inappropriate in respect of degree, occasion, or object.

The *logos,* or rational principle, to which correct feelings and choices will conform resembles a mathematical ratio in that it has no spatiotemporal location but can be instantiated in countless different behavioural or psychological episodes: its presence is what makes each episode into an ex-

26. This tripartite account of the structure of Platonic–Aristotelian ethics is drawn from Alasdair MacIntyre, *After Virtue: A Study in Moral Theory* (London: Duckworth, 1981), p. 52.

27. *"Broad* agreement": a more detailed discussion would perhaps need to consider their different attitudes to the role of tradition in moral rationality.

28. Plato, *Republic* 403c5–6.

29. Ibid., 401d5–402e4.

30. Aristotle, *Nicomachean Ethics* 1104b30–1105a16; and compare *Metaphysics* 1029b5–8: "*Just as in conduct our work is to start from what is good for each and make what is good in itself good for each,* so it is our work to start from what is more intelligible to oneself and make what is intelligible by nature intelligible to oneself" (trans. W. D. Ross, in Jonathan Barnes, ed., *The Complete Works of Aristotle* (Princeton: Princeton University Press, 1984), vol. 2, p. 1625; emphasis added).

31. Aristotle, *Nicomachean Ethics* 1106b5–1107a2.

emplar of the kind of response demanded by the relevant moral virtue. It can also be present in an individual soul, insofar as the latter is educable or "has reason" *(logon echei)*. Once installed there through upbringing, it ensures that where there was previously nothing but a pool of psychic energy of a certain kind (say, the disposition to retaliate against injury), there will now be a disposition to manifest that energy in an ethically informed way.[32] Hence to undergo formation is to come to have in (the desiderative part of) one's soul the same structure—the same *logos* or system of *logoi*—as anyone else who exemplifies correct judgement (or who "*is* the truth," as in §2 above) in regard to ethics. And when the virtue of an individual agent is expressed in action, it is this structure that is externalized, or embodied, in a concrete course of events: a certain *logos* is, as it were, communicated by the "soul" of the agent to the socially significant "matter" that will be reorganized by his act.[33]

4

The idea that in order to qualify as a practically rational person, I need to have my mind (or "soul") informed by the same *logos* that informs the minds of other such persons, or to come to instantiate a *universal* form or type, will take on a renewed importance in Part III when we come to consider certain recent ("postmodernist") moves in regard to the opposition of "sameness" and "difference." For the moment, though, the interest of this idea lies in the implication that *logos* can serve as a counterweight to the uncodifiability of the virtuous person's knowledge—the knowledge

32. In the case of retaliation, the relevant disposition will be the virtue of good temper, *praotês*, which is a "mean relating to anger" (ibid., 1125b26).

33. J. L. Stocks ("*Logos* and *Mesotês* in the *de Anima* of Aristotle," in *Journal of Philology,* 33 [1914], pp. 182–194) draws a parallel between Aristotle's accounts of action in the *Nicomachean Ethics* and of sensation in the *de Anima:* in each case a separable form or *logos* passes between mind and matter with the assistance of a *meson* or "medium." "In action the process starts with the *logos,* which, by determining a *meson* in *pathos* and *praxis,* is able to produce an act: in sensation we start from an object, which is able, by influencing a *meson,* to produce the *logos* which is sensation" (pp. 193–194). He adds that the comparison is "one more proof of the fact that Aristotle was saturated with Platonism . . . [T]he principle involved is simply the Platonic doctrine of the *apeiron* and the *peras,* that quantitative determination makes formed matter possible and that through number the creator brought order out of chaos," and cites Plato, *Timaeus* 53ab. For the idiom of "externalization," see also Jonathan Lear, "Inside and Outside the *Republic,*" *Phronesis,* 37/2 (1992), pp. 184–215.

that directs the feelings and actions of such a person "occasion by occasion." Although we are supposing this knowledge to be unrepresentable in terms of a code of practice providing explicitly for every contingency, it still belongs on the side of "form" in that it expresses a principle of internal (psychological) order—an established capacity to find one's way around within the space of ethical reasons. Plato and Aristotle hold that it is thanks to such a principle—whether established through active intellectual attention to the realm of "ideas"[34] or through the ordinary process of upbringing—that good citizens can be relied on to see for themselves not only how to behave in their private lives, but also what detailed social measures may be needed from time to time[35] or what course of action would be in accord with a particular statute.[36]

Aristotle uses a strikingly literal form of words in connection with the last example: he says that someone with the quality of "equity," *epieikeia*, will know how to remedy the inevitable abstraction of the law by supplying "what the lawmaker himself would have said if he had been there [that is, if he had had experience of the case now at issue], and would have included in his law if he had known." What makes it the case that there is anything in particular that the lawmaker "would have said" about a situation he never envisaged? Evidently the attempt to *determine* what he would have said can be expected to make as little headway on the basis of mere biographical information, supposing we have any, about the man in question as Wittgenstein does (in another passage on the theme of intention: compare §1 above) in trying to remember what he was going to say on the basis of evidence drawn from his "stream of consciousness."[37] Just as the latter reveals nothing but a scattering of disconnected psychological data, which on their own—that is, in isolation from the determinacy conferred on his state of mind when it is retrospectively identified as the intention *to say that p*—yield nothing intelligible or "readable," so the question of what the lawmaker intended with regard to the present (unforeseen) situation

34. See Plato, *Republic* 500b8–d9.

35. Ibid., 425d7–e2.

36. See Aristotle, *Nicomachean Ethics* 1137b11–24 (and compare Chapter 2, note 16). The same theme appears in Plato, *Statesman* 294b–296a.

37. See *Philosophical Investigations* §635: "'I was going to say . . .'—You remember various details. But not even all of them together show your intention. It is as if a snapshot of a scene had been taken, but only a few scattered details of it were to be seen: here a hand, there a bit of a face, or a hat—the rest is dark. And now it is as if we knew quite certainly what the whole picture represented. As if I could read the darkness."

demands that we look beyond the contingencies of that person's life history and enter into the *logos* or "rational principle" expressed in the original law; for only then can *our* sense of how to apply the law be relied on to replicate that of its author. In each case we have the contrast between (first) a psychological state with a content capable of being entertained by more than one subject and of being transferred from one context to another, and (second) the indeterminate *(apeiron)* character of the contexts themselves, construed as unrepeatable and unshareable. (Or: in each case we find *logos* serving as a vehicle of "sameness," a principle enabling a thought or intention to be replicated in a new context.)

In one way, then, the *logos* that informs the "soul" of the Platonic–Aristotelian virtuous person anticipates the role assigned, within an updated virtue ethics, to the idea of "immersion in a culture": each points to something "in," or attributable to, the individual moral subject that cancels or redeems the inability to make explicit provision in advance for every possible context of deliberation. But in another way the suggestion of kinship between these two ideas is a jarring one. For we have been treating virtue ethics in its modern variant as a product of philosophical quietism—that is, of a mode of thought that rejects theory in favour of the attempt to "command a clear view"[38] of linguistic and social practice. And the idea of virtue as a determinate form or structure realized in individual human "souls" by the right sort of education is by no means an obvious instance of this mode of thought. In fact, it has been plausibly argued that the Socratic "virtue-is-knowledge" doctrine—the point of departure for the tradition with which we are now concerned—amounts, precisely, to a (causal or explanatory) *theory* about the origins of virtuous action. Thus according to Terry Penner, "When Socrates asked 'What is bravery?' and so forth, he did not want to know what the meaning of the word 'bravery' was, nor what the essence of bravery was, nor what the universal *bravery* was. His question . . . was not a request for a conceptual analysis . . . [It] was rather the *general's* question, 'What is bravery?'—that is, 'What is it that makes brave men brave?' The general asks this question not out of interest in mapping our concepts, but out of a desire to learn something substantial about the human psyche."[39]

The thesis that it is through immersion in a culture that we become re-

38. See ibid., §122.

39. Terry Penner, "The Unity of Virtue," *Philosophical Review*, 82 (1973), pp. 35–68; quotation from pp. 39–40.

ceptive to the force of ethical reasons is not the fruit of a desire to "learn something substantial about the human psyche." It belongs, rather, to the study of what already "lies open to view."[40] From the point of view of this study, a search for the supposed principles of psychological organization that *make* us act bravely will already have succumbed to what Wittgenstein identifies as a characteristic hazard in philosophy: "The difficulty—I might say—is not that of finding the solution but rather that of recognizing as the solution something that looks as if it were only a preliminary to it. 'We have already said everything.—Not anything that follows from this, no, *this* itself is the solution!'"[41] For example, in recording the process by which a child learns to count,[42] we may describe "what the teacher says and does and how the pupil reacts to it"; and we may also be inclined at a certain point to remark on our own account that the pupil "can count now," or "has understood the numeral system." But in making this kind of remark we are not necessarily saying something without which the rest of the story would be incomplete: "Whether this or that belongs to a complete description will depend on the purpose of the description,"[43] and so, therefore, will the content of a catalogue of "what happens."

This is the light in which a philosophical quietist can also be expected to view the process of moral upbringing. We know that that process includes a variety of different kinds of human interaction—at one extreme the use of physical constraint and the issuing of orders, at another such experiences as having one's attention directed in a certain way or being struck by a certain adjective (or anecdote, as in Diamond). And no doubt there are ethical contexts that generate a practical purpose for utterances analogous to "Now he can count." An example might be the statement, made in a letter of recommendation, that a student "has an unwavering respect for the evidence": this serves to tell some interested audience that the person in question has succeeded in acquiring a certain (intellectual) virtue. But to look beyond the "physiognomy" of the student's evidence-respecting pattern of behaviour for a mental "principle" or "structure" that would explain this behaviour is to make one of those moves that would be regarded

40. Wittgenstein, *Philosophical Investigations* §126.

41. Wittgenstein, *Zettel*, ed. G. E. M. Anscombe and G. H. von Wright, trans. G. E. M. Anscombe (Oxford: Basil Blackwell, 1981), §314.

42. Ibid., §310.

43. Ibid., §311.

by the quietist as an "unnecessary shuffle."[44] If *nothing* is concealed[45] in the way in which classical virtue theory invites us to picture the harmony, or other desirable formal properties, of the virtuous "soul" as being concealed—that is, by being such as to disclose themselves only to substantial psychological enquiry—then the place to call a halt in answering the question "What happens when someone acquires an ethics?" will be the one we reach when (or if) we succeed in giving an adequate survey of the forms of "ethical" instruction actually in use.[46] Ethics will thus become a part of life in which there is no more temptation to introduce an *explanatory* psychological principle of "practical wisdom" than there is to refer what goes on between, say, Wittgenstein and his tailor to an analogous principle of "taste." People gain a certain amount of experience of wearing clothes, making decisions about the length of their trousers and so on, and some of them, eventually, reach the point of not having to defer to anyone else's authority about such things: *"That is all that happens."*[47] And if we could come up with an appropriate reference for "That," we might say the same about ethics.

5

These considerations suggest a certain view of the relationship between classical virtue ethics and the kind of practical reason account developed here, which has made sensitivity to the force of ethical reasons a component of "second nature" (Chapter 2, §1). They suggest that such an account is a lineal descendant of the classical one—but with a difference attributable to the more thorough-going naturalism of its philosophical context.[48] The relevant line of descent is marked by a continuing recognition, in relation to ethical life, of something characterizable as "form." So to adopt the practical reason approach will be to remain within the tradition described by Henry Staten when he says that "the crucial boundary for Aristotle and

---

44. Wittgenstein, *Philosophical Investigations* §213.

45. Compare ibid., §435.

46. Such a survey might, of course, need to address the question of when someone counts as having got the message.

47. Compare Wittgenstein, *Zettel* §310.

48. The context is that of what McDowell has called a "naturalized" as opposed to a "rampant" Platonism about reasons for action: see John McDowell, *Mind and World* (Cambridge: Harvard University Press, 1994), p. 110.

for philosophy generally does not pass between thought and thing or between word and thing *but, within each of these, between form and formlessness or indefiniteness.*"[49] But it will also be to depart from that tradition in
respect of the particular conception of form invoked. For instead of postu-
lating a certain psychological arrangement or structure of which virtuous
conduct would be the actualization, our version of the practical reason
view is content to point to a phenomenological counterpart of this idea—
that is, to the *manifest* form conferred on human action by the internaliza-
tion of shared standards of conduct, and beyond that, by a more diffuse
feeling for ethical significance or saliency.

Acknowledging the reality of this kind of form involves no violence to
the methodological principle expressed in the statement that "what is hidden . . . is of no interest to us."[50] For it does not take us beneath the (physical) surface of that totality of phenomena in which humanly intelligible
forms, or patterns, are to be found. It does not imply that in learning to
add and subtract (or to avoid hurting people's feelings, or to criticize the
performance of a string quartet) we need to do more than acquire the capacity for certain kinds of intelligent response to our sensory input—any
more than we need to get beyond the surface of the paper in order to see a
face in a picture. Yet if we are going to point to *immersion in a culture* as
the material basis of our sense of value and of its normative bearing on action, then it would seem that we remain committed to a character ideal in-
extricably linked with the concept of form—a concept that reappears in
the setting of "relaxed" (nonreductive) naturalism in the guise of that ethically significant form to which the virtuous person is attuned. The process
of immersion is what corresponds, in this new setting, to what Plato and
Aristotle imagine as a process of formation of the *psuchê*. And this corre-
spondence means that the metaphor of ethical "formation" still has point
in the new setting, since here too, as the thesis of uncodifiability reminds
us, successful communication depends on a "likemindedness" that outruns
what can be expressed in any finite list of beliefs or principles; it depends
on whether the raw human material originally presented in each of the relevant parties has been *turned into something,* or equipped with a "second
nature," sufficiently in agreement with that of others to make good the in-

49. Henry Staten, *Wittgenstein and Derrida* (Oxford: Basil Blackwell, 1985), p. 7; emphasis in original. (It is unclear why Aristotle rather than Plato should get so much of the credit
for this feature of philosophical thought, but Staten's discussion rises above that peculiarity.)
50. Wittgenstein, *Philosophical Investigations* §126.

herent limitations of conventional signs. Only we must remember that the likemindedness recognized by the quietist will not be called upon to play a role in any constructive theory, but will slot into a place opened up by the negative thought that mutual intelligibility—about ethics or anything else—rests in part on factors not subject to human control.

The "nothing-is-hidden," antipsychologistic tendency of our updated conception of practical reason also promotes a different understanding of the teleological theme in virtue ethics. Instead of assuming the *telos* of formation, or upbringing, to be determined by a timelessly fixed human nature, it leads us to recognize as part of the distinctive "natural history" of our species the fact that, as humans, we possess a "second" nature as well as a "first," and hence (at the risk of paradox—but this particular nettle is one we must go ahead and grasp) that it is natural to us to participate in a history that is more than *merely* natural.[51] With this dual nature in view, we can acknowledge that the work of formation is governed by a *social* teleology in which one generation sets itself the goal of initiating the next into a common repository of wisdom about "what is a reason for what." And the point of view from which that goal is visible can now be recognized, in turn, as a construct of upbringing—which means that it is no more of a "natural" given than is the already determinate "second nature" of the parents and teachers who direct us towards it. No more, and no less: but the first of these thoughts is the one that brings out the contrast between ancient and modern. For by historicizing our conception of practical wisdom, it prepares us for a return to the characteristically modern idea of morality as a zone of *contention*. In order to feel the force of this idea, we must recognize that when we appeal (as in the positive phase of quietism: §2 above), to the actual existence of people who exemplify the sought-after quality, we make no progress at all—except perhaps by the chance occurrence of some emotionally suggestive image—towards resolving any actually existing *difficulty* in moral epistemology. If practical wisdom per-

---

51. I believe this idea of the natural capacity of human beings for self-transcendence (though not the historicist inflection of it introduced in the text above) is present in Plato's picturesque statement that humanity is the "offspring not of earth, but of heaven" (*phuton ouk engeion alla ouranion: Timaeus* 90a). Julia Annas's gloss on this passage, in which she finds the thought that "it is in transcending our human nature, *not fulfilling it,* that we find happiness" (*Platonic Ethics, Old and New,* pp. 57–58; emphasis added), seems to me to underplay the dynamic and self-transforming aspect of our existence—Platonically construed—in contrast to that of other animals.

tains to our second (social) nature, then the question of its content (in terms of particular moral beliefs or sensibilities) will be exactly as problematic, within any given society, as that of *who should count* as exemplifying the rationalist character ideal for ethics.

Since quietism is not meant to be a form of idealism (compare Chapter 1, §3), the quietist should be as ready as anyone to acknowledge the dialectical relation between submitting one's own judgement to correction by authority, and relying on it to determine how far any self-styled authority actually deserves one's allegiance in a particular case. The existence of this tension is a harmless point of phenomenology. It does not imply that any of the autonomous thinking we currently do about (for example) ethical questions can be delegated to someone else; so it provides no epistemic short cuts. But on the other hand it is in no way hostile to the thought that what governs our alternation, as individual thinkers, between the receptive and the critical mode is an effort towards *knowledge*—both substantive knowledge and, connectedly, knowledge about the credentials of particular judges. In the next chapter I want to say something about the particular social interests that direct the work of ethical upbringing, and especially about the role played in it by our partly epistemic interest in reliability, trustworthiness, and the like.

Teleology

Why Be "Serious"? The Natural Basis of Our Interest in a "Rational Self"

1

Part I of this book has been devoted to the task of expounding, as plausibly as I know how, a certain variant of what I have called the "practical reason" view of ethics. In what follows, the tone of the discussion will become more critical—not necessarily in the sense of being destructive (since for me the motive to investigate this kind of ethical theory is precisely that I find it the best on offer), but rather in the sense of enquiring into the commitments, allegiances, loyalties, disloyalties, denials, and so forth that are implicit in *becoming* an "ethical" subject as represented in the account now before us. In spelling out these commitments more clearly, I shall be seeking to make the practical reason view accessible to the kind of negative considerations brought forward since the 1960s against positions in moral and political philosophy which inherit the values and assumptions of the classical rationalist tradition—I mean the universalist, hierarchical, and teleological values associated with Platonism and with some modern varieties of rationalist politics. However, before those negative themes can be introduced I want to look more closely at the "physiognomy," or natural aspect, of our participation in ethics: that is, at the place occupied by ethical interests and concerns within the life of our species, considered as one animal species among others. How exactly are we proposing to hold open a place for talk about moral "virtues" and "sensibilities," and about an ideal of practical rationality, while at the same time adhering to a fully naturalistic approach (in the sense just indicated) to language and other expressive behaviour?

One natural interest that seems to find expression in the work of moral upbringing is an interest in being able to *rely* on the future availability of certain goods. This point is implicit in a well-known passage of Aristotle in which he argues that virtues of character, like technical skills, are acquired by practising the relevant outward forms of behaviour.[1] As with technical capacities, so with moral ones, we have to make the transition from a state of understanding in which all we can do is reproduce particular actions selected for us from time to time by more competent practitioners—"press this key now," "say thank you"—to one in which we ourselves embody the competence encountered in our teachers' (at first opaque and unpredictable) commands. The way we do this is through the repetition, over a long enough period and with a sufficiently varied input of examples, of the actions characteristic of a particular skill or (moral) virtue. The effect of this repetition is to bring it about, imperceptibly for the most part, that behaviour which initially figured in our lives only under the aspect of compliance with authority comes instead to express something inward and enduring; or to put the point another way, that such behaviour comes *actually* to express the evaluative attitudes or concerns which it is (conventionally) *apt* to express.[2] Of course, as Aristotle points out,[3] the technical case differs from the moral one in that the value of skills lies in their results, and a desired result produced "more by luck than judgement" is no less materially useful than the same result delivered by an expert; action considered from a moral point of view, by contrast, loses its value for us if we learn that it did not express any good disposition of the will—that is, if it turns out that an act seemingly inspired by a fixed attitude of esteem for the "noble" had some other, latent motive or was no more than an impulsive gesture. However, in both cases the goal of instruction is to transform the learner into someone who, subject to human limitations, can be *relied*

1. Aristotle, *Nicomachean Ethics* 1103a31–b2.

2. I do not mean to suggest that the cut-off between "natural" and "conventional" forms of expression is always a sharp one. Think for example of Charles Taylor creating "rapport" with a stranger on a train in hot weather: if the stranger is likely to be an English speaker he can say "Whew, it's hot in here"; if not, "I just smile, look towards him, and say 'Whew!', wiping my brow"—much the same social end being achieved in both cases ("Theories of Meaning," in Taylor, *Philosophical Papers*, vol. 1 [Cambridge: Cambridge University Press, 1985], pp. 248–292; quotation from p. 264). There may well be some specifically ethical "attitudes or concerns" whose expression can fall into the intermediate zone with respect to this contrast (benevolence, perhaps, as manifested in sympathetic joy or sadness); but most ethical expression is not of this kind.

3. Aristotle, *Nicomachean Ethics* 1105a26–33.

on to secure certain values through his or her way of dealing with particular situations as they arise. The worth of technical experts corresponds to our need to be able to rely on continuous production of crops, running of machines, and the like (that is, I suppose, on the stability of what counts for us as the "expedient"); the worth of the "virtuous person" corresponds to our need for assurance that the cultural artefact, "morality," will be sustained in existence by the unfolding sequence of individual choices.

In relation to moral upbringing, the value set upon predictability is registered both by ancient virtue ethics through the notion of form, and also—to recall the parallel for which I argued in Chapter 3—by our own practical reason approach insofar as it appeals to the idea of a norm-governed (or rule-governed) social practice.[4] Just as the atemporal principle of unitary "form" serves as a guarantee of the faithful transfer from one context to another of whatever is essential to, say, just or brave action,[5] so the descriptive study of the use of the word "rule" reveals it to be interwoven with that of the word "same":[6] following a rule means carrying on in the same way, or extending a previously established pattern.[7] And this conti-

---

4. See Chapter 2, note 57 for an attempt to forestall possible confusion over the meaning of "rule." In using this word from now on, I shall be referring to rules in the informal sense of norms or standards of correctness, not to rules as algorithms.

5. That form should be what enables us to *do* the same—to produce one more token-action identifiable under a certain description, say "fair distribution" or "suitably warm welcome"—is a corollary of the idea that it is what enables us to *think* the same: that is, to produce one more token-thought identifiable as a thought *of* some object that is also capable of being represented in the thought of another person, or in our own at another time. Thus Henry Staten (*Wittgenstein and Derrida* [Oxford: Basil Blackwell, 1985], p. 150), expounding Derrida's concept of "presence": "That which is capable of being known must be so under the form of presence, and this presence must be thinkable, repeatable as the same, apart from the existence of any empirical knower. *What is* can only be what it is *as such* if it is in principle capable of persisting even though I disappear . . . The form of presence makes possible the definition of the essence of man as wakeful rationality, because the idealized fullness of living consciousness can be conceived only as the correlate of a presence that transcends the absences to which a merely empirical subject is susceptible (forgetfulness, lapses of attention, sleep, death)."

6. Ludwig Wittgenstein, *Philosophical Investigations*, trans. G. E. M. Anscombe (Oxford: Basil Blackwell, 1967), §225.

7. A more complete version of this story would also embrace "concepts," which Kant (*Critique of Pure Reason*, trans. N. Kemp Smith [London: Macmillan, 1933], A106) holds to be tantamount to rules: "[A] concept is always, as regards its form, something universal which serves as a rule." This seems to represent an intermediate moment in the philosophical development by which "forms" give way to "rules."

nuity is unsurprising in that we can see both ideas ("form" and "rule") as rooted in a belief that there are some questions to which the correct answers are *determined in advance;* some facts whose significance is *there to be appreciated* by an intelligent mind.

But "predictability" as such, though a useful characteristic of human as well as of natural environments, does not adequately specify the aim of moral upbringing. For that aim is not to make human action predictable in the same way as the workings of *mere* nature—nature as the "realm of law," as McDowell would put it[8]—but rather in a way that passes through what we know (or assume) about the motivational dispositions of individual agents, and through the assumption of their intentional control over their own actions. In particular, we want to be able to conduct social relationships on the basis of an expectation of widespread respect for the demands both of justice and, ideally, of the other social virtues (on one hand, for the duties of law-abidingness, promise-keeping, and refraining from injury or deceit; on the other, for those of social solidarity or "refraining from indifference").[9] But we want this expectation to be borne out not just by the existence of a suitable system of conditioned reflexes, but by the fact that (enough of) those with whom we have dealings have *adopted* the relevant values or principles as their own, so that their behaviour is, in the relevant respects, predictable *in the particular way associated with that fact.* This is the desideratum that Aristotle seems to have in mind when he characterizes a moral virtue as a "fixed and unchangeable" disposition to pursue certain ends,[10] this disposition being grounded in a "true apprehension" of the ultimate human good;[11] alternatively, the same desideratum can be invoked by saying that virtue "belongs to the will,"[12] or even—in a

8. See John McDowell, *Mind and World* (Cambridge: Harvard University Press, 1994), p. 71. The realm of law is demarcated "by the way its proper mode of intelligibility contrasts with the intelligibility that belongs to inhabitants of the space of reasons" (ibid.), the latter kind of intelligibility being dependent on teleological notions such as that of the point or purpose of an action (see Chapter 1, §1).

9. This bipartite conception of obligation is based on Onora O'Neill, *Towards Justice and Virtue: A Constructive Account of Practical Reasoning* (Cambridge: Cambridge University Press, 1996): see especially the schema on p. 205. A more distant ancestor is Kant's contrast between strict and broad duties: see *The Metaphysics of Morals*, ed. Mary Gregor (Cambridge: Cambridge University Press, 1996), p. 153.

10. Aristotle, *Nicomachean Ethics* 1105a32–33.

11. Ibid., 1142b31–33.

12. See Philippa Foot, *Virtues and Vices* (Oxford: Basil Blackwell, 1978), pp. 4–6; quotation from p. 4.

more Kantian vein—that adopting a moral end is a "volitional act," albeit "one that you can only do gradually and perhaps incompletely."[13] So the particular kind of predictability aimed at in moral upbringing is one that will allow us to form expectations about the future conduct of others on the basis, not merely of their place in the causally organized system of nature, but of the values or goals they have set before themselves—where the question of *what these are* is one to which a normal (mature) human being is assumed, in her own case, to have some measure of reflective access.

A society whose practices of upbringing are designed to make the actions of its members predictable in the way just mentioned—that is, to turn out people who can be relied on to follow certain (socially desirable) lines of conduct, not on the basis of their participation in nature as the "realm of law," but because they have made it their policy to do so—can be seen as conforming to a time-honoured view about the psychological basis of accountability. This is the idea of upbringing as a process that creates a unitary character out of the various motivational "fragments" present in us from day one in the form of transient impulses, and so gradually enables us, as this character gains definition, to *speak as one person*, self-consistent over time (or sufficiently so, by human standards) in our desires, beliefs, and habits of judgement. The same process can also be seen as one that enables us to *represent* ourselves to others as holding certain beliefs or attitudes; whereas those on whom it fails to work, and who to that extent remain deficient in the virtues, do not have the same right to speak in this way on their own behalf, since they lack the psychological consistency that would give weight to what they say.[14] The capacity for self-representation,

13. Christine M. Korsgaard, "Morality as Freedom," in her *Creating the Kingdom of Ends* (Cambridge: Cambridge University Press, 1996), pp. 159–187; quotation from p. 180.

14. See Plato, *Republic* 442c: the (rightfully) ruling part of the mind is that which knows what is in the interest of *each* part, and of the whole comprising them (and compare 428cd: in a society constituted in accordance with nature, the role of the guardian class will be to take thought for the welfare of the whole). Note that I am speaking here of the "psychological basis of responsibility" in an ideal, not an empirical sense: on the view I am outlining, one does not need actually to exemplify the perfectly integrated character in order to be held responsible for one's actions, but rather to be someone who can reasonably be *treated* as capable of representing herself to others. I have argued elsewhere ("Meaning What We Say: Feminist Ethics and the Critique of Humanism," in *New Left Review*, 220 [November/December 1996], pp. 98–115) that our failure, as empirical beings, to actualize this particular "idea of pure practical reason"—our exposure, for example, to skeptical reflections like those of Jacques Lacan about the "function of *méconnaissance* that characterizes the ego in all its structures"—cannot be taken in a practical (forensic) context to entail that what looks and

so understood, emerges from the process of internal division and organization whereby we learn to resist immediate impulses for the sake of longer-term goals (say, to resist aggressive impulses for the sake of not quarrelling, as we have to learn to do in the name of the virtue of "good temper"); it is in proportion to our success in this that we gain the right to make statements, of the particular sort that constitute declarations of intention, about our own future behaviour. Only on condition that I have, for example, sufficient self-control (or courage, or energy) to carry out some declared intention of mine can I credibly give myself out as *someone who is going to act in that way* ("Don't worry, I won't get into an argument about . . ."); if the condition is not met, others will do better to disregard my words in favour of whatever locally relevant knowledge they may have of my involvement in the "realm of law" (say, the number of drinks, hours or minutes of dinner party, or whatever that it usually takes to crack my thin veneer of cool).

2

In describing this quest for predictability in human behaviour, we might take a cue from Nietzsche and say that it involves an attempt to transform each new entrant to the community into "an animal with the right to make promises."[15] In Essay II of the *Genealogy of Morals,* which is the source for the phrase just quoted, Nietzsche trawls the depths of an imagined prehistory for the origins of this "right" and postulates a "mnemotechnics" of torture and sacrifice whose imprint is still traceable in the gestures of historical humanity.[16] But, characteristically, he does not make this "torture

feels like the *recognition* of certain words and deeds as our own is really a "misrecognition". The arguments against drawing this inference are parallel to those that would be available within a Kantian framework against supposing that as natural (and therefore imperfectly rational) beings, we cannot recognize, but only "misrecognize" ourselves as subject to the moral law. (Of course, there will still be room for local exemptions from moral responsibility on grounds of either short- or long-term psychological abnormality: see P. F. Strawson, "Freedom and Resentment," in his *Freedom and Resentment and Other Essays* [London: Methuen, 1974], §IV.) See also Chapter 6, §3.

15. Friedrich Nietzsche, *On the Genealogy of Morals,* trans. Walter Kaufmann and R. J. Hollingdale (New York: Random House, 1969), Essay II, §1; p. 57.

16. Ibid., Essay II, §3; p. 61: "'If something is to stay in the memory it must be burned in: only that which never ceases to *hurt* stays in the memory' . . . One might even say that wherever on earth solemnity, seriousness, mystery, and gloomy coloring still distinguish the life

and sacrifice" into a ground of condemnation. For he also speaks with approval of the "emancipated" or "sovereign" man in whom it bears fruit—whose "mastery over himself also necessarily gives him mastery over circumstances, over nature, and over all more short-willed and unreliable creatures."[17] The same man, conscious of the achievement distilled into these qualities, measures others by what he values most in himself—the ability to answer for one's future actions, confident that one will have the strength to keep one's word even "in the face of fate"—and is "bound to reserve a kick for the feeble windbags who promise without the right to do so, and a rod for the liar who breaks his word even at the moment he utters it."[18]

I think this Nietzschean notion of the "sovereign" or "masterful" utterance—despite the obvious complications posed by its setting within a wider philosophy of "lightness," "dance," "dangerous play," and the like—can add something to our conception of an ethics of practical reason. Recall the suggestion (made in §1 above) that we hope to find in the behaviour of people around us a reliability grounded not in any merely law-like regularity of emotional response, but in a moral personality determined by the adoption of certain ends or values rather than others. With this point in mind, and recalling also the Aristotelian contrast between mere imitation (of a given kind of virtuous behaviour) and behaviour sustained by actual possession of the relevant virtue, we can think of moral upbringing as seeking to establish a particular relationship between the learner and the words or gestures with which she is becoming conversant.[19] The relationship to be established is one that seems to create an opening for the language of *seriousness:* what is required of the learner is that her participation in the prevailing system of "language games" should come to display, in some appropriate range of contexts, the quality we register when we say that a linguistic (or other conventionally expressive) act was "really meant," or that a speaker was "serious" in uttering certain words. This quality is of interest to us because it is the ostensibly "serious," or really meant, compo-

---

of a man and a people, something of the terror that formerly attended all promises, pledges and vows on earth is *still effective:* the past, the longest, deepest and sternest past, breathes upon us and rises up in us whenever we become 'serious'."

17. Ibid., Essay II, §2; pp. 59–60.

18. Ibid., p. 60.

19. For reasons considered earlier (Chapter 2), it would be unwise to assume that this educational effort relates to any clearly delimited range of "moral" contexts.

nent of someone's expressive output that is to be compared with their subsequent conduct in order to determine where they stand on the scale of value we noticed just now in Nietzsche—a scale whose extremes are occupied, on one hand, by the condition of "self-mastery" or full competence to represent oneself to the rest of the world; on the other, by the "feeble windbag who promises without the right to do so." Moral upbringing has to teach us that sooner or later, we too must submit to evaluation on this scale, and that for the purpose of such evaluation there has to be a more or less determinate boundary around the class of utterances for which, as speakers, we can properly be called to account. This requirement is what Nietzsche invites us to see as transmitting to our own lives some echo of the terror that originally went into "breeding" a conscientious species of animal.

So what constitutes this "seriousness" which may or may not characterize the relation of a speaker to her own expressive acts? Perhaps we need to describe it more carefully. Or do we? Isn't it obvious what is meant by speaking "seriously?" Isn't that simply our *usual* way of speaking? J. L. Austin, for example, in an early chapter of his book *How To Do Things with Words* (in which he introduces the concept of "performative" utterances),[20] distinguishes the *ordinary circumstances* of language use from a class of *special circumstances* such as those in which words are "said by an actor on the stage, . . . introduced in a poem, or spoken in soliloquy."[21] The point of the distinction is that "language in such circumstances is in special ways—intelligibly—used not seriously, but in ways *parasitic* upon its normal use—ways which fall under the doctrine of the *etiolations* of language."[22] Austin remarks that these etiolations can affect (or indeed, to use his own word, "infect") *all* utterances,[23] but with regard to performatives

---

20. J. L. Austin, *How To Do Things with Words* (Oxford: Clarendon Press, 1962). Austin explains the term "performative" by saying that "the issuing of such an utterance is the performing of an action—it is not normally thought of as just saying something" (ibid., pp. 6–7). He acknowledges later, however, that performative utterances are not rigorously distinguishable from assertoric or "constative" ones (ibid., p. 149).

21. Ibid., p. 22.

22. Ibid. (emphasis in original); and compare p. 121, where *joking* is mentioned as a further instance of the nonserious. (This part of Austin's work has attracted particular attention in recent years as a result of the criticism devoted to it by Jacques Derrida: see Chapter 5.)

23. Ibid., p. 21.

in particular, his point is that the cases cited can be excluded from consideration as falling outside the range of the "ordinary." What makes them other than "ordinary" is that in such cases, someone is speaking in a way or a context that insulates her utterance from the normal practical consequences of speech. Perhaps she is speaking not *as herself* but in an "implied," poetic voice or in a dramatic character. Or perhaps her words were not intended to be made available to an audience at all. The idea seems to be that these are all contexts in which, for one reason or another, my uttering certain words does not really constitute doing what I *would* be doing if I were to come out with the same words in an "ordinary" context—say, praising or cursing someone, expressing grief or joy, or putting forward an opinion for consideration.[24] Conversely, an "ordinary" context is one in which I do not merely go through the motions but actually make a move in some "language game," a move for which I must be prepared to take responsibility in a way that the stage actor, for example, does not have to.[25]

Austin, then, thinks of the ordinary circumstances of language use as those in which we speak "seriously." Is there an alternative to this picture? Yes, there is. The alternative would be to see "serious" utterance, not as the norm from which acting and the rest are deviations, but as an achievement to be set against the background of the less-than-accountable in linguistic behaviour—a background represented by the merely imitative way in which Aristotle thinks young people first begin to produce action "in accordance with the virtues." The thought which can defamiliarize Austin's picture is that "really meaning" what we say or do is an attitude we *learn* to adopt, and that the lesson belongs to an extended course of instruction in *why it matters* whether this attitude is present or absent. Let me now try to develop this thought in more detail.

24. This interpretation does not really work for the case of "soliloquy," since if someone happens to overhear me cursing him *sotto voce* it would hardly be convincing to say that what he overheard was not really an instance of my cursing him, just because I believed myself to be out of earshot at the time. Nevertheless, I think the general point Austin is aiming at is the one indicated in the text, namely, that in each of the contexts he mentions here, speech is disconnected from the normal business of getting on with life—either through its absorption into an activity of imaginative play or make-believe, or in the case of soliloquy, through the (physical or psychological) withdrawal of the speaker.

25. I do not mean that acting is not an occupation in which moral decisions sometimes have to be made—only that it is, in an obvious sense, "not my fault" if a character whose part I am performing says something false or obnoxious.

3

Wittgenstein writes: "Someone might learn to understand the meaning of the expression 'seriously *meaning* what one says' by means of a gesture of pointing at the heart. But now we must ask: 'How does it come out that he has learnt it?'"[26]

This question is meant to induce us to do something for which a parallel is provided by Wittgenstein's treatment of the distinction between voluntary and involuntary movement:[27] that is, it is meant to induce us to abandon the search for a special sort of mental *origin* that would qualify an utterance as "really meant" (or a movement as *willed*), and to look instead at its "surroundings." (*Zettel* §577 says that "[w]hat is voluntary is certain movements with their normal *surrounding* of intention, learning, trying, acting"; *Philosophical Investigations* §628 gives as an example the fact that "voluntary movement is marked by the absence of surprise.") As Stewart Candlish points out, Wittgenstein's aim in these passages is to weaken our attachment to the idea that the voluntary–involuntary contrast must lie "in the presence or absence of an *extra* element of willing";[28] for Wittgenstein "this whole conception of the will as something prior to the bodily act"— whether an experiential phenomenon, or something nonexperiential and ineffable—"is mistaken."[29]

The analogy that interests Candlish, following a hint by Wittgenstein that he sees the two topics as connected,[30] is between *willing a bodily movement* and *meaning (or intending) one thing rather than another* by something one says or does. Within the same family of "language games," the one that interests me here is that between *willing* and *"really" or "seriously" meaning* (in contrast to saying something in a way that falls short of the "serious"). In this case too, there may be some point in looking away from

26. Wittgenstein, *Philosophical Investigations* §590.

27. Ibid., §§611–628; and compare Ludwig Wittgenstein, *Zettel,* ed. G. E. M. Anscombe and G. H. von Wright, trans. G. E. M. Anscombe (Oxford: Basil Blackwell, 1981), §§577–599.

28. Stewart Candlish, "Das Wollen ist auch nur eine Erfahrung," in Robert Arrington and Hans-Johann Glock, eds., *Wittgenstein's Philosophical Investigations: Text and Context* (London: Routledge, 1991), pp. 203–226; quotation from p. 224 (emphasis added).

29. Ibid., p. 217.

30. *Zettel,* §590: "The connection of our main problem [namely, the problem of meaning: see Candlish, 'Das Wollen', p. 226, note 13] with the epistemological problem of willing has occurred to me before."

the spot where we imagine the essence of the problematic item to be located, and turning instead to the apparent *in*essentials of its surroundings.

The surroundings of what we call "seriousness"—that is, the phenomena with which we have to make ourselves at home in order to become competent judges of whether the speech acts of others are "seriously meant"—can perhaps be best understood by reference to the *natural interest in gathering correct information about our environment.* This interest belongs as much to "first" as to "second" nature: that is, it can be attributed not only to organisms that have, but also to those that lack, the capacity to attribute it to themselves; for the value of such information lies in the fact that it "enable[s] behaviour to be suited, in the light of needs or goals, to the way the environment actually is,"[31] and is therefore conducive to survival. The interplay of needs (or goals) and information, thus abstractly characterized, persists through the evolutionary event of the emergence of a "second nature." For example, just as there can be survival value for a nonhuman animal in suiting its behaviour to that of other animals present in its habitat, so human beings can promote their own survival (along with many of their more local interests) by taking into account in their deliberations the foreseeable actions of their own animal neighbours, among whom the most significant are usually other humans. And as language users—that is, as creatures endowed with intentional control over our expressive (and hence over our representational) behaviour—we are in a position actively to cooperate with one another and to engage in a mutual promotion of interests by pooling information, not least by telling others from time to time how we intend to act. Such declarations of intention, if reliable, provide our audience with an "epistemic surrogate"[32] for actual

31. John McDowell, "Meaning, Communication, and Knowledge," in Zak van Straaten, ed., *Philosophical Subjects: Essays Presented to P. F. Strawson* (Oxford: Clarendon Press, 1980), pp. 117–139; quotation from p. 129.

32. Ibid., p. 134: "When the communicative process functions properly, sensory confrontation with a piece of communicative behaviour has the same impact on the cognitive state of a perceiver as sensory confrontation with the state of affairs which the behaviour, as we may say, represents; elements of the communicative repertoire serve as epistemic surrogates for represented states of affairs." It is worth emphasizing that what is provided in this passage is a purely generic account of the production and uptake of representational behaviour, unmarked as yet by the obvious contrast between, say, the merely functional or *de facto* "warning" conveyed to its fellows by the anxious squawk of a bird (McDowell's example: ibid., p. 129), and on the other hand the human production of a speech act intended to be recognized by its audience as, precisely, a warning ("They're behind you!")—the latter form of

sensory confrontation with the state of affairs that consists in our performing the relevant action. (Since this state of affairs is, by hypothesis, not yet actual at the time of our declaration, a verbal surrogate is nearest the audience is going to get, at that moment, to being confronted with it.)

But if information about deliberatively relevant circumstances is (so far as it goes) a natural good, the lack of such information is equally a natural evil, and the benefit or harm we can incur from these sources brings communicative behaviour within the scope of ethics. Of course, to say that some bit of information now at my disposal is potentially of interest to some other person to whom I could communicate it is not yet to specify the nature of that interest: it could be a matter of life and death, or again, something merely curious or amusing. (It could also be of less interest to them to receive it than it is to me to transmit it: "I'm drowning!," for example.) Indeed, a large part of the discipline we learn to impose on ourselves in the matter of communication centres on the withholding of information that others can be assumed *not* to want, that is, on refraining from boring people. Failure to acquire this species of communicative virtue[33] reveals itself in a (surely culpable) lack of attention to the pleasure and displeasure of our audience. But there is a different kind of fault which consists in lack of empathy with the interest of one's audience in knowing

words being a good candidate for the specification of what constitutes a warning proper, that is, one pertaining to the realm of second nature. But in any case, once we start to consider the way in which a developed natural language answers to the epistemic interests of its users, we see that the matching of individual states of affairs with individual utterances that represent them is just the tip of an iceberg. In particular, the recognition of objective logical relationships among those utterances to which we grant the status of *assertions* creates the scope—and to some extent the need—for continual monitoring of the doxastic commitments and entitlements of people within one's communicative environment (not excluding oneself, as I go on to mention in the text). This process, to which Robert Brandom has given the name of "deontic scorekeeping" ("deontic" because of the normativity of the underlying concepts of commitment and entitlement), figures in his own philosophy of language as the basis for a systematic "conceptual-role semantics" which seeks to explain the phenomenon of semantic content—both in principle and in its actual diversity—by reflection on the social practice of giving and asking for *reasons*. See Robert B. Brandom, *Making It Explicit: Reasoning, Representation and Discursive Commitment* (Cambridge: Harvard University Press, 1994), pp. 141–143.

33. Aristotle offers a few pages on what his translator W. D. Ross calls the "virtues of social intercourse," namely, "friendliness," "truthfulness," and "ready wit" (*Nicomachean Ethics* 1126b11–1128b9). We need not linger over this discussion, except to note that the account of "truthfulness" diverges considerably from Christian or post-Christian preoccupations.

what it will *damage* them not to know. This may result—as before—from inattention or stupidity. But it may also be due to the prospect of gain from the ignorant or misinformed state of the other party. The latter case takes us to the heart not just of the "ethics of communication" but of ethics as such: "Deceit and violence—these are the two forms of deliberate assault on human beings," writes Sissela Bok.[34] The centrality of deceit may be due to the fact that it touches on the same mutual vulnerability that fuels our concern with violence itself: if "the weakest [human being] has strength enough to kill the strongest, either by secret machination, or by confederacy with others,"[35] it must be at least equally true that the weakest is capable of deceiving the strongest.[36]

Just as we can incur (material) harm from the bad ethical dispositions displayed by others in their communicative dealings with us, so we can hope to *avoid* harm through the competent appraisal of those dispositions—of people's honesty, reliability, disinterestedness, conscientiousness in observation, and the like. On this appraisal will depend, in part,[37] the future ordering of our relations with the relevant others in point of trust—as expressed, say, in a readiness to enter into joint undertakings with them— and probably also in point of social approach or avoidance.

This seems to be the natural setting of the concept of "seriousness" as it figures in the contrast between an utterance that is, and one that is not, "seriously meant." Our most basic incentive to master this contrast lies in the possibility of incurring harm through incompetence in the kind of appraisal I just mentioned. What we learn when we learn the concept of "seriously meaning" seems to be a technique for evaluating certain kinds of evidence about the beliefs and attitudes of others, the purpose of this technique being to assist in the correct ordering of our relations to these others with a view to our own "good life as a whole." In particular, we

34. Sissela Bok, *Lying: Moral Choice in Public and Private Life* (London: Quartet Books, 1980), p. 18.

35. Thomas Hobbes, *Leviathan,* ed. C. B. Macpherson (Harmondsworth: Penguin, 1968), p. 183.

36. The communicative "fault" discussed in this paragraph is that of *unprovoked* (or, in general, gratuitous) deceit. I do not mean to deny that deceit, like violence, may on occasion be justified—for example, in self-defence or in the defence of another.

37. Not exclusively, of course. Other things being equal, we prefer to associate with those whom we can regard as amusing, charismatic, life-enhancing, and so forth—that is, as possessing "virtues" of a not clearly ethical kind. (Sometimes we prefer this even when other things are not equal.)

have to learn to place the expressive phenomena of the present moment in their true relation to a more temporally extended pattern of behaviour—a skill in which young children are trained by such devices as teasing and role-playing. Wittgenstein's "gesture of pointing at the heart," supposing it could actually convey to someone what is meant by "seriously meaning," would presumably have its effect against this sort of background: one criterion of someone's having successfully understood the expression—one answer to the question "How does it come out that he has learnt it?"—might be that he takes the pointing gesture as an invitation to go back *later* to the person who makes it and expect a certain line of action from them.

But a full account of this aspect of upbringing would have to mention not only the judgements we learn to make about others, but also those we learn to assume that others are making about ourselves. For example, as an adjunct to the topic of not entering lightly into promises (or, later, contracts), we are taught to monitor our own linguistic behaviour from the point of view of a notional audience whom we must think of as subjecting *us* to the scrutiny we apply to others when we raise the question of their "seriousness." This scrutiny has to do with the integration (or lack of it) of particular utterances of ours into a pattern of behaviour which can be treated as indicative of the ends we have adopted (see §1 above), and can thus come to figure in a certain way in the deliberations of the imagined audience.

4

One thing we have to learn, then, in the name of social viability is to protect ourselves against the dangers arising from actions of our own that may create false expectations about our future behaviour. Our protection against these dangers lies in an awareness of the *conventions* that mediate between our words and gestures, on one hand, and on the other the impressions formed by other people of our (projectible)[38] attitudes and beliefs. One of these conventions is noticed by Austin when he says that "saying or stating that the cat is on the mat commits me to saying or stating 'The mat is underneath the cat' just as much as the performative 'I define X as Y' . . . commits me to using those terms in special ways in future dis-

---

38. By "projectible" attitudes and beliefs I mean those about which others are entitled to assume that we will not change them whimsically or arbitrarily.

course"—to which he adds the comment: "We can see how this is connected with such acts as promising."[39]

Perhaps the connection Austin has in mind can be put like this: when we promise, we declare to one or more other persons that we are willing to be held to account for nonperformance of what we promise to do; that is, we concede in advance the justice of their resentment, and of the infliction of whatever would be socially accepted as appropriate sanctions, if we should fail to perform. Similarly when we make an assertion—assuming the absence of those *special* circumstances in which language undergoes a "sea change"—we implicitly consent to be held to account for any inconsistency between our actual future behaviour and the behaviour, such as it may be, to which our assertion "commits" us. In Austin's cat-on-mat example, the inconsistency will be a matter of failure to respect relations of entailment: the analogy with promising evidently lies in the fact that in both cases the speaker subsequently disappoints the legitimate expectations of others ("legitimate" because those expectations might have been formed by any reasonable person in response to her words).

Austin backs up the analogy by referring to his earlier review of the "infelicities" that can affect performative utterances. By "infelicities" Austin means, in his own words, "things that can be or go wrong on the occasion of such utterances."[40] His account of these takes the form of a statement of six rules, or rather three pairs of rules, to which performatives are subject. The first two pairs relate, respectively, to the conditions allowing the act to be performed at all (A.1, the existence of a procedure; A.2, the suitability of persons and circumstances) and to the execution of the act itself (which

---

39. *How To Do Things with Words*, pp. 135–136; compare p. 50, "The insincerity of an assertion is the same as the insincerity of a promise . . . to say 'I promise', without intending, is parallel to saying 'It is the case' without believing"; also p. 89 on definition. (I assume that Austin's claim about a *commitment to saying or stating* that the mat is underneath the cat is not intended quite literally, but means: this is what one has to say if one ventures an opinion on the matter.) Brandom rightly points out that asserting is *unlike* promising in that "assertional commitments . . . can be withdrawn without penalty by the asserter who undergoes a change of mind" (*Making It Explicit*, p. 264), whereas a promise would not be a promise if it could be treated in this way. This, however (he continues), does not discredit the idea that someone performing an assertoric speech act thereby undertakes a commitment which remains in force until such time as it *is* voided or withdrawn, and while in force, "has a significance for the deontic score" (ibid., p. 265; compare note 32 above).

40. Austin, *How To Do Things with Words,* p. 14.

must be both correct, B.1, and complete, B.2). The third pair, Austin's Γ rules, are the ones of particular interest to us. They state that

(Γ.1) Where, as often, the procedure is designed for use by persons having certain thoughts or feelings, or for the inauguration of certain consequential conduct on the part of any participant, then a person participating in and so invoking the procedure must in fact have those thoughts or feelings, and the participants must intend so to conduct themselves, and further

(Γ.2) must actually so conduct themselves subsequently.[41]

The difference between the A and B rules and the Γ rules is that whereas the violation of one of the former results in the nonperformance of the relevant act (for example, a marriage is void unless conducted by someone empowered to do so; the ceremony "misfires"), the violation of a Γ rule does not—the act takes place, but constitutes an "abuse" of the procedure (though we are told "not [to] stress the normal connotations of this word").[42]

In spite of this disclaimer, which is evidently meant to safeguard the dispassionate or value-neutral character of Austin's study, much of the work of *ethical* formation can arguably be summarized under the heading of his two Γ rules. Γ.1 underlies such warnings as we may receive against expressing attitudes or beliefs which we are conscious of not really holding; that is, against expressing ourselves *insincerely.* Γ.2 on the other hand underlies a different kind of lesson, having to do with the avoidance, in future, of conduct that will disappoint any legitimate expectations created by our present speech act.[43] For example, I am taught that if I make sympathetic noises to *X* about the shameful behaviour of *Y,* I should not (under Γ.2) subsequently engage in the same kind of behaviour myself. This teaching, which relates (in Austin's terms) to the avoidance of the "breach" rather

41. Ibid., p. 15.

42. Ibid., p. 16.

43. This discussion abstracts from the possibility of a "no-fault" scenario in which we disappoint people's expectations as a result of some (defensible) change in our own moral outlook. I take it that since the moral content of upbringing (the "that," as Aristotle calls it) is not usually supposed to be a mere matter of taste or opinion, there is no harm at this stage in proceeding on the (admittedly somewhat artificial) assumption that what upbringing communicates to us is a stable and substantively determinate morality, about which we have no business to entertain doubts; this assumption, however, will be suspended in Part III.

than of the "insincerity" form of infelicity[44] in ethical discourse, is different from the teaching that takes place in respect of Γ.1 because, while the question that arises under Γ.1 is presumably supposed to be one that I can settle by introspection (do I really disapprove of what Y did?), the question that arises under Γ.2 is not of this kind: introspection may confirm that I do feel disapproval of Y, but it cannot determine whether, despite this disapproval, I am in danger of behaving as badly as Y myself in future.

The latter question also calls for self-examination, but of a more objectifying and historical kind. It calls into play, in relation to a speech act of one's own, the kind of critical scrutiny which I said (in §3 above) might figure in an answer to Wittgenstein's question about "seriously meaning": "How does it come out that he has learnt it?" Specifically, the process by which we learn to purge our own speech acts of Austin's Γ.2 (or "breach") form of infelicity consists, I think, in the acquisition of a certain power of self-appraisal: in this case, the power to determine whether or not a certain ethically significant gesture (say, an expression of sympathy with X over Y's conduct: "That is a truly disgusting way to behave!") stands in the right sort of relation to the temporally extended behavioural pattern that defines one's moral personality. We could think of the object of appraisal here as the *functional* (as opposed to the introspectible) *sincerity* of an utterance.

This application of the idea of "functional sincerity" exploits Austin's willingness to regard assertions, along with more mainstream performatives, as susceptible to the "breach form of infelicity"—the form that can be diagnosed when I fail to "say" (or, presumably, assent to) what one of my assertions commits me to "saying." For Austin, assertion can give rise to "breaches" because in asserting something, one uses a form of words that is conventionally apt to express not just a thought, but also an intention—the intention to "say" whatever is entailed by (and nothing that is inconsistent with) that particular thought, and moreover (by Γ.2) to "conduct oneself subsequently" in a way that is consistent with it.

The idea now before us is that a "serious" assertion is, functionally speaking, like a promise in that to perform either of these speech acts is to undertake a commitment. Any assertion—"special circumstances" apart—places one under obligations to a linguistic community. Nothing has been said as yet about the boundaries of this community, and we might suppose that it is only the original addressee(s) of my assertion that, say, the cat is

44. Austin, *How To Do Things with Words*, pp. 39; 135.

on the mat with whom that utterance brings me into the relevant norm-governed relationship. But there are obvious epistemic advantages to be derived from a discursive regime under which speakers learn to think of such relations as springing into existence, whenever they make a "serious" assertion, between themselves and *anyone* to whom that speech act may be reported (allowing, of course, for relativization to particular times, cats, and mats): such a regime sets a standard for assertion which—to the extent that it is adhered to—makes hearsay a more reliable, and hence more deliberatively useful, source of information. So where consideration is given to this common interest in enlarging the range of adequate epistemic surrogates for personal experience, there will be pressure towards that form of conscientiousness embodied in the principle that *only what is epistemically good enough for anyone is good enough for one's present audience.*[45]

This looks like, and no doubt is, an intimidating constraint on assertion. Yet it is no more than a corollary of the idea of rational subjectivity as involving the capacity discussed earlier in this chapter (§1)—that of *representing oneself to others.* When Plato and Aristotle maintain that the rational self is the *true* self,[46] they are responding to what we can also think of as a social need for individuals to submit to the discipline of responsibility for their own utterances—the need for them to become "animals with the right to make promises." The "true self" of rationalism is, as it were, constructed out of all the answers (as long as they are given in the right spirit—that is, "seriously"!)[47] which a particular person would give to questions of the form "What do you (really) think (or intend to do) about . . . ?" It is thus controlled by the demand that in any context identifiable as a "serious" one, we say only what we are prepared to be called to account for.[48] And in view of the powers of self-criticism called into play by

45. I am passing over the fine tuning that might be carried out on this principle even by those broadly committed to it—for example, in order to legitimize a policy of selectiveness in what one communicates to children.

46. See Plato, *Republic* 611bd (and compare *Phaedo* 66b–67b, 79cd); Aristotle, *Nicomachean Ethics* 1166a16–17, 1168b31–1169a3, 1177b31–1178a3.

47. How would we know whether or not that was the case? This question throws us back on the holistic considerations of §3. For "the most explicit expression of intention is by itself insufficient evidence of intention" (Wittgenstein, *Philosophical Investigations* §641).

48. As was acknowledged in note 43 above, complying with this demand does not mean never changing one's beliefs or intentions once formed. It does, however, mean not doing so inadvertently or surreptitiously—a practice condemned by Plato as incompatible with dialectical enquiry.

the demand for accountability—powers that depend on our mastery of the social practice of reason-giving—it makes sense that the label "rational" should be attached to a construct arrived at in this way.

What we have been considering in this chapter, then, are the natural origins of a certain ideal that manifests itself in our philosophical tradition. The contrast between "serious" and "nonserious" speech, I have suggested, deserves to be regarded as central to this topic. It is not simply that among the many things we have to master in the course of moral upbringing is a system of conventions bound up with this contrast—conventions having to do with the normative consequences of "serious" speech, or in other words, with the claims or expectations that can arise out of it. The further, and more striking, point is that these conventions seem to be the very ones presupposed by the psychological construction of a responsible "self"—of something that is *authorized* to speak and judge on behalf of the person as a unitary subject. The continued presence within our "language game" of Austin's "serious"/"nonserious" contrast seems to point to the survival, as a component of upbringing, of the demand that we graduate from mere opportunism or short-term expediency in the production of speech acts to a capacity for assuming full *authorship* of such acts—"authorship" here being an implicitly ethical notion, internally related to accountability. In the next chapter I want to say some more about this concept of authorship, and to try and use it to shed light on one of the more surprising products of ethical rationalism—the Socratic thesis that wrongdoing is due to ignorance.

FIVE

On Being the Author of
a Moral Judgement

1

In the last chapter I was concerned with the normative idea of "serious" or responsible utterance. I suggested that this idea rests upon our natural interest in effective deliberation; that the importance of the contrast between "serious" and "nonserious" speech acts has to do with our need to find a certain sort of *predictability* in the behaviour of other persons whose actions may impinge on our own; and that the presence within ethical upbringing of disciplines designed to enforce sensitivity to that contrast—for example, by instilling conscientiousness about the content of what one asserts in "serious" contexts—reflects the enhanced value we attribute to a given individual once their words (and other forms of self-expression) have been shaped by these disciplines into reliable indicators of their future actions.

This picture, so far as it goes, is not a reductive one with regard to the ethical. For although it posits a connection between ethical upbringing and human interests, it does not restrict the relevant interests to those we would have anyway, without benefit of upbringing: among the concerns and objectives in regard to which we want reliable indications of the attitude of others are some that we entertain specifically as "moral" beings, that is, as creatures capable of being motivated in the more than (merely) prudential way which I described earlier[1] in setting out the "practical reason" view. For example, insofar as we need collaborators in morally motivated activity we shall want to know to what extent a given other person is accessible to motivation of that kind.

1. See especially Chapter 1, §2.

Now it is precisely in connection with the demand for *moral* predictability that we might expect the discipline of "serious" utterance to be most insistently applied. To see why, we can recall Aristotle's conception of the virtuous person as someone who has learned to respond not just to the demands of the "pleasant" and the "expedient," but also to those of the "noble" (see Chapter 3, §3). This schema draws attention to the relative remoteness of moral demands from instinct: to find in the "noble"—or perhaps more likely, in the "base"—an incentive to give up some available pleasure or advantage, let alone to face death in battle, is a mark of the triumph of "second" over "first" nature at just those points where "first" nature can be expected to put up the fiercest resistance. Alternatively, we can make use of the idiom introduced in Chapter 4, §4 and say that moral assertions (along with other, less-than-assertoric indications of moral attitude—"the expression of admiration, a smile or a gesture"?)[2] present a particular challenge to the learner who is required to achieve "functional sincerity" in producing them. The reason for this is that these speech acts (or gestures), insofar as they exhibit the promise-like character we have attributed (following Austin) to assertion in general, represent a promise that we are particularly at risk of breaking; that is, it is particularly difficult, in connection with them, to avoid the "breach form of infelicity" (the violation of Austin's Γ.2 condition, which does not invalidate, but constitutes "abuse" of, a performative). Ethical formation has to turn us into "animals with the right" to make the kind of functional, or implicit, promise contained in a moral assertion (or other act of moral expression). Or again, it has to make us capable of producing such acts, not merely as imitators, but as authors—where it is only through the ability to answer for one's future adherence to the values expressed in them that one is genuinely *authorized* to produce them.

2

What seems to be emerging here is an *ideal* conception of the authorship of expressive acts—that is, a conception under which one will not count as (really) the author of such an act simply by producing the appropriate

---

2. See Chapter 2, §4 above. (The quoted words are from L. Wittgenstein, *Lectures and Conversations on Aesthetics, Psychology and Religious Belief*, ed. Cyril Barrett (Oxford: Basil Blackwell, 1970), p. 10, §32.)

visible or audible signs, but only insofar as one satisfies some more de-manding psychological criterion relating to the (temporally extended) "surroundings" of one's expressive behaviour. Although this idea undoubt-edly possesses something of the "strangeness" with which our discussion began (see Chapter 1, §1), I believe it is worth exploring on two counts. The first of these is the close relation it bears to a bit of doctrine that is one of the most puzzling candidates for transfer from ancient to mod-ern thinking about practical reason: I mean the Socratic thesis that *the vir-tuous, or practically wise, person sees the world in a way that is guaranteed to issue in morally appropriate action.* And in case this should sound like a point of historical rather than of current philosophical interest, the sec-ond is that I hope to show—perhaps contrary to expectation—that a "re-laxed naturalism" about practical reason can extend to the Socratic thesis something of the same hospitality with which it has already received the "strange" postulate of a category of objective, unconditional reasons for action.[3] I will argue, not that Socrates' alleged view is one that we *must ac-cept,* but that it is one whose philosophical motivation we ought to ac-knowledge as, at any rate, not alien to us, since it incorporates a conception of the ideal outcome of ethical formation for which a counterpart can be found within our own account of that process—the rationale for the term "counterpart" here being that in each philosophical context it is the *quality of our relation* to the moral judgements we produce that determines the *quality of the grounds there are* for confidence in the future conformity of our actions to our words.

First, however, some background. Our Socratic thesis has been the point of departure for a whole subgenre of speculation within moral philoso-phy—a genre kept alive today by the production of student essays on the "problem of acrasia," or weakness of will. The main sources for the thesis are two Platonic dialogues, the *Protagoras* and *Meno,* in which Socrates ar-gues respectively for the propositions that:

   (i) "No one, either knowing or believing that a different course of ac-tion is better than the one he is pursuing, and is open to him, per-sists in his present course of action, when the better one is avail-able" (*Protagoras* 358b7–c1); and
   (ii) "No one wants what is bad" (*Meno* 78a6).[4]

   3. On the qualification "unconditional," see Chapter 1, note 6 and accompanying text.
   4. A related passage of argument occurs at *Gorgias* 466a–468e: see esp. 468d5–7 (if some-one is doing what is in fact bad for him, then he is not doing what he wants).

Either of these claims, if accepted, will enable us to argue (by *modus tollens* or contraposition) that if you do pursue a course of action that is in fact bad (or *not good enough,* or worse than another that is open to you), then you cannot (really) have known or believed that this was the case—that is, that your actually chosen course *was* flawed in any of these ways. Of course, on the face of things, we often see people behaving in ways which they are quite prepared to say—and to say in good faith—that they know or believe to be bad for them; this is the experience that gives rise to what is described in the *Protagoras* as the view of the "many,"[5] namely, that we behave in that way from time to time because we are "overcome" by pleasure, pain, anger, or the like. But the Socratic thesis entails that we ought, precisely, *not* to take such phenomena at face value, but rather to redescribe them as cases in which the person in question does not really know (or believe) that the choice they are making is a bad (or not good enough, or less than optimal) one, even though they may *believe* that they know (or believe) this. In other words, it entails that in such cases a person's cognitive state—not just their state of knowledge but, crucially, their state of belief also[6]—is something on which they do not have full authority to pronounce.

The thesis as I have just stated it refers solely to the pursuit of one's own interest or welfare: it says that failure to pursue whatever it is that actually constitutes these things is always attributable to a failure of knowledge. However, this can be combined with another claim advanced by the Platonic Socrates, namely, that the soul is the most authentic and precious element in the person and that one's own welfare consists primarily in the welfare of that element (which can be achieved only by living a morally good life).[7] This combination gives us the uncompromising moral ratio-

5. Plato, *Protagoras* 352b2, d5.

6. Although Plato sets great store, on general epistemological grounds, by the contrast between knowledge and mere belief (see for example *Meno* 97e–98a, *Republic* 475d–541b, *Timaeus* 51de), that contrast is passed over in the *Protagoras* passage cited as (i) above in favour of the thought that one cannot *in practice* do more, at any given moment, than act in pursuit of the good according to one's own lights (see *Republic* 505d11–e4; and compare Aristotle, *Nicomachean Ethics* 1146b27–31, which asserts the legitimacy of treating "knowledge" and "belief" as interchangeable with respect to the puzzle posed by acratic action). There are obvious fallibilistic reasons why we cannot claim perfect authority concerning our own states of *knowledge,* but the shortfall in authority concerning our own states of *belief* is a point that may not yet have been fully assimilated, and that underlies the considerations still to come in this chapter.

7. See for example *Crito* 47e–48a.

nalist position which maintains that not just failure to promote what would count in commonsensical terms as one's own interests, but also failure to *do the right thing* or to act as moral virtue commands, is a mark of ignorance or error in the agent.

3

We thus arrive at the classical formulation of what has been labeled "internalism" in moral theory—the view (already touched on in Chapter 1, §1) that motivation is internal to moral judgement.[8] In its unqualified form, this view entails that if you judge that (all things considered) you ought to do action *a*, then you will necessarily be moved to do *a*—that is, moved in such a way as actually to do it unless physically prevented. An "externalist," by contrast, adheres to the Humean tradition according to which two agents could be in complete agreement on an "ought" judgement relating to a situation in which they both found themselves, while differing in their motivation (or lack of it) to perform the relevant act.

A more modest, but still recognizably internalist, thesis would be that if you judge that (all things considered) you ought to do *a*, then you will be moved to do *a unless* you suffer from some lapse in practical rationality (for example, from acrasia) at the crucial moment. This thesis asserts a *defeasible* internal connection between moral judgement and motivation to act.[9] By contrast, the full-blooded Socratic view maintains that the connection is *indefeasible;* it therefore allows us to treat the nonperformance

8. The "internalism requirement on normative practical reasons" is spelled out as follows in a recent overview of the subject: "[A] normative reason for me to φ must be a consideration my awareness of which would motivate me to φ if I were thinking about it rationally and with full knowledge" (Garrett Cullity and Berys Gaut, eds., *Ethics and Practical Reason* (Oxford: Clarendon Press, 1997), Introduction, p. 3). Note that I shall be concerned in this chapter only with moral judgement *qua* practical—that is, with what we think we ought to do (or must do) all things considered: I shall not be considering the kind of *pro tanto*, but practically inconclusive, reasons that we couch in terms of "thick" moral predicates (see Chapter 1, note 40). I shall also confine myself to talking about judgements as to what we ought to do *on particular occasions,* since unless we disavow the reasoning of Chapters 2 and 3 and postulate the existence of moral principles that are both fully explicit and exceptionless, these seem to be the only moral judgements that give rise to indisputable cases of acratic action.

9. I am using "motivation" here as the nominal equivalent of "being moved," though in some contexts it may be necessary to draw a distinction between these ideas.

of the act (in what would popularly be regarded as cases of acrasia) as a basis for the *modus tollens* argument mentioned earlier and to conclude that the judgement itself, contrary to appearances, cannot strictly speaking have been made, or cannot have been fully adhered to throughout the acratic episode.

The latter view forms part of an account of moral motivation which has been defended since the 1970s by John McDowell, and which I mentioned in Chapter 1, §2, where it was meant to shed light on the idea of a mode of awareness that would be both objective and practical. At that stage of the discussion, my concern was simply to make this idea intelligible, and so the only element in McDowell's account that mattered to us then was his suggestion that for a virtuous person, the perception of objective features of a situation—that is, of *facts*—may constitute a source of *unconditional reasons* why this or that action is required. But now I want to bring into play the more distinctively Socratic thought that when a virtuous person perceives a fact of the relevant kind, *action* (or inaction, as appropriate) *necessarily follows* (again, unless it is physically prevented)—a thought which McDowell elaborates by saying that if virtue does (in the agent's eyes) demand a particular course of action, then considerations which would otherwise have told against that course of action (such as pleasure or personal convenience) will be "silenced":[10] that is, they may still be recognized in a detached or contemplative way, but they will not be allowed to play any part in the virtuous person's deliberations.

---

10. John McDowell, "Are Moral Requirements Hypothetical Imperatives?" in *Proceedings of the Aristotelian Society,* supp. vol. 52 (1978), pp. 13–29. McDowell suggests (p. 26) that "the dictates of virtue, if properly appreciated, are not weighed with other reasons at all, not even in a scale which always tips on their side. If a situation in which virtue imposes a requirement is genuinely conceived as such, according to this view, then considerations which, in the absence of the requirement, would have constituted reasons for acting otherwise are silenced altogether—not overridden—by the requirement." (A precursor of this thought is to be found in Gary Watson, "Free Agency," in *Journal of Philosophy,* 72, no. 8 [April 1975], pp. 205–220, Section II.) In fact, I suspect Jonathan Dancy is right to point out (in a critical discussion of McDowell) that the phenomenon of silencing is "not peculiar to ethics," and that the virtuous person is best deployed in the theoretically unambitious role of "someone in whom opposing considerations are silenced when they should be, and not when they shouldn't" (see Dancy, *Moral Reasons* [Oxford: Blackwell, 1993], pp. 54, 52; and compare Chapter 1, note 32). However, all that is needed for present purposes is the concession that there are some circumstances in which moral considerations are entitled to silence nonmoral ones in determining how we ought to act.

It is of course phenomena such as acrasia—along with depression, apathy, and other forms of emotional disengagement—that constitute the obvious difficulty for the thesis. One writer who has drawn attention to this difficulty is Michael Smith in his book *The Moral Problem*,[11] to which I am indebted for the distinction drawn at the beginning of this section between weak and strong variants of internalism. Smith maintains that the strong variant has consequences which are "manifestly implausible," indeed "quite incredible," in the face of everyday experience: in particular, "it is a commonplace . . . that when agents suffer from weakness of the will they may stare the facts that used to move them square in the face, appreciate them in all their glory, and yet still not be moved by them."[12] Interestingly, although this criticism is directed at McDowell, it issues from a position in moral philosophy that has some important points in common with his. Like McDowell, Smith holds that moral requirements are unconditional or "categorical" requirements of reason;[13] moreover, he too wishes to defend a form of internalism, since he insists on the "practicality" of moral judgement.[14] Yet he claims that such judgement is "quite evidently"[15] practical only in the weak, other-things-being-equal sense associated with the idea of a *defeasible* internal connection (between the judgement and the action it demands), and reaffirms the Humean view that "[d]esires are . . . the only states that can constitute our motivating reasons."[16]

The immediate target of these remarks is the discussion by McDowell which we revisited just now, and in which it is argued that a complete answer to the question why someone acted in a certain way can consist simply in a statement of some fact about the circumstances of the action, a fact the agent happens to be perceptive enough to have noticed ("Why don't you get *N* to join in the karaoke?"—"Because he's shy and sensitive.")[17] Smith works towards his Humean conclusion about motivating reasons by way of criticism of McDowell's example of the virtuous (in this case, pre-

11. Michael Smith, *The Moral Problem* (Oxford: Blackwell, 1994).

12. Ibid., pp. 61, 123.

13. Ibid., p. 91.

14. Ibid., p. 6 and elsewhere. See also Chapter 1, note 4 and accompanying text.

15. Ibid., p. 120.

16. Ibid., p. 125.

17. See McDowell, "Are Moral Requirements Hypothetical Imperatives?" p. 21: "[I]n urging behaviour one takes to be morally required, one finds oneself saying things like this: 'You don't know what it means that someone is shy and sensitive.'"

sumably, the kind or socially attentive) person who does, and the boorish one who does not, appreciate the practical significance of the point mentioned in this exchange. He objects that McDowell tacitly builds on our willingness, as morally like-minded readers, to assent to the conditional proposition that *if someone is virtuous,* and conceives of another person as shy and sensitive, then they will be disposed to show certain kinds of consideration towards that person. But this, he argues, is inadequate as a basis for McDowell's position because all it says is that there is a necessary connection between conception and action "in the restricted case where the believer [the subject of the thought '*N* is shy and sensitive'] is a virtuous person"; and "if, as the Humean will claim, someone counts as a virtuous person only if she has certain desires . . . then we see immediately that the necessary connection is an artefact of that restriction. The virtuous person is a regular believer and desirer after all."[18]

If this criticism is to succeed, however, the hypothesis that a certain person is virtuous can be no more than externally, or contingently, related to the hypothesis that they perceive *N* as shy and sensitive; in other words, it must be possible to perceive this irrespective of whether or not one has the characteristic desires of the virtuous person. For otherwise the "restriction" mentioned by Smith will not (as he implies) be arbitrary, and so will not create an opening for the charge that McDowell's necessary connection is established by sleight of hand. And the idea of a merely contingent connection between these two hypotheses is precisely what the "anti-Humean" would challenge. For the crucial anti-Humean, or Socratic, move is to deny that one can, strictly speaking, *be* a subject of the relevant beliefs in the first place unless one is suitably motivated. (That is: unless, when the moment comes, one is moved in such a way as actually to do *a* if not prevented.)

At this point, Smith's argument with McDowell grinds to a halt. For he seems to hold the Socratic picture, and hence the "indefeasibility thesis"— the idea of an indefeasible, as opposed to a defeasible, internal connection between moral judgement and action—to be sufficiently discredited by holding up for inspection certain passages in which McDowell concedes that this picture involves a departure from "ordinary" or empirical canons of evidence. Thus we have, first, the admission that "[f]ailure to see what a circumstance means, in the [morally] loaded sense, is of course compatible with competence, by all ordinary tests, with the language used to describe

18. Smith, *The Moral Problem,* pp. 122–123.

the circumstance"; and second, the statement that despite appearances "the relevant conceptions are not so much as possessed except by those whose wills are influenced appropriately."[19] The very fact that McDowell is forced by the unfavourable outcome of applying "ordinary" tests to retreat to a mode of argument that puts his proposals beyond the reach of such tests suggests to Smith that "[i]ronically enough, . . . it is McDowell's anti-Humean view [about the nature of the virtuous person's motivation] that has turned into a dogma, not the Humean view that it was supposed to replace."[20]

4

Smith is right to comment on the curious indifference to the "facts of experience" that is implicit in the indefeasibility thesis. This indifference, though, may be more understandable if we can provide the right kind of context for the idea with which the thesis stands or falls, namely, that if someone fails to act on one of their supposed moral beliefs—as in acrasia—then that belief could not strictly speaking, or at the relevant moment, have been "one of theirs." Let us now introduce a thought that might serve to create this context: it is that only insofar as someone instantiates the rationalist character ideal for ethics (Chapter 1, §2) do they *really*, as opposed to *ostensibly*, hold the kind of belief which the (moral) acratic is said to act against.

This thought is, on the face of it, an implausible one. It seems easier to concur with a quite different account of what we normally mean by "holding a moral belief," and to say that we associate this concept with a fairly loose cluster of criteria which would include assenting verbally to the truth of the relevant judgement, acting on it without hesitation, feeling pleased or displeased with oneself depending on whether one acts on it or not, and much more. There would probably be widespread support for the view that while no single one of these conditions is either necessary or sufficient, still "the satisfaction of some disjunction of conjunctions"[21] of them *is* sufficient, to warrant the attribution to me of (say) the belief that it

---

19. McDowell, "Are Moral Requirements Hypothetical Imperatives?" pp. 22, 23.

20. Smith, *The Moral Problem*, p. 124.

21. See C. C. W. Taylor, "Plato, Hare and Davidson on Acrasia," *Mind*, 89 (1980), pp. 499–518; quotation from p. 516.

is my duty to respond to a certain request for help. And no doubt Smith's acratics (the clear-sighted depressive, and so forth) do satisfy some appropriate subset of our cluster of criteria. (It is possible to do *that* while still failing, on a given occasion, actually to perform.)

Yet the indefeasibility thesis invites us to reject this cluster concept of "judging" or "holding a belief" in favour of an ideal concept, such that in those who fully instantiate the concept—but *only* in them—the connection between judgement and action would be unbreakable. As a paradigm of *really holding the belief,* it offers us the "virtuous person," the complete embodiment of the (local) rationalist character ideal; imperfectly virtuous people only approximate, in varying degrees, towards this paradigm. (Thus McDowell argues that Aristotle's doctrine of the special coerciveness of the conclusions of practical wisdom "leaves him no option but to suppose that if someone in a way achieves one of those conclusions but does not act accordingly, what he achieves is at most a *flawed approximation* to the conclusion.")[22]

The view that someone who fails to act on a moral belief must somehow fall short of really holding the belief exemplifies, I think, a phenomenon discussed by Wittgenstein:[23] the production of what are, formally speaking, *a priori* propositions about objects (in our case, beliefs and the way they connect with action), but "really" *(eigentlich)* "avowal[s] of adherence to a form of expression." An adherent of the indefeasibility thesis will refuse to entertain the possibility of a state of affairs that would satisfy the criteria for a genuine instance of acrasia: that is, she will refuse in advance to recognize any state of affairs as correctly describable in that way. Hence, I suppose, the accusation of dogmatism.

It is undeniable that to adopt this attitude is to place the indefeasibility

22. John McDowell, "Incontinence and Practical Wisdom in Aristotle," in Sabina Lovibond and S. G. Williams, eds., *Essays for David Wiggins: Identity, Truth and Value* (Oxford: Blackwell, 1996), pp. 95–112; quotation from p. 104 (emphasis added). (But the idea of a defective approximation to the cognitive state that constitutes true moral sensitivity is already present at pp. 334–335 of McDowell, "Virtue and Reason," *Monist,* 62 (1979), pp. 331–350—an account endorsed by David McNaughton in his *Moral Vision: An Introduction to Ethics* [Oxford: Blackwell, 1988], pp. 127–130. Compare also McDowell, "Are Moral Requirements Hypothetical Imperatives?" p. 28: "[I]n a view of what genuine virtue is, idealization is not something to be avoided or apologized for.")

23. Ludwig Wittgenstein, *Zettel,* ed. G. E. M. Anscombe and G. H. von Wright, trans. G. E. M. Anscombe (Oxford: Basil Blackwell, 1981), §§441–442.

thesis beyond the reach of empirical falsification. And by our standards, if not by those of Socrates and Plato,[24] any such move will clearly debar the thesis from featuring in a psychologically informative theory about the origins of virtuous action. But what if it was never meant to play that kind of role? What if it was intended, rather—in a spirit of "rebellion against the priority of psychology" (see Chapter 1, §1)—to cut the Socratic paradox[25] free from any semblance of grounding in a substantive psychological theory, and to make us look at it afresh against the background of a purely phenomenological method: one that "simply puts everything before us, and neither explains nor deduces anything"?[26] For example (since phenomenology may draw, among other materials, on those supplied by our ethical interests): does the ideal notion of "believing" or "judging" belong to a form of expression to which, in our ethical capacity, we might feel that we had some *incentive* to adhere?

5

I want to approach this question by asking whether there is any variant of the (cognitive) concept of *believing* that is internally related to the overtly ethical (or juridical) concepts of "functional sincerity" or "being authorized to speak"—that is, to those concepts which we can recognize (or so I argued in Chapter 4) as regulating the process of upbringing. This enquiry seems to fall into place within the ongoing philosophical effort to mediate or mitigate the opposition of "fact" and "value"; my proposal, at any rate, is that we should investigate the potential of the idea of *authorship* to contribute to that mediation. The way in which I think this idea can help to dispel the air of dogma or arbitrariness surrounding the Socratic position is by helping us to do justice to an element of indeterminacy which already, in our prephilosophical thinking, attaches to questions of moral conviction—for example, to the question: am I (Lovibond) one of those people

24. See Chapter 3, §4 above.

25. By "*the* Socratic paradox" I mean the thesis that virtue is knowledge and, consequently, that all wrongdoing is due to ignorance. However, commentators sometimes recognize a number of distinct Socratic paradoxes: see for example Gerasimos Xenophon Santas, *Socrates: Philosophy in Plato's Early Dialogues* (London: Routledge and Kegan Paul, 1979), chap. 6.

26. Ludwig Wittgenstein, *Philosophical Investigations*, trans. G. E. M. Anscombe (Oxford: Basil Blackwell, 1967), §126.

who *really believe* that to perform (or omit to perform) action *a* in the present situation would be morally impossible?

We can begin by turning to Aristotle's commentary, in Book VII of the *Nicomachean Ethics*, on the Socratic denial of acrasia. In particular, I would like to take up the idea (which I borrow from a discussion by Myles Burnyeat)[27] that Aristotle's solution to the problem involves an account of the acratic state of mind as involving *regression* to a more primitive, instinct-dominated condition. And I want to make the relevant concept of regression more concrete by understanding it as the converse of a *progression* towards genuine authorship of the moral judgements of which one gives oneself out as author.

Perhaps the best way of explaining what I mean by this is to apply it to the interpretation of Aristotle's own treatment of acrasia in *Nicomachean Ethics* VII, 3. Consider his famous comparison of the acratic to someone reciting the verses of Empedocles while drunk; or alternatively to someone who has just learned something, and can reproduce it verbally, but does not yet understand it.[28] (The comparison refers to the familiar fact that people often find themselves thinking—or saying—"I know I shouldn't be doing this," but doing it anyway.) These analogies are driven home by saying that, in contrast to the person whose moral knowledge has "become part of their nature," acratic agents are "like actors"—obviously in respect of their incomplete mental engagement with any conscientious thoughts they may express during the acratic episode. But now, what about a positive characterization of the condition that unites the virtuous agent, the student in full command of a bit of theory, and the sober performer of Empedocles? This is where the notion of authorship comes in. For we can

27. See M. F. Burnyeat, "Aristotle on Learning to be Good," in A. O. Rorty, ed., *Essays on Aristotle's Ethics* (Berkeley: University of California Press, 1980), p. 85: "We must account for [the acratic's] present condition in terms of stages in the development of his character which he has not yet completely left behind . . . on Aristotle's picture of moral development, as I have drawn it, an important fact about the better syllogism [the verbal reconstruction of the thinking that issues in the virtuous person's, in contrast to the acratic's, action] is that it represents a later and less established stage of development." Note that one element in the Aristotelian position that I have omitted to discuss is the distinction between the "continent" person, who does the right thing despite being tempted to do otherwise, and the virtuous person who is free from such inner conflict. The distinction undoubtedly holds some interest, but if, as here, (true) virtue is understood as the ideal end point of a developmental process, it can only be one of degree.

28. Aristotle, *Nicomachean Ethics* 1147a18–24.

locate the resemblance between the acratic and the drunken performer in the fact that each of them regresses from *being in a fit state to present himself as the author of the words* to just *serving as a mouthpiece for them.*

It may sound fanciful to say that in reciting Empedocles one "presents oneself as the author" of his words: we can hardly think of the reciter as pretending actually to *be* Empedocles. But this is to take the suggestion too literally. If the significant thing about reciting Empedocles when drunk is that although you know the words you do not (at that moment anyway) understand them, then what the drunken performer lacks will be the ability to *take on, for present conversational purposes, the role of Empedocles* by expounding or explaining his verses and thereby, as it were, speaking on his behalf. To be able to do this would be to display a capacity prized by Plato, and captured in his doctrine that the way to take intellectual possession of something—some discursive item—is by making oneself competent to answer questions about it, and so to act as its protector in the sphere of discussion;[29] it would be to prove oneself capable of the kind of *mimêsis* of Empedocles (or whomever) that consists in an *enactment,* as opposed to just a replication of the external record, of his thought processes.[30]

When this ability is present, then even though the person who utters a verse of Empedocles—or any other remark—may not be its author in the sense of the first person to think the thought in question, they can still be seen as its honorary "author" by virtue of having appropriated it mentally and so made it theirs. When the relevant ability is absent, on the other hand, the words uttered by the speaker revert to expressing a thought that is *someone else's*—not necessarily that of some definite individual (such as Empedocles), but often "someone else's" in the merely negative sense of "not the speaker's own." In the case of the acratic who even at the moment of action says "This is awful, I should not be doing this," and the like, the utterances that express her supposed convictions revert to being the vehicle, not of convictions of the agent's own (though insofar as the acratic behaviour is out of character they will *approximate* towards this function in her life), but (usually) of beliefs figuring in the particular moral consensus on which her upbringing has been based.[31] So the "regression" involved in

29. See Plato, *Meno* 85bd, 98a; *Republic* 534bd; *Phaedrus* 275d–277a.

30. For "enactment" as one of the meanings of *mimêsis,* see Stephen Halliwell, *Aristotle's Poetics* (London: Duckworth, 1986), chap. 4.

31. R. M. Hare seems to have found this idea suggestive at the time of writing *The Language of Morals* (Oxford: Oxford University Press, 1952): he notes for example that "it is . . . possible to use 'ought' and other value-words, as it were, *unconsciously in inverted commas*"

acratic behaviour will be from a later to an earlier stage in the evolution of our relation of authorship to the relevant moral opinions. (It will consist, as Anthony Price has written, in "a form of transient insincerity" in which practical judgement "loses contact with one's psychology.")[32] And the indefeasibility thesis will now be tantamount to the claim—*a priori* as ever—that *we do not act against those practical beliefs, or morally loaded "conceptions" of our circumstances, of which we have achieved full authorship,* but only against those we have appropriated in a more partial or opportunistic way.

This interpretation seems to accord with the spirit of Socratic intellectualism. At all events, it makes Aristotle's account of acrasia look entirely pertinent to the difficulty found by (Plato's) Socrates in the common-sense approach to the subject—a difficulty that relates to the larger topic of *self-contradiction*. Thus, suppose we suspend judgement about the cluster conception of moral "believing" (§4 above) and assume that whatever other propositional attitudes we may or may not be able to attribute to the acratic, we can at least attribute to her one that is a verbal representation of the very course of action she in fact adopts—say, "It would be all right for me to break my promise to *N*."[33] Now if we also see fit to dignify with the

(p. 167, emphasis added), and contemplates a future treatment of the problem of acrasia based on the admission that "there are *degrees of sincere assent,* not all of which involve actually obeying the command [assented to]" (pp. 169–170, emphasis added—and compare the interesting passage [pp. 125–126] on cases in which it is "difficult . . . to say" whether a judgement carries evaluative content or merely "[pays] lip-service to a convention"). His subsequent discussion in *Freedom and Reason* (Oxford: Oxford University Press, 1963) retains the idea that there are different states of mind, not all equally "robust," which can be grouped under the heading of *thinking that one ought to do something* (p. 77); but "insincerity" as such makes only a brief appearance (p. 83) in the relevant chapter, and (so far as I can detect) is no longer mentioned in connection with acrasia in Hare's *Moral Thinking: Its Levels, Method and Point* (Oxford: Clarendon Press, 1981).

32. A. W. Price, *Mental Conflict* (London: Routledge, 1995), p. 132. Price's interpretation of this passage of Aristotle leads him to suggest a few pages later (p. 137) that "[w]here knowledge is practical, a failure of desire brings with it a kind of ignorance"; but he concludes his discussion (p. 144) by voicing the worry that "[p]racticality cannot, without equivocation, be at once a feature of the *content* of practical judgement, and a matter of its *effect*." The view entailed by the indefeasibility thesis (as understood here) could perhaps be elucidated as saying that what pertains to the *content* of a practical judgement (or proposition) is "practicality" in the sense of *aptness to express* a judgement which, if someone attains to full authorship of it, will be practical in its *effect*.

33. This assumption might be regarded as a corollary of the view that knowledge or belief is "commanding" (*hêgemonikon* or *archikon*: Plato, *Protagoras* 352b4); it is also the idea to

title of "belief" those states of moral consciousness which, according to the cluster conception, can exist in the absence of (effective) motivation, we shall find ourselves compelled to attribute to a single subject two conflicting attitudes to the same thought content (since the subject in our example will now count as holding the belief: "It would *not* be all right to break my promise to *N*," inferred—in the absence of any exceptional circumstances—from "One must not break one's promises"). But this defeats understanding[34] (since it involves representing a rational being as committed to two propositions that are related to one another as "*p*" and "not *p*") and so necessitates, intellectually, a redescription of the case. Aristotle's contribution can be read as a proposal about the form this redescription should take: the proposal that the inoperative "belief" should be seen as not having been definitively converted from an *interpersonally available thought content* (the status such thoughts possess for us in our initial encounters with them) into a *thought content to which the utterer is related as author*. For in this case the subject, or originator, of the moral judgement that is violated in acratic action will not be precisely the same as the subject of the action itself:[35] the judgement will retain, from the point of view of the acratic agent, something of the foreignness with which moral demands and prohibitions naturally present themselves to us as learners.

6

Let us review the present state of the discussion. We have before us, first, a particularly surprising item in the repertoire of ideas available to a contemporary practical reason approach to ethics—the idea of an indefeasible internal connection between moral judgement and action. We also have the Socratic thesis from which this idea is derived, namely, the thesis that

which Hare appeals at the beginning of *The Language of Morals* (p. 1) when he says that the best way to find out what someone's moral principles are is to study what he *does*.

34. Compare Donald Davidson, *Essays on Actions and Events* (Oxford: Clarendon Press, 1982), p. 42: "[The acratic] recognizes, in his own intentional behaviour, something essentially surd."

35. In what sense "not the same," since we have recognized that the acratic agent may actually utter the words "I should not be doing this" (or equivalent)? Evidently the proposed view of acrasia involves a certain exercise of imagination, a characteristically "philosophical" refusal to acquiesce in outward appearances: compare the intimately related idea (touched on in Chapter 4, §4) that the "true self" is (not the physically manifest person, but) the subject of rational thought.

no one acts against their own better judgement. And finally we have a modified version of the Socratic view, suggested by Aristotle's commentary upon it. This version distinguishes the virtuous from the morally mediocre person no longer in baldly cognitive terms, but in terms of the more or less satisfactory outcome of a process of social reproduction, the aim of that process being to constitute a fully autonomous subject of moral thought and speech. This subject embodies the ideal paradigm of authorship which I have suggested can replace, or anyway serve as a gloss upon, the Socratic ideal of perfect ethical knowledge.

At this point, someone may ask: why should the Socratic thesis be any more convincing when couched in terms of authorship than it was in its original, cognitive, formulation?

My concern, however, is not so much to mount a direct defence of the thesis as to crack the code in which it presents what is really a cultural or educational ideal—that of the perfect integration, within the life of any given individual, of particular instances of moral expression (whether explicit or otherwise) with entrenched states of character. We can see that such an ideal might be arrived at by extrapolation from the measure of success actually achieved by human societies in equipping their members with an ethically informed "second nature." To that extent it would resemble the Socratic conception of (practical) knowledge or belief, since the latter too looks beyond everyday morality by denying that most of the people whom we would ordinarily accept, say, as *believing that they ought not to do such and such a thing* really do believe this: it sets a standard for "really believing" of which most apparent instances of the concept, in the case of ethics at least, will fall short. But the idealism associated with the work of formation, or with the process of establishing a moral sensibility as "part of our nature,"[36] diverges from that of the Socratic conception in that it wears on its sleeve—as the other does not—the demand that it addresses to us to endorse a certain scheme of purposive social activity.

Now I am aware that our response to this demand may well be less than whole hearted; nor do I see that as necessarily a bad thing, as I hope will become clear in Part III. Indeed, it is precisely because our sense of ourselves and of our own beliefs and attitudes is not orientated exclusively to-

36. See Aristotle, *Nicomachean Ethics* 1147a22. Note that whereas in Chapter 1, §3 "idealism" was to be understood in the sense current in epistemology (meaning the view that mind or thought is ontologically prior to reality), I am using it here, more informally, to refer to the orientation of thought *towards an ideal*.

wards the ideal of integrated subjectivity, but takes into account also the expressive (including the linguistic) behaviour of the natural creature that each of us empirically is, that the cluster conception of *holding a belief* must strike us as closer to common sense than the Socratic conception.[37] Yet in the face of this commonsense identification with the actual, our thinking about the relation in which we stand to our own speech acts seems nevertheless to be subject (as I also suggested in §4 above) to a certain idealist pressure, which contemporary philosophy may be in a particularly favourable position to register.

The point may become clearer if we turn our attention away from the *rational* moral subject, who inevitably takes centre stage in a "practical reason" account of ethics, and fix it on the material with which moral upbringing has to work—that is, on the *incompleteness* or *imperfection* that characterizes our actual (empirical) relation to much, at least, of our own moral expression. This will lead us on to the terrain of a critique of "psychologism" whose target is no longer just the Humean account of motivation—the account that has prompted some people to a "rebellion against the priority of psychology"—but more ambitiously, an entire "philosophy of consciousness," a satisfactory line of escape from which was perhaps the main desideratum of twentieth-century European thought.

I would like in particular to look at the Socratic thesis—or rather at its quasi-Aristotelian successor, formulated in terms of authorship—in relation to certain insights about language deriving from poststructuralist theory. Poststructuralism reminds us that what makes linguistic signs into more than mere noises or marks—what enables them to communicate meaning—is their public character, their ability to be taken up and used successively by different subjects. However, it also maintains that this same publicity makes any thought of mine potentially detachable from *me* and transferrable, without any necessary loss of communicative power, to other contexts in which *my* particular intentions in producing the relevant signs will be of no account; and this attribute of not being *essentially* mine affects my words, my utterances, even at the moment of my most complete intellectual engagement with them. As competent users of a language, we

---

37. Indeed, the difficulty of coming to terms with Socratic rationalism in its pure—or crude—form may explain the move to a more psychologically complex view in Book IV of Plato's *Republic*, where the doctrine of the tripartite soul is developed.

know how to bend the available symbolic resources to our own intended meanings, but the "iterability" of the sign—that is, its inbuilt capacity for being *repeated-with-a-difference*—"already at the moment of utterance, makes it structurally incapable of full permeation by the intention of the speaker."[38] The particular sentences I construct, in speaking or writing, represent what I as an individual have been able to accomplish in the way of self-expression[39] on the basis of the collective "mindedness" embodied in English (or some other natural language); but this "mindedness" existed before me, and although I can draw upon it more or less creatively, I cannot wholly rid it of the alterity that consists in its being *available,* not just to me but to any English speaker, for the expression of meaning.

One of the classic texts in which this idea of alterity is explored is Jacques Derrida's "Signature Event Context," first delivered as a conference paper in 1971.[40] Significantly for us, the positive content of this paper emerges in part from a (not unrespectful) critique of the thought of J. L. Austin as presented in *How To Do Things with Words,*[41] the book to which I referred in Chapter 4 as a source for the idea of the "functional sincerity" (or otherwise) of an assertion. Derrida's discussion seems to me to offer that element of drama that occurs when one experimentalist locates a particularly suggestive oversight or blind spot in the work of another, and since the diagnosis in this case has a bearing on our current theme of authorship, I think it is worth considering in some detail.

38. Henry Staten, *Wittgenstein and Derrida* (Oxford: Basil Blackwell, 1985), p. 125. See also Simon Glendinning on the logical connection, with respect to significant or "readable" patterns of behaviour, between "public intelligibility" and "structural anonymity" (*On Being with Others: Heidegger, Derrida, Wittgenstein* [London: Routledge, 1998], p. 143). The moment of difference within "iterability" will surface again in Chapter 9.

39. The concept of *expression* is, strictly speaking, inadmissible in the context of anti- or posthumanist considerations about the nature of signs. I have made no attempt at terminological rigour on this point; nor, conversely, would I object on humanist grounds to the characterization of moral discourse as a "sign system" (*pace* H. P. Grice, who says firmly that "some [bearers of non-natural meaning] are not signs (e.g., words are not)": see his "Meaning," in P. F. Strawson, ed., *Philosophical Logic* [Oxford: Oxford University Press, 1967], p. 41. This claim evidently rests upon an ordinary-language sense of "sign" which, for better or worse, has long been sidelined by philosophy of language in the Saussurean tradition.)

40. Jacques Derrida, "Signature Event Context," trans. Samuel Weber and Jeffrey Mehlman, in *Limited Inc,* ed. Gerald Graff (Evanston: Northwestern University Press, 1988), pp. 1–23.

41. J. L. Austin, *How To Do Things with Words* (Oxford: Clarendon Press, 1962).

According to Derrida, the fruit of Austin's "patient, open, aporetical"[42] and constantly self-transforming investigations in *How To Do Things with Words* is an unintended encounter with the "writerly," or *graphematic,* character of locution in general—that is, with its indebtedness to the physical production of the sounds or marks that we tend to regard as mere "vehicles" of thought. The encounter is unintended because Austin himself assumes, in his account of the performative and its possible "infelicities," that a *normal* speech act can claim as one feature of its total context—"and not one among others," adds Derrida—"the conscious presence of the intention of the speaking subject in the totality of his speech act,"[43] enabling the act to constitute "an absolutely meaningful speech [*vouloir-dire*] that is master of itself."[44] Yet it is also rendered inevitable by Austin's admission that (not only performatives, but) *all* utterances are vulnerable to features of their context which are such as to make them "*in a peculiar way* hollow or void"[45]—these being the sort of circumstances in which, as we saw earlier, Austin takes language to undergo a "sea change" from its normal ("serious") use to a different one that is "parasitic" or "etiolated." For this admission reveals the dependence of even a successful speech act on the "general iterability"[46] that enables us to identify certain forms of words as conforming to a particular linguistic model—the model for, say, launching a ship or tendering an apology; and as a consequence, it suggests that the condition of "parasitism" (relative to a supposedly authentic utterance located elsewhere) is not a "failure or trap into which language may *fall*"[47] so much as a structurally "necessary possibility"[48] for it. This possibility of giving the lie to its own ostensible "seriousness" is, in Derrida's view, "the very force and law of [the] emergence"[49] of language.

Once this "necessary possibility" is recognized (the argument continues), Austin's inclination to suppress it by representing the "nonserious" as

---

42. Derrida, "Signature Event Context," p. 14.

43. Ibid.

44. Ibid., p. 15; words in square brackets supplied by the translators.

45. Ibid., p. 16; quotation from Austin, *How To Do Things with Words,* p. 22 (emphasis in original).

46. Derrida, "Signature Event Context," p. 17.

47. Ibid. (emphasis in original).

48. Ibid., p. 15.

49. Ibid., p. 17. Staten (*Wittgenstein and Derrida,* chap. 3) draws attention to the parallel with Wittgenstein, *Philosophical Investigations* §641.

external to the ordinary can be attributed to a conception of the "ordinary" itself which is shaped by a kind of (not fully self-conscious) moralism[50]—a conviction that *ideally,*[51] one would be able to certify the context of an utterance as being free from any of those factors that give rise to "infelicity," including the hazard of (either introspectible or functional) insincerity on the part of the speaker. Since the fulfillment of this ideal would require, among other things, that the conscious intention of the speaker should be "totally present and immediately transparent to itself and to others"[52] within the relevant context—a condition that is at variance with the "structural unconsciousness"[53] of the sign—the best we can do is to maintain an explicit awareness of the idealization at work in Austin's conception of the "ordinary," a conception which, though unstable, is the nonaccidental product of an "ethical and teleological discourse of consciousness."[54] The teleology in question here is already familiar to us as the one that regulates the business of upbringing, viewed now under the aspect of a process designed to turn out individual language users as (really) the authors of their own linguistic (or other expressive) performances. Some of these performances, namely, those touching on our interest in the "good life as a whole," fall within the province of what we have been calling *ethical* formation.

7

I said at the beginning of this chapter—reflecting on the account offered in Chapter 4 of our interest in "serious" utterance—that this account, "so far

50. Derrida applies this word to Austin's theory of speech acts in respect of the opposition it sets up between "normal" and "parasitic" uses of language. See "Limited Inc abc . . .," trans. Samuel Weber, in Derrida, *Limited Inc,* pp. 29–110, at p. 97: "I am convinced that speech act theory is fundamentally and in its most fecund, most rigorous and most interesting aspects . . . a theory of right or law, of convention, of political ethics or of politics as ethics . . . [However,] this "theory" is compelled to reproduce, to reduplicate in itself the law of its object or its object as law; it must submit to the norm it purports to analyze. Hence its fundamental, intrinsic moralism and its irreducible empiricism."

51. Derrida ("Signature Event Context," p. 17) cites *How To Do Things with Words,* pp. 72–73, on "the 'pure' statement [as] a goal, an ideal, towards which the gradual development of science has given the impetus, as it has likewise also towards the goal of precision."

52. Derrida, "Signature Event Context," p. 18.

53. Ibid. See also note 38 above and accompanying text.

54. Ibid.

as it went," was not a reductive one with regard to ethics. I now need to ask whether the same can be said of it once it has been informed or modified by deconstructionist considerations about the "serious" or "really meant." Could there be a *virtuous person*—not some irony-entangled counterpart of that person, but the real thing—to whom our implication in a teleology of authorship (in this case, the authorship of morally expressive action) was fully transparent? Can we maintain even of that spectacularly counterintuitive bit of moral philosophy, the indefeasibility thesis, that it offers no more than a perspicuous representation of something that is there anyway (if only sporadically and ambivalently) in our attitude to the ethical; and that no "constructive" or "sideways on" philosophy (see Chapter 1, §4) is needed as a basis for it?

Let's consider, or rather attempt to reconstruct, Derrida's own attitude to this question. Turning once more to "Signature Event Context," we find that his aim is not to abolish the distinctions that prompt Austin to speak of language undergoing a sea change, but to remove these from their traditional setting and relocate them within a philosophy of the signifier. He writes as if from a desire to see Austin emancipate himself more fully from the authority of uncriticized or "fetishistic" oppositions such as those of truth and falsity or of fact and value.[55] What Austin must do in order to complete this emancipation, Derrida suggests, is to look again at the conception of linguistic activity as comprising a "serious" core—the class of speech acts saturated by the conscious intention of their producer—and, separate from these, the "nonserious" residue of what is merely cited or trotted out. Against this presumption of an unmitigated opposition of "serious" and "nonserious," we should think of the "citationality" or "iterability" which allows linguistic signs to be grafted—however irresponsibly—into new contexts as the very thing that makes possible, not just those speech acts that deviate from the norm of "seriousness," but the *totality* of contexts within which we can make out a relative contrast between those speech acts that do, and those that do not, exhibit authorial "presence" and intention.

> [The] iterability of the mark is neither an accident nor an anomaly, but is that (normal/abnormal) without which a mark could not even have a

55. For the idea of these oppositions as "fetishes," see Austin, *How To Do Things with Words,* p. 150, quoted by Derrida, "Signature Event Context," p. 22, note 5.

function called "normal". What would a mark be that could not be cited? Or one whose origins would not get lost along the way?[56]

Derrida therefore argues that "[r]ather than oppose citation or iteration to the noniteration of an event [that is, to the ontologically self-contained fact of a bit of behaviour that encapsulates and expresses a speaker's intention: "event" is emphatic], one ought to construct a differential typology of forms of iteration"[57]—a typology within which "the category of intention will not disappear," but "will no longer be able to govern the entire scene and system of utterance [*l'énonciation*]."[58]

This disavowal by Derrida of any ambition to make the category of intention "disappear" is of a piece with his subsequent claim that "the value of truth (and all those values associated with it) is never contested or destroyed in my writings, but only reinscribed in more powerful, larger, more stratified contexts."[59] It seems to suggest the makings of a stable philosophical position that would place the phenomena of moral expression in a ("relaxed") naturalistic setting, while at the same time licensing us to continue in a participatory (as opposed to "sideways on") attitude to such expression—for example, to the giving or receiving of ethical reasons. For while we may accept that the full saturation of signs by the conscious intention of their users provides only an imaginary *telos* for the work of upbringing, we can still argue—at any rate so long as upbringing remains at the service of a truth-orientated discursive practice—that this particular product of the collective imagination is imposed on us by a kind of transcendental necessity: that, in fact, beings who are to exist within a space of reasons *need* "really judging," or "meaning what one says," in the role of

56. Derrida, "Signature Event Context," p. 12.

57. Ibid., p. 18. The passage continues: "assuming that such a project is tenable and can result in an exhaustive program, a question I hold in abeyance here."

58. Ibid. Derrida agrees with Austin on the "relative purity" of the category of performatives, since the citationality involved in naming a ship (and the like) is of a different type from that involved in, say, acting on stage or quoting a philosophical text. "But this relative purity does not emerge *in opposition to* citationality or iterability, but in opposition to other kinds of iteration within a general iterability which constitutes a violation of the allegedly rigorous purity of every event of discourse or every *speech act*" (ibid.).

59. Derrida, "Afterword," trans. Samuel Weber, in *Limited Inc*, pp. 111–160; quotation from p. 146.

what Kant would call a "regulative idea."[60] They need it because their up-bringing has to convert them into viable members of a community within which the continual effort to adjust one's thinking to the deliverances of experience (Chapter 1, §4) proceeds in part through acceptance of the as-sertions of others as "epistemic surrogates" for actual confrontation with some aspect of reality (Chapter 4, §3); and also because one thing they have to do in the name of this process of conversion is to develop a certain sensitivity to the promise-like character of the act of assertion, a require-ment whose influence we have seen at work in the classical rationalist equation of the "true self" with the seat or ground of our capacity to justify ourselves to others.

Now, someone might object that to describe this position as a stable one is premature. For while it may be possible to give a nonreductive interpre-tation to the idea of an "ethical and teleological discourse of conscious-ness," the reasoning that gives rise to this idea also has its subversive side. One way of explaining what I have in mind here is by reference to the con-trast between "immanence" and "transcendence" which was mentioned in Chapter 3 (§2) in connection with Plato's theory of forms. So far in this discussion we have been influenced mainly by the neo-Aristotelian con-ception of ethics, or rather of the exchange of ethical reasons and observa-tions, as an "already going concern."[61] This has led to an emphasis on the *immanence in culture* of moral sensibility, and hence (assuming the thesis of the "unboundedness of the conceptual": Chapter 1, §4) on the *imma-nence in the world* of the values and disvalues which that sensibility allows us to recognize. By contrast, Derrida's critique of the idea of authorial "presence" might make us wonder whether our confidence has been mis-placed. For we might ask: doesn't this critique suggest the more pessimistic thought that moral beliefs[62] are inherently elusive (or *transcendent*) with

60. Kant says of the "ideas of reason" that "they have an excellent, and indeed indispens-ably necessary, regulative employment, namely, that of directing the understanding towards a certain goal upon which the routes marked out by all its rules converge, as upon their point of intersection"—even though this point is "a mere idea, a *focus imaginarius,* from which, since it lies quite outside the bounds of possible experience, the concepts of the understand-ing do not in reality proceed" (*Critique of Pure Reason,* trans. Norman Kemp Smith [Lon-don: Macmillan, 1933], A644/B672).

61. John McDowell, *Mind and World* (Cambridge: Harvard University Press, 1994), p. 125.

62. Moral ones among others—but I take the point to be particularly significant in rela-tion to morality, with its "difficult," potentially ego-threatening subject matter.

respect to their supposed subjects? And wouldn't this in turn mean that the "second nature" on which our version of the practical reason approach depends is itself not *present* in us in an unqualified way? Such questions seem to impose a strain on our "quietist" principles, which were said to call for *acquiescence* in the measure of rationality that our upbringing has succeeded in transmitting to us (Chapter 1, §4). Are the principles at fault? Or the questions?

It is worth remembering here that pessimism about our entitlement to count certain moral beliefs as "ours," and thus to claim authorship of them, is nothing new in itself. One might even argue that it forms the ideological basis of the original Socratic paradox. If we are to believe Plato, the "commonsense" attitude toward acrasia in his time, as in ours, was one of willingness to go with appearances and say that, under various emotional pressures, people often do act against their better judgement; as noted earlier (§2), Socrates in the *Protagoras* calls this the view of the "many." But probably we are meant to understand, not just that this attitude is widely held, but also—pejoratively—that it is a *vulgar* one. And it may be that this verdict rests on an ethical insight that is detachable from the uglier manifestations of Platonic snobbery. For perhaps there *is* something presumptuous in the idea that, just because I assent to a certain practical judgement "with all the sincerity at my command" and have a record of acting, most of the time, in the spirit that it represents, I am entitled to say categorically that I *hold* the relevant belief. To make that claim might be to negate the distance between myself and some other person who would continue to act in the same spirit under much sterner tests than I should; perhaps "all the sincerity at my command" is not, as it happens, enough to give me the right to call the belief one of *mine*. For it is not subjective, or introspectible, sincerity alone that confers this right but functional sincerity.

We saw just now that the idea of ethical formation as governed by an "imaginary" rather than by an empirically manifest *telos* still leaves room for a *mitigated* contrast between "serious" and "nonserious" usage, and for a concept of *relative* success in acquiring a second nature modeled on that of the virtuous person. Yet it too seems to justify a certain pessimism about the credentials of ordinary "morality." Indeed, the switch from a speculative philosophical psychology to a method centred on the public domain of "language games" or "signifiers" makes this attitude, if anything, more compelling than before. For it recalls our attention to a familiar (because deeply traditional) set of worries about the natural intractability of the material that has to be *made* "moral" through human upbringing—that is, about the difficulty of turning creatures like ourselves into beings who can inject even a measure of functional sincerity into the forms of moral expression they have learned. This point is taken up in some remarks of Henry Staten's on Derrida. Staten says that Derrida opposes to "modern Anglo-American clean-mindedness or sincerity . . . a more archaic moral rigor that insists on reminding us of the residue of darkness in man's intention." And he continues: "If there is any skepticism in Derrida, it is a moral, not an epistemological, skepticism—not a doubt about the possibility of morality but about an idealized [that is, unrealistic] picture of sincerity that takes insufficient account of the windings and twistings of fear and desire, weakness and lust, sadism and masochism and the will to power, in the mind of even the most sincere man."[63] These "windings and twistings" bear witness to a continuing tension, even in the most "sincere" or fully finished human product of formation, between the behavioural constraints imposed by the promise-like aspect of ethical expression, and on the other hand the pre-ethical sources of motivation on which these operate—the psychological *apeiron* of classical virtue ethics.

63. Staten, *Wittgenstein and Derrida*, pp. 126–127. These comments occur in the summing-up of Staten's discussion of "Signature Event Context" and of the ensuing debate between Derrida and John Searle.

SIX

The "Intelligible Ground
of the Heart"

I concluded, after some hesitation, that the position reached at the end of the last chapter (§7) could in a certain sense be regarded as philosophically stable—the reason being that our involvement in the practice of giving and seeking reasons already implicitly commits us to drawing the kind of distinctions among speech acts that Derrida seems to envisage when he advocates replacing Austin's contrast between "serious" and "nonserious" utterance with a "differential typology of forms of iteration." This stability was qualified by a pessimistic thought which is apt to suggest itself once we start to reflect on the "structural unconsciousness" or anonymity of conventional signs, namely, that what we like to think of as "our" moral values and convictions are less fully present in us than the humanist philosophical tradition has supposed. We did however find one of Derrida's Anglophone commentators, Henry Staten, maintaining that the pessimism in question is itself internal to morality, not something brought into play from outside (or in our idiom, from "sideways on"); Staten's claim was that it is "a moral, not an epistemological skepticism," and hence not a legitimate basis for doubt about the possibility of morality as such. And we also saw that that claim enjoys the backing of Derrida's own statement that "the value of truth (and all those values associated with it) is never contested or destroyed" in his writings.

It is possible to imagine feeling somehow cheated by the outcome of this discussion. Someone who felt this way might protest that if the public character of language poses an *a priori*, or structural, obstacle to the complete transcendence by any speaker of the "actorly" relation to the signs that they use (Chapter 5, §6), then although it may be a fact of experience that speech acts exhibit varying degrees of functional sincerity, there is nevertheless a point of view from which one wants to say that no one "really," "strictly speaking," *believes in* anything—that even to suffer for a cause is merely to be an unusually loyal or disciplined mouthpiece for some currently available ideology. For every thought, every belief, will now be "someone else's" in the sense fixed by its dependence on a system of representation: this after all is the feature to which we appealed in Chapter 2 (§4) when we noted that questions such as "Why don't I like *N*?" can sometimes be resolved—not arbitrarily, but in a spirit of respect for the "reasons that there are"—by embracing as our own an answer that originates elsewhere.

Would this persistent critic be demonstrating a simple lack of understanding of the "quietist" stance as presented so far? Or would she be showing a commendable determination to get the full measure of any intellectual adjustments that may be needed in order to bring ethics into line with a modern (or "disenchanted")[1] conception of nature? In this chapter I want to give her the benefit of the doubt, and to test the power of a "relaxed" naturalism to articulate the distinctive (and, it may be thought, indispensable) form of anxiety associated with moral introspection and self-scrutiny.

A natural opening move in response to the critic who feels cheated would be to reactivate some of the sorts of consideration that favour a quietist reading of the later Wittgenstein. For example, we can note that the attitude expressed by this critic is like one that occurs in *On Certainty*[2] in the course of a train of thought dedicated to breaking the spell of constructive epistemological theory. Wittgenstein is moved to rebel against G. E. Moore's commonsense rebuttal of skepticism ("I *know* that this is a hand!"), but feels that just as Moore's position is tainted by (the wrong kind of) "philosophy," so is his own rejection of it:

§407. For when Moore says "I know that that's . . ." I want to reply "you don't *know* anything!"—and yet I would not say that to anyone who was

1. See John McDowell, *Mind and World* (Cambridge: Harvard University Press, 1994), p. 70.

2. Ludwig Wittgenstein, *On Certainty,* ed. G. E. M. Anscombe and G. H. von Wright, trans. Denis Paul and G. E. M. Anscombe (Oxford: Basil Blackwell, 1969).

speaking without philosophical intention. That is, I feel (rightly?) that these two mean to say something different.

§553. It is queer: if I say, without any special occasion, "I know"—for example, "I know that I am now sitting in a chair", this statement seems to me unjustified and presumptuous. But if I make the same statement where there is some need for it, then, although I am not a jot more certain of its truth, it seems to me to be perfectly justified and everyday.

§554. In its language-game it is not presumptuous. There, it has no higher position than, simply, the human language-game. For there it has its restricted application.

But as soon as I say this sentence outside its context, it appears in a false light. For then it is as if I wanted to insist that there are things that I *know*. God himself can't say anything to me about them.

In the interval that separates these passages, Wittgenstein has summarized the situation by saying:

§482. It is as if "I know" did not tolerate a metaphysical emphasis.

A *metaphysical* emphasis: this is what seems to occur in the suggestion that, on the view we are entertaining, no one "really believes in" any of the values promoted by ethical upbringing. Accordingly, and bearing in mind the negative Wittgensteinian connotations of the word "metaphysical," it is open to a defender of that view to attribute the suggestion to a typically philosophical neglect of what goes on within the "language game": for example, of the fact that for practical purposes (such as distinguishing one's own views from another person's) it is sometimes *not* presumptuous to say that we hold certain moral beliefs, just as it is "not presumptuous" to say *without* a "metaphysical emphasis" that we know certain things. With facts such as these in clear view, it can be argued, the "structural idealism"[3] underpinning our conception of "serious" utterance need not be taken to en-

3. Compare Jacques Derrida, "Afterword," trans. Samuel Weber, in *Limited Inc* (Evanston: Northwestern University Press, 1988), p. 120: "I do not believe I said that this 'goal of language or of interpretation' [that is, the goal implicit in the ideality of concepts in general] reveals itself to be 'illusory' . . . Illusion is so little involved here that indeed the structural idealism of which we have just spoken constitutes the condition of a certain classical value of what is called scientific truth."

tail the nihilistic doctrine that in our various states of incomplete psychological integration, we are all as bad as each other.

There is, however, a question that arises *within* the ethical "language game" and yet that is liable to draw us, despite ourselves, towards its outer limits. This question is linked with the function attributed to ethical upbringing in Chapter 4, §1, namely, that of leading us to conform to a certain standard of predictability in social interaction—the desired predictability being based not on our participation in the "realm of law" but on a scheme of values in which we have come to share through a (perhaps gradual and imperfect) act of will.

To want to know when such an act can properly be said to have taken place, and when, therefore, we can regard the use of ethical signs by a particular speaker as amounting to more than mere performance, is not an obvious example of the kind of question—"metaphysical" in a bad sense—in respect of which language is "like an engine idling."[4] That something of practical importance is at stake here seems, after all, to be confirmed by the presence in ordinary language of a concept of "seriously meaning" which is grounded in our interests as agents—this concept (to repeat) being one that we have to master in order to deliberate effectively in an environment containing other subjects who can, but are not guaranteed to, make their mental states apparent to us through language. Yet as we learn the techniques of appraisal (and self-appraisal) demanded by this deliberative environment, we can hardly fail to notice the *historical contingency* of the circumstances in which any given moral personality is manifested, and to reflect that these circumstances leave many gaps in our knowledge. Just as certain mathematical procedures suggest counterfactual questions which we are inclined to express in realist terms,[5] so the techniques just mentioned suggest questions about how someone would behave, or would have behaved, in some imagined counterfactual situation—questions we are in-

4. Ludwig Wittgenstein, *Philosophical Investigations,* trans. G. E. M. Anscombe (Oxford: Basil Blackwell, 1967), §132: "The confusions that occupy us arise when language is like an engine idling, not when it is doing work."

5. For example, "Does the group 7777 occur in the decimal expansion of π?" (see Wittgenstein, *Philosophical Investigations* §352) is a realist formulation of the counterfactual question, "If we were to develop π . . . , would we ever find ourselves writing down this group?," which—if the dots are filled in by specifying "to n decimal places" for some finite n—does have a sense internal to the "game."

clined to express by asking whether that person is *really* brave, incorruptible, committed to such and such a cause, or whatever.

This kind of speculation may be sparked off by a problem which, in the aftermath of a much discussed exchange between Thomas Nagel and Bernard Williams, has come to be known as that of "moral luck."[6] The crux of the debate about moral luck is whether we should recognize the existence of such a thing in the first place, or whether on the contrary the characteristics by which a person legitimately incurs *moral* judgement must—logically—be subject to his or her will. If moral luck exists, however, then we can agree with Nagel that one form it will take is that of "luck in one's circumstances."[7] Nagel's immediate purpose in mentioning this idea is to affirm its influence on "ordinary moral attitudes," as attested for instance by our acceptance of the good luck that consists in not having been exposed to certain political crises with their attendant risks of moral failure.[8] But he also notes that however successful we may be in representing people's ostensibly moral choices as effects of external determination, "ordinary moral attitudes" also bear the mark of a refusal, or inability, to abandon the "internal view that we extend to others in moral judgement—when we judge *them* rather than their desirability or utility," and when we "accord to

6. See Thomas Nagel, "Moral Luck," in his *Mortal Questions* (Cambridge: Cambridge University Press, 1979), pp. 24–38; Bernard Williams, "Moral Luck," in his *Moral Luck: Philosophical Papers 1973–80* (Cambridge: Cambridge University Press, 1981). Williams's *Shame and Necessity* (Berkeley: University of California Press, 1993) offers more extended criticism of the idea of unconditioned agency, and argues that the ancient conception of moral responsibility had more in common with our own than modern scholarship, under the influence of Kant, has been able to recognize.

7. Nagel, "Moral Luck," p. 33.

8. Ibid., p. 34: "Ordinary citizens of Nazi Germany had an opportunity to behave heroically by opposing the regime. They also had an opportunity to behave badly, and most of them are culpable for having failed this test. But it is a test to which citizens of other countries were not subjected, with the result that even if they, or some of them, would have behaved as badly as the Germans in like circumstances, they simply did not and therefore are not similarly culpable." Nagel also recognizes a form of circumstantial moral luck in the face of which personal virtue seems to be impotent—for example, during the Vietnam War of the 1960s and 1970s "even U.S. citizens who had opposed their country's actions vigorously from the start often felt compromised by its crimes," and could consider themselves morally unlucky to be American at that historical moment (ibid., note 10)—but the case we need to consider here is that in which events simply happen to spare us certain tests of character.

them selves like our own."[9] It is this side of Nagel's antinomy that asserts itself in the wish to be able to say in advance—about ourselves at any rate—that if such and such a situation arose, we could emerge from it without disgrace. And from the standpoint of a practical reason approach to ethics, this is a wish that we ought not to be without, since it is the only incentive we have to devote ourselves *unconditionally*—that is, without regard to our actual prospects of escaping some of the painful choices we know others have faced—to the amendment of our own character.

But to say that we ought not to be without it is not to say that it is fulfillable. And in fact we are already in a position to see why, for a philosophy committed to remaining within the "zone of mere signification,"[10] it cannot be so. The reason why we cannot, within such a philosophy, get into a position to say categorically that we have acquired the necessary moral qualities has to do with the rejection, in that context, of a certain traditional view of the concepts of *will* and *intention*. Whereas on the rejected view these concepts were understood in a way that gave too much credence to the substantive form of the words that denote them, the alternative approach suggested by Wittgenstein's *Investigations* and *Zettel*[11] (Chapter 4, §3) was that we should break with the habit of picturing either as a distinctive kind of *thing*—a species of some genus such as "experience" or "psychological origin"—and concentrate instead on describing the "physiognomy" of those acts that are *called* "voluntary" or "intentional."

This change of approach is bound to affect our account of ethical formation. It will have an impact, first, on the idea that formation seeks to ensure the adoption of ethical values by an *act of will* on the part of the learner; and second on the idea that it seeks to draw the learner into a mode of ethical expression in which the signs she uses come to be saturated, so far as their public nature allows, by her own (serious) *intention*.

Perhaps the best way to describe this impact is by summoning up—as it were, for a backward glance—the picture from which Wittgenstein's

9. Ibid., p. 37.

10. See Henry Staten, *Wittgenstein and Derrida* (Oxford: Basil Blackwell, 1985), p. 111 (where Staten argues that just as Derrida focuses on "the moment of signification, the moment during which the availability of the knowable undergoes storing up in signs," so Wittgenstein's philosophical practice likewise "takes place in this zone of mere signification").

11. Ludwig Wittgenstein, *Zettel*, ed. G. E. M. Anscombe and G. H. von Wright, trans. G. E. M. Anscombe (Oxford: Basil Blackwell, 1981).

reasoning is meant to liberate us.[12] In the case of the decimal expansion of π, Wittgenstein imagines our inclination towards a dogmatic realism (about the occurrence or nonoccurrence of the group "7777") coming out in a thought on the lines of "God sees—but we don't know."[13] The same thought can be invoked in support of that realism about ethical dispositions to which we implicitly reach out when we feel the need to believe in the existence of reliable defences against "moral danger."[14] For if I consider the process by which genuinely virtuous action emerges from a merely imitative habit of action *in accordance with* the virtues, and if I then wonder how far I personally have got beyond square one in that respect, I may be drawn to the idea that the answer to this question—though inaccessible to me—nevertheless exists within a hidden "ethical reality"; and this may in turn suggest the idea of a subject with cognitive powers appropriate to the "reality" in question.[15]

This pattern seems to be traceable in a late work of Kant entitled *Religion within the Limits of Reason Alone*,[16] which aims to establish a purely ethical (and hence, in Kantian terms, rational) basis for religion. In that work we find a contrast between the moral "revolution" or "change of heart" that is necessary in order to make ourselves pleasing to God (and because necessary, possible: its possibility is a "postulate of pure practical reason"),[17] and on the other hand the "gradual reform" that is the most we can claim, *from experience,* to be able to accomplish. And as an adjunct to

12. Wittgenstein, *Philosophical Investigations* §115: "A *picture* held us captive."

13. Ibid., §352.

14. See Chapter 1, note 30 and accompanying text.

15. I believe there is a parallel here with the dialectic noted by Staten according to which a sense of the limitations of human consciousness (through "forgetfulness, lapses of attention, sleep, death") leads, first, to the postulation of objects that are capable of persisting (in all their determinacy) even in the absence of a thinking subject; and subsequently to a conception of the essence of man as "wakeful rationality," the ideal correlate of that "presence" which was itself conceived in reaction against the fact of our frequent cognitive *absences*. See Chapter 4, note 5.

16. Immanuel Kant, *Religion within the Limits of Reason Alone*, trans. Theodore Greene and Hoyt Hudson (New York: Harper and Row, 1960).

17. "Because necessary, possible": of course, it would be fallacious to say that just because something is necessary as a means to some arbitrary end—say, my traveling from England to China within the next two minutes—it must therefore be possible. The idea is, rather, that making ourselves pleasing to God is not an arbitrary end, but one that is constitutive of moral effort as such. (Kant's strictly rationalist conception of the deity is in evidence here.) In other words, if it were not possible to make ourselves pleasing to God, morality would be

this contrast we are invited to postulate a point of view to which our true moral orientation (change of heart or no change of heart?) would be disclosed.

> [A man] can hope in the light of that purity of the principle which he has adopted as the supreme maxim of his will [*Willkür*], and of its stability, to find himself upon the good (though strait) path of continual *progress* from bad to better. For him who penetrates to the intelligible ground of the heart (the ground of all maxims of the will) and for whom this unending progress is a unity, i.e., for God, this amounts to his being actually a good man (pleasing to Him); and, thus viewed, this change can be regarded as a revolution. But in the judgement of men, who can appraise themselves and the strength of their maxims only by the ascendancy which they win over their sensuous nature in time, this change must be regarded as nothing but an ever-during struggle towards the better, hence as a gradual reformation of the propensity to evil . . .[18]

Wittgenstein's discussion of will and intention suggests a way of thinking that would make it possible to renounce both the God who "penetrates to the intelligible ground of the heart," and the correlative idea of the existence of such a "ground," where this is construed as something set in place by a temporally determinate "act of will"—the act of resolving to be, say, a just or a charitable person. If we consent to do without ethical "super-concepts"[19] and to understand the voluntary in terms of "certain movements with their normal *surrounding* of intention, learning, trying, acting,"[20] then we shall see a person's status in respect of ethical formation—and hence her presumable level of immunity to (circumstantial) moral bad luck in future—as turning, not on anything reserved for the eyes of a transcendent God, but on certain facts about the unfolding course of that person's life: facts of the same general description, perhaps, as those Kant has in mind when he speaks of the "ascendancy which [we] win over [our] sensuous nature in time."[21] Adopting a moral end will then be like grasping the for-

an illusion. But morality cannot be an illusion. So it must be possible to make ourselves pleasing to God.

18. Kant, *Religion within the Limits of Reason Alone*, p. 43.

19. Compare Wittgenstein, *Philosophical Investigations* §97.

20. Wittgenstein, *Zettel* §577.

21. But for further consideration of what may or may not be implied by the "God" idiom, see §2 below.

mula for the continuation of a series: "It would be quite misleading [to call the words "Now I know how to go on"] a 'description of a mental state'.— One might rather call them a 'signal'; and we judge whether it was rightly employed by *what he goes on to do*."[22]

2

Now we can comment that since the question of whether such a signal is rightly employed *is* often, in fact, settled by "what he goes on to do," there should be no objection from the standpoint of "quietism" to the claim that at a certain moment a person may indeed become entitled to say he knows how to go on—even if, as the quietist will maintain, there is nothing analytically illuminating to be said about what it is that has come to be true of him at that moment.[23] And we can add that since the question of whether someone has adopted a certain moral end is often settled, for all practical purposes, by what they go on to do in the sort of circumstances in which that end makes a claim on us, the quietist should likewise agree that there may be a moment in the course of a person's upbringing when they do indeed become entitled to think of themselves (and others to think of them) as having adopted such an end. It is true that the "surroundings" that would warrant this thought will consist in part of a sequence of (future) historical events, and will therefore not be present at the moment when the thought is entertained or expressed. But if it is the case that this sequence of events will in fact be forthcoming, then we will be able to say in retrospect that whoever entertained or expressed the thought at that moment was right to do so.

Should we conclude, then, that Kant's talk of a God who can "penetrate to the intelligible ground of the heart" merely gives a picturesque form to a certain intellectual permission that we get from the quietist—the permission to say "Yes, sometimes a person does really grasp a rule (or adopt a moral end)"? One commentator who seems to hint at this interpretation is Christine Korsgaard. In a paragraph expounding "Kant's explicit view" in *Religion within the Limits of Reason Alone*, she writes:

22. Wittgenstein, *Philosophical Investigations* §180 (emphasis added).

23. Compare Wittgenstein, *Philosophical Investigations* §393, "'When I imagine that someone who is laughing is really in pain I don't imagine any pain-behaviour, for I see just the opposite. So *what* do I imagine?'—I have already said what."

You cannot, just by making a resolution, acquire a virtue or recover from a vice. Or better still, we will say that you can, because you are free, but then we must say that *only what happens in the future establishes whether you have really made the resolution or not.* I do not mean that only the future will produce the evidence: I mean that only what you do in the future will enable us to correctly attribute a resolution to you. There is a kind of backwards determination in the construction of one's character.[24]

As far as this goes, there might be no more to the God's-eye view than to that of an observer who can already see (at the moment when you are supposed to have understood, or resolved) what you will in fact go on to do—someone for whom the historical sequence in virtue of which a finite observer could agree, *in retrospect,* that you were entitled to say you had done these things is present for inspection all at once.

There does seem to be a difference at this point, however, between the Kantian conception of practical reason and a fully naturalist one. The difference is that the former, but not the latter, incorporates the idea of a moral world order—that is, of a "supreme cause of nature which has a causality corresponding to the moral intention."[25] Kant argues that only if we assume the existence of such a principle can we regard as possible the realization of the highest (or "perfect") good—that is, of morality combined with the happiness it merits;[26] and that unless we regard this as possible we cannot, as morality demands, undertake to promote it through our actions. "Therefore, it is morally necessary to assume the existence of God."[27] In fact, "the concept of God is one which belongs originally not to

---

24. Christine M. Korsgaard, "Morality as Freedom," in her *Creating the Kingdom of Ends* (Cambridge: Cambridge University Press, 1996), pp. 159–187; quotation from pp. 180–181 (emphasis added).

25. Immanuel Kant, *Critique of Practical Reason*, trans. L. W. Beck (Indianapolis: Bobbs-Merrill, 1956), p. 130. Regrettably, a book that has come to hand too late to be an influence on this chapter is Gordon E. Michalson, Jr., *Kant and the Problem of God* (Oxford: Blackwell, 1999), which argues that "Kant's ties to nineteenth century post-Hegelian atheism are stronger than typically supposed" (quotation from p. viii). Belief in a moral world-order, however—at any rate in the strong sense envisaged by Kant—seems to me to be a no-go area for any self-respecting atheist. (A more modest, holistic successor to the idea of divine providence is defended by Rosalind Hursthouse (*On Virtue Ethics* (Oxford: Oxford University Press, 1999), pp. 264–265.)

26. Kant, *Critique of Practical Reason*, p. 130; and compare pp. 114–115.

27. Ibid., p. 130.

physics, . . . but to morals";[28] this concept, says Kant, "really arises *solely* from the consciousness of [moral] laws and from the need of reason to postulate [a power capable of enforcing them]."[29]

It is by another application of the ought-implies-can thesis—that is, of the idea that what is morally required must also be possible—that Kant establishes the claim of *immortality* to be a "postulate of pure practical reason." His argument here is that "complete fitness of the will to the moral law," while practically necessary, is "a perfection of which no rational being in the world of sense is at any time capable"; therefore, practical reason must presuppose what is required in order to fill the gap and to make that perfection possible for such beings; so it must presuppose an "*endless* progress to that complete fitness," and this in turn implies the "infinitely enduring existence and personality of the same rational being," or in other words the immortality of the soul.[30]

A conception of practical reason as part of our "second nature" has no obvious use for either of these postulates—that is, neither for God nor for immortality. The overall view of nature in which it is embedded in no way requires us to assume that virtue and vice are bound to receive the rewards they deserve, except insofar as we think of ethical formation itself as bringing the subjective capacity for pleasure and pain into conformity with the demands of virtue (Chapter 3, §3).[31] And since the practical reason view, as developed here, has not committed itself to a conception of the (unconditioned) ethical subject as belonging to a wholly different ontological "world" from the (conditioned) human animal, an adherent of this view— while acknowledging, with Kant, a certain inbuilt resistance on the part of ("first") nature to the teleology of formation—will not see such resistance as threatening to reduce ethics to a state of pragmatic self-contradiction,

---

28. Ibid., p. 145.

29. Kant, *Religion within the Limits of Reason Alone,* p. 95 (emphasis added).

30. Kant, *Critique of Practical Reason,* pp. 126–127 (emphasis added).

31. This exception is not a trivial one, since ethical formation cannot be said to have succeeded with someone who remains untroubled by crimes in which they have no fear of being detected: one of its central aims is, after all, to turn us into people for whom the consciousness of wrongdoing is in itself a source of unhappiness. All the same, one might well be at a loss to argue—without recourse either to divine justice or to an empty moralism— for the proposition that things cannot fail to turn out well for the virtuous. Hursthouse (*On Virtue Ethics,* chap. 8, especially pp. 182–185) strikes a sane neo-Aristotelian balance on this point.

nor, therefore, as calling for any special theoretical measures (such as a postulate of immortality) to rescue it from that state.

With these points in mind, let us return to the metaphor of God's penetration to the "intelligible ground of the heart." My suggestion is that if we wish to accommodate this metaphor to our own version of the practical reason view, we must be prepared to register the effect of an ideological shift whereby "the world as a whole" (in contrast to certain natural beings within it) has ceased to be understood as purposive. By renouncing this idea, we lose the incentive to posit that *infinitely enduring* personal existence which Kant, in particular, considers to be needed if we are to fulfil the "moral destiny of our nature."[32] We may then say to ourselves in connection with the hidden (that is, not *now* present) reality of moral character: "Don't imagine an imaginary kind of description of which you have really no idea!"[33] And the effect of this maxim will indeed be to limit our conception of a "God's-eye" view of character—for example, in regard to someone's having adopted or failed to adopt a certain moral end—to a view embracing the sum total of information contained in the historical sequence of what she actually does. For we do not really know what more to imagine being available for inspection than the whole of this sequence of events. To suppose that there are determinate answers to our counterfactual questions ("What if I had been there? Would I have done any better?")—even where these answers are not settled, for a person of exemplary moral sensitivity, by the material occurring within the sequence—is to succumb to the same impulse that makes us want to invoke the law of excluded middle over such questions as the occurrence of "7777" in the expansion of π. "'God sees—but we don't know.' But what does that mean?"[34] Kant thinks of God, precisely, as a being to whom the "unending progress" (or lack of progress) realized in an infinitely enduring personal life can present itself as a unity. But for "God" to be a legitimate metaphor-

32. Kant, *Critique of Practical Reason*, p. 127; and compare p. 128, "[A creature] cannot hope here or at any foreseeable point of his future existence to be fully adequate to God's will, without indulgence or remission which would not harmonize with justice. This he can do only in the infinity of his duration which God alone can survey."

33. Compare Ludwig Wittgenstein, *Lectures and Conversations on Aesthetics, Psychology and Religious Belief*, ed. Cyril Barrett (Oxford: Basil Blackwell, 1970), p. 35, §11 (with reference to the idea of a supposedly precise specification of aesthetic attitudes in terms of the muscular sensations that accompany them).

34. Wittgenstein, *Philosophical Investigations* §352.

ical device within a naturalized epistemology, the powers ascribed to "him" must always—to adapt a remark of Michael Dummett's about the realistic treatment of counterfactuals—"bear a recognizable relation to the powers which we in fact possess; they must be analogous to, or an extension of, our actual powers."[35] And there is, as it happens, at least one context in the *Philosophical Investigations* where Wittgenstein seems to apply this principle to "God": he says that "If God had looked into our minds he would not have been able to see there whom we were speaking of."[36]

Some questions about the character of any given person will be left undecided by the finite sequence of events that constitutes that person's life history. This is the source of that circumstantial moral luck which some of us have reason to accept with gratitude. No doubt we may also feel, in a spirit of moral rigorism, that the mere luck of not being tested in certain ways is a gift we should be able to do without. And this feeling may suggest that in the name of (ultimate) justice there would have to exist a point of view for which the undecidability of the relevant counterfactuals was removed. Yet on the basis of our recent reflections about moral character, we ought to resist that suggestion. For we are supposing that the act of will by which someone may be said to have adopted a moral end is no more available for inspection than the rest of their life can make it; and that any question not resolved within this frame will fall into the category of things about which we must concede that, if "God" were to survey the evidence, "he" would be none the wiser. Hence we no longer have any justification for picturing the ethical "ground of the heart" as fully intelligible even to "God" (where "God's" powers of observation are taken to be limited to those that form a recognizable extension of our own).

It seems, then, to be a consequence of exchanging Kantian transcendental idealism for a more consistent naturalism that we must accept not just the inaccessibility to our own limited powers, but the absolute unavailability, of a final verdict on what Kant calls our "moral happiness": the happiness derived from confidence in "the reality and constancy of a disposi-

35. Michael Dummett, "What is a Theory of Meaning? (II)" in Gareth Evans and John McDowell, eds., *Truth and Meaning: Essays in Semantics* (Oxford: Clarendon Press, 1976), pp. 67–137; quotation from p. 100.

36. Wittgenstein, *Philosophical Investigations*, Part II, p. 217. The lines immediately preceding the quoted sentence suggest that we are meant to picture God as "looking into our minds" without benefit of any of the "surroundings" which may, in practice, enable *us* to answer the question.

tion which ever progresses in goodness (and never falls away from it)."[37] Just as Kant maintains that even those who have the best (autobiographical) grounds for *hope* with regard to their inner disposition can still only *conjecture* that it is as they would wish it to be,[38] so his successors should acknowledge that even those who have the best grounds for hope that their future actions will continue to be directed towards "the good life as a whole"[39]—people whose good character is amply confirmed "for all practical purposes"—can still only *conjecture* that it will not give rise to some counterpart of Wittgenstein's "1004, 1008" case (Chapter 3, §1); for this case too was specified as involving someone who was confirmed, for all practical purposes, as a reliable negotiator of the relevant "space of reasons." The difference is that a philosopher committed to the reintegration of "reason" with "nature" will decline to postulate that transcendent point of view—the point of view of a knowing subject located outside space and time—from which such questions could receive a more than conjectural answer.

The (rigorist) desire for *unconditional* confidence that we will not deviate from the line of virtue looks like one more effect of adopting the "internal" view of ourselves (see §1 above)—the view according to which our genuinely moral qualities cannot be regarded as products of external determination. This desire expresses an understandable, and admirable, reluctance to acquiesce in a condition that is indeterminate with respect to "moral happiness." But as Kant already indicates through the less-than-cognitive language of "hope" and "conjecture," it may be that "moral happiness"—so far as this is part of anyone's experience—is one of those things that will not "tolerate a metaphysical emphasis." If anyone is inclined to say of themselves that they have (really) made some moral end

37. Kant, *Religion within the Limits of Reason Alone*, p. 61.
38. Ibid., p. 62.
39. I mean towards a life that actually deserves this description, not just one that appears to them to do so (for the distinction see Aristotle, *Nicomachean Ethics*, 1113a15–1113b2). (Of course, there is also plenty of scope in ethics for failing to pursue what one would be perfectly willing to call the "apparent good"; this is what gives rise to the problem of acrasia, and so to the considerations of Chapter 5. But if acrasia is held, on Socratic grounds, to be unreal, this will in a sense discredit anything the (ostensibly) acratic agent may say about how the good "appears" to her, since the Socratic position entails that such "appearances" cannot diverge from effective motivation.)

their own, then we may feel equally inclined to retort: "You don't *know* anything!"—or, in the words of a Biblical text recalled by Kant: "Work out your own salvation with fear and trembling!"[40]

3

In the *Critique of Practical Reason* Kant lists three "postulates of pure practical reason," or ideas that play a structurally indispensable role in moral thinking: "those of immortality, of freedom affirmatively regarded (as the causality of a being so far as he belongs to the intelligible world), and of the existence of God."[41] The first and third of these, I have suggested, will no longer occupy the role of "postulates" within a naturalized account of practical reason. But the second, that of freedom, looks more durable. The reason for this claim will, I hope, become clear if we recall once again the idea of ethical upbringing as directing us towards the goal of full authorship of a certain genre of expressive action (Chapter 5).

The progress of an individual learner towards this goal, I said, could be represented as a passage from mere imitation of the target forms of speech (and related behaviour) towards a use of those forms in which they would become, at the limit, fully "serious," or fully permeated by the conscious intention of the user. What we should notice, though, is that imitating the words and gestures of others is not portrayed in this account as a clearly delimited phase of life, eventually to be superseded by another clearly delimited phase in which speech and action are strictly attributable to their ostensible subject. Rather, a still partly opportunistic relation to (what passes for) one's own ethical expression *coexists*—in normal adult human beings, and to some extent also in children—with the condition, or forensic status, of responsibility for one's actions. Returning to Aristotle, we could say that such a relation coexists with the state of being a fit object of

---

40. Philippians 2:12; quoted by Kant, *Religion within the Limits of Reason Alone*, p. 62.

41. Kant, *Critique of Practical Reason*, p. 137. To regard freedom "affirmatively" would be to think of it not just as the absence of constraint, but as the subject's own power of self-determination—though there is certainly also a negative side to this coin, since in arguing for the postulate of freedom in the *Groundwork* Kant says that "[r]eason must look upon itself as the author of its own principles *independently of alien influences*" (*Groundwork of the Metaphysic of Morals,* trans. H. J. Paton as *The Moral Law* (London: Hutchinson, 1948), p. 448 (Prussian Academy numbering); emphasis added).

praise and blame for what one does voluntarily, or for behaviour of which the "moving principle" is in oneself.[42] For the voluntary movements of children, however heedless, nevertheless create an opening—as those of nonhuman animals do not—for moral guidance or teaching.[43] Even when we are still far from being capable of originating actions in the way proper to a rational adult (that is, of exhibiting full *prohaeresis* or "preferential choice"), we can begin to be held to account (or "praised and blamed") for them "like parents for their children."[44] In so treating us, our teachers will be deferring to the idea of what we are destined, as human beings, to *become* through the completion of the educational process: they will be exercising a kind of judgement that is applicable to us, not as the instinctually motivated creatures which (to a greater or lesser extent) we still are, but as creatures who are supposed to be emancipated from instinct and in possession of a reflectively adopted "object for noble living."[45] So for Aristotle, as later for Kant, moral praise and blame are *practical* notions: they bear upon voluntary agents not simply as such (for then they would apply equally to many nonhuman animals),[46] but just insofar as these agents are (generically) of a kind to be measured by the standard of practical reason. And "except in exceptional cases" (say, where normal mental functioning is compromised or where some essential human attribute is felt to be lacking), the relevance of praise and blame is unaffected by theoretical considerations—in particular, by our awareness of the

42. Aristotle, *Nicomachean Ethics* 1110a17–18. The formula about the "moving principle" partially explains what Aristotle means by "voluntary" (though only partially, since movements caused by some internal bodily spasm would not be included by him in this category: a voluntary action is also one of which it can be said that it was "up to us" whether we did it or not (ibid., 1113b6–17)). He regards not only adult humans, but also children and other animals, as capable of acting voluntarily.

43. To represent Aristotle in these terms is to follow the traditional humanist practice of affirming psychological discontinuity at the expense of continuity between ourselves and other species: the educable versus the (at best) tameable or trainable. A more nuanced account of the relationship, featuring an evolutionary scale in which human subjectivity emerges from animal "proto-subjectivity," is offered by McDowell in *Mind and World*, Lecture VI, esp. p. 117. See also Chapter 1, note 70.

44. Aristotle, *Nicomachean Ethics* 1113b18–19.

45. Aristotle, *Eudemian Ethics* 1214b8.

46. Compare Aristotle, *Nicomachean Ethics* 1111b8–9.

shortcomings, in point of practical rationality, of this or that human being or of human beings generally.[47]

The point I have just been making relates to moral *formation* or education, viewed as a dynamic and unfinished process. That process, I have argued, aims to convert us into people whose good actions are not just felicitous bits of copying or recycling, but express dispositions which are fully ours; at the same time, however, and precisely by placing this state of affairs before us as a *goal*, it acknowledges that we still have some distance to travel and that we can and should undergo further episodes of character change in future. The case is different with *morality* or *virtue* itself, these being not processes but abstract entities from which certain demands can be seen as flowing. For morality makes its demands upon the people we actually are—that is, upon natural beings who possess certain moral capacities and who can therefore be addressed, in more or less idealizing fashion, as members of a community of interest in the relevant forms of value (this community being, perhaps, the naturalized counterpart of Kant's "kingdom of ends").[48] In fact, we already have grounds for believing the element of idealization here to be ineliminable: I mean, of course, the considerations adduced in Chapter 5 (§6) about the structural impossibility of *completing* the process of upbringing, if completing it is taken to be a matter of transcending once and for all the alterity of ethical signs. But this is, once again, a finding to be accepted "quietly." For unless we consent to live with this idealizing manœuvre and to think of morality as addressing us in the way just mentioned, we shall forfeit our participation in the kind of life to which ethical *formation* is relevant at all, and allow our status to lapse from that of recipients of upbringing to that of mere matter for conditioning. Only "under the Idea of freedom,"[49] as Kant would put it, can we un-

47. See Chapter 4, note 14.

48. Compare Bernard Williams, *Ethics and the Limits of Philosophy* (London: Fontana Press, 1985), p. 193 (emphasis added): "The *fiction* of the deliberative community is one of the positive achievements of the [Kantian] morality system." However, Williams thinks it "certain" that a "reflective and nonmythical understanding of our ethical practices" would impose some change of style on the negative, or judgemental, component of this work of fiction. Ibid., p. 194. I find this claim hard to evaluate, mainly because of the difficulty of convincing oneself that some such reflective understanding is not already present in "ordinary" (unphilosophical) consciousness.

49. Kant, *Groundwork of the Metaphysic of Morals*, p. 448.

derstand ourselves as proper objects of the internal (judgmental) point of view adopted by our educators; and conversely, only under that "Idea" can we find a rationale for adopting the judgmental point of view towards anyone else. In this sense, freedom is as much a "postulate" for a naturalized as it is for a "pure" practical reason.

Counter-Teleology

CHAPTER
SEVEN

The Determinate Critique of Ethical Formation

1

My aim in Part II was to bring out the inherently teleological character of the concept of ethical formation. In calling this concept a teleological one, I had in mind the thought that if we recognize an *ideal* condition of receptivity to the "reasons that there are" (for responding in one way rather than another to the course of our experience), then—by implication—we acknowledge this condition as the goal (*telos*) of a certain intellectual and educational effort. However, I also suggested in Part I (Chapter 3, §5) that the teleological story undergoes an important variation as we pass from classical virtue ethics to its putative modern successor—that is, to a position designed to overcome the scientistic "disenchantment" of nature and to restore reason to its proper setting within a certain form of animal life. In the classical model, pride of place is given to the idea of a timeless structure of rationality (both theoretical and practical), which is taken to set the standard for individual development; and this despite the fact that, given the distinctive characteristics of our species, the only way in which we can make any progress towards that standard is through assimilation into an ordered community such as the Greek city-state. Our proposed successor to this model, on the other hand, concentrates in the first instance on the business of upbringing itself—on the need for each of us individually to enter into a historically specific culture of giving and asking for reasons: the question of how this local culture might compare, for better or worse, with others of its kind is one for which this different view sets the stage rather than one about which it can make any assumptions *a priori*. So my suggestion was that by reclaiming the Aristotelian conception of human beings as creatures with not only a "first" but a "second," socially acquired nature, while at the same time giving more explicit recognition to the historicity of the process by which this second nature is set in place, we can come to see in the work of formation a purposiveness of the kind that is typical of historical agents—the purpose in this case being to initiate our successors into our own particular form of "mindedness."

I argued in Chapter 5 (§§1 and, with reservations, 7) that the move to this more concrete conception of the teleology of upbringing is not in itself a reductive one. For as long as we adhere to the policy of looking at our own cognitive activity from an immanent rather than a "sideways on" point of view, we should have no difficulty in entertaining the thought that—as McDowell puts it—"immersion in a tradition might be a respectable mode of access to the real."[1] And if we do acknowledge "immersion in a tradition" as a worthy (because potentially truth-disclosing) object of human effort, we should also be able to admit to having a stake in any teleological notions that may be needed to support it. In particular, the discovery of our own implication in an "ethical and teleological discourse of consciousness" (to recall a phrase from Derrida: Chapter 5, §6) looks as if it might simply pave the way to a recognition of this discourse as grounded in our practical epistemic interests: for all its implicit "moralism,"[2] the "serious"/"nonserious" contrast may still be a product of concerns and purposes which we cannot plausibly disown, and which we can even acknowledge as integral to the activity of "symbolic reproduction." And this suggests that there is no purely philosophical reason why the naturalist (or, consequently, the historicist) turn should make us any less conscientious in our pursuit of that activity. Perhaps we do implicitly believe we have a duty to play our part in the conservation of a certain culture of responsiveness to reasons; and perhaps the raising of this belief to consciousness will not, and should not, make it go away.

But there is another kind of conscientiousness—no doubt especially characteristic of modern human beings—which is evoked not so much by the idea of conservation as by that of *freedom* (the only one of Kant's "postulates of pure practical reason," or so I suggested in Chapter 6, §3, to

1. John McDowell, *Mind and World* (Cambridge: Harvard University Press, 1994), p. 98. Note that this thought, as it stands, is quite a modest one. The point is not that a living tradition of thought can be expected to resolve all epistemological problems, but that it should be credited with some epistemological value rather than none. See (again) Chapter 3, §5.

2. See Chapter 5, note 50 and accompanying text.

retain its place within a secular world view). This too—like the kind concerned with maintaining established norms of rational receptivity—involves an attitude of vigilance. But the shortcomings of which it stands ready to accuse itself are different. They relate not to our possible failure to be all that other (decent, morally upright) people in our social milieu expect us to be, but rather to a possible failure to subject these very social expectations to the scrutiny they deserve. The message of the "emancipatory" conscience is that insofar as we fail to do this latter thing (a failure whose causes we may see fit to describe in terms of credulity, complacency, vested interest, and the like) we condemn ourselves, and others who could benefit from our collaboration in the work of critical reflection, to a condition of avoidable "heteronomy" or subservience. And in this way we acquiesce in the exposure of our lives to unchecked social and ideological determination.

An overtly historicized account of the process of ethical formation raises new questions for the emancipatory conscience. The element of novelty that it introduces lies not in the idea of social determination as such (since this is merely one of many traditionally recognized grounds for skepticism about the freedom of the will), but rather in the way we are now invited to see that determination as working. Traditional causal determinism, responding to the influence of the experimental sciences, fixes its attention—so far as "nurture," or social causality, is concerned—on the genesis of this or that type of *behaviour,* treating the subject of the behaviour as standing in an ontologically external relation to the relevant causal factors. For example, it might suggest the hypothesis that individuals placed in particular sorts of circumstances (high-rise apartment blocks, boarding schools, broken homes, or whatever) are more likely than a control group to behave in certain ways, but it would picture these individuals as having already "become who they are" by the time they enter the situation, or the set of relationships, that figures in the given hypothesis. By contrast, with the idea of mental activity in general as resting on initiation into a socially realized sum of "wisdom about what is a reason for what,"[3] we get a picture of subjectivity itself—that is, of the condition of *being a subject* of thought or of (intentional) action—as "socially (or discursively) constituted."

Applied to thought and action under their ethical aspect, this picture clearly owes something to the classical notion of *form as essence*—spe-

3. McDowell, *Mind and World,* p. 126.

cifically, of a person's ethical identity as determined by the "disposition," or arrangement, of elements in their *psuchê;*[4] but it insists more strongly on the idea that this disposition in turn is brought about by our involvement in social relationships, the very relationships that the traditional determinist saw as operating upon us from outside. This involvement provides the substance of that "immersion in a culture" which we said would be the successor, within an updated practical reason view, of the rational principle or *logos* that serves as a guarantor of Platonic–Aristotelian moral virtue (Chapter 3, §§3–4).

The new questions mentioned just now had to do with the way in which an "overtly historicized" account of ethical formation might interact with the modern commitment to freedom. That this account can be taken to call human freedom into doubt is shown by its association with an idea of the subject as a *function* or *effect* of social order, and especially of language. Recalling what was said in Chapter 5 about the struggle to achieve *full authorship* of (what count for us as) ethically exemplary judgements, we might recognize some of the antecedents of that discussion in a certain (negative) line of thought laid down by Roland Barthes in the 1960s with reference to the concept of literary authorship ("For [Mallarmé], for us too, it is language which speaks, not the author"),[5] and by Michel Foucault when he proposes to displace the "solid and fundamental role [in the history of ideas, literature, and science] of an author and his works" in favour of an enquiry into how the "author-function" is determined within specific discursive practices.[6] But the word "antecedents" is probably misleading, for already at that date some more general considerations are in full view. Foucault concludes his essay[7] by asking: "Is it not possible to reexamine, as a legitimate extension of this kind of analysis, the privileges of the subject?" and by suggesting that while the subject "should not be entirely abandoned," it "must be stripped of its creative role and analysed as a complex and variable function of discourse"—no longer pictured, for example, as

---

4. See Chapter 2, note 18 and accompanying text.

5. Roland Barthes, "The Death of the Author," in Barthes, *Image—Music—Text,* trans. Stephen Heath (Glasgow: William Collins, 1977), pp. 142–148; quotation from p. 143.

6. Michel Foucault, "What is an Author?" in *Language, Counter-Memory, Practice: Selected Essays and Interviews,* ed. Donald Bouchard, trans. Donald Bouchard and Sherry Simon (Oxford: Basil Blackwell, 1977), pp. 113–138; quotations from pp. 115, 130.

7. Ibid., pp. 137–138.

"animating the rules of discourse from within," but as occupying a position made available within a certain discursive order.

The proposal to "strip the subject of its creative role" sounds like a recipe for bringing thought to a standstill; but it may be that in resorting to this image, Foucault has exposed the idea of creativity to what was described in Chapter 6 (§1) as a questionably "metaphysical emphasis." Avoiding such an emphasis and returning to the standpoint of "quietism," we can think of our own creative role as subjects of thought and intention not as a problematic theoretical construct standing in need of validation, but as something displayed from moment to moment in the exercise of spontaneity—that is, in the effort to respond rationally to the state of the world. The quietist, we might say, is already equipped to live with the idea of the subject as a "complex and variable function of discourse." For this form of words can serve to express a point that is implicit in the thesis of the "unboundedness of the conceptual." We saw in Chapter 1, §4 that someone who regards the conceptual as "unbounded" will picture the continuing adjustment of thought to reality as aiming at the goal of identity between the content of (declarative) thought, on one hand, and on the other the content of "what is so";[8] and we said that on this view the latter (the thing that "is so") must already contain all the conceptual determinations a true declarative thought can find in it, since otherwise "the world," or "reality," would not be able to provide rational grounds for just that thought. What we need to notice at this stage is that the same picture commits us, further, to a conception of the *subject* as owing its openness to reality—a reality which, to repeat, we are supposing *not* to lie outside the bounds of the conceptual—to the possession of a repertoire of concepts in terms of which it can represent the various sorts of fact disclosed to intelligent awareness (for example, the "fact that *p*," where *p* can contain as much conceptual structure as we please). Now, it is reasonable to assume that "possession of a repertoire of concepts" entails possession of a language.[9]

8. Compare Ludwig Wittgenstein, *Philosophical Investigations,* trans. G. E. M. Anscombe (Oxford: Basil Blackwell, 1967), §95: "When we say, and *mean,* that such-and-such is the case, we—and our meaning—do not stop anywhere short of the fact; but we mean: *this— is—so.*"

9. McDowell (*Mind and World,* p. 125) sees entry to the "space of reasons"—which he equates with the "space of concepts"—as being accomplished, in effect, through learning to talk. See also ibid., p. 120, where he extends the picture outlined in the text to subjectivity in

So it would seem that we are already committed by our quietist principles to a conception of the (thinking) subject as "discursively constituted"— but committed, also, to understanding this conception in such a way that its outward pessimism is counterbalanced by an *internal,* or participatory, point of view which provides for the emergence of spontaneity.

McDowell insists on the possibility of applying our own (discursively constituted) powers of thought to the critical evaluation of the system of (discursive) norms under which we acquired those powers: for him, the cognitive tradition embodied in a particular natural language is "subject to reflective modification by each generation that inherits it."[10] (He expresses the point elsewhere by saying that in this respect all thinking is in the same boat, namely, "Neurath's boat," which has to be repaired on the open sea.)[11] But he offers no detailed account of the nature of this process, since for him "reflective thinking about specific norms [is] an activity that is not

the more intuitive sense of an "inner world," or of a way things are for one subjectively, by treating this as a limiting case of the legitimate application of the "structure of awareness and object": located at the limit because "the object of [first-person] awareness is really nothing over and above the awareness itself," but still legitimately subsumed within that structure—and this is where the enabling role of language comes in—because the states of affairs given to first-person, present-tense awareness are also *thinkable in other persons and tenses.* And compare Jacques Derrida, *Limited Inc* (Evanston: Northwestern University Press, 1988), p. 148: "What I call 'text' implies all the structures called 'real,' 'economic,' 'historical,' socio-institutional, in short: all possible referents. That does not mean that all referents are suspended, denied, or enclosed in a book . . . But it does mean that every referent, all reality has the structure of a differential trace, and that one cannot refer to this 'real' except in an interpretative experience." (For some observations on the protoconceptual capacities of non-language-using animals, however, see Alasdair MacIntyre, *Dependent Rational Animals* [London: Duckworth, 1999], esp. chap. 5.)

10. McDowell, *Mind and World,* p. 126. Compare the view of Hilary Putnam that reason is "both transcendent and immanent" with respect to social practice ("Why Reason Can't Be Naturalized," in Kenneth Baynes, James Bohman and Thomas McCarthy, eds., *After Philosophy: End or Transformation?* [Cambridge: MIT Press, 1987], pp. 222–244; quotation from p. 242. The naturalism alluded to in Putnam's title is, of course, of the reductive kind). See also Chapter 3, note 51 and accompanying text.

11. McDowell, *Mind and World,* p. 81. See also John McDowell, "Two Sorts of Naturalism," in Rosalind Hursthouse, Gavin Lawrence, and Warren Quinn, eds., *Virtues and Reasons: Philippa Foot and Moral Theory* (Oxford: Clarendon Press, 1995), pp. 149–179, esp. §§9–12. The idea is that while different regions of thought—say, ethics and natural science—have their own distinctive epistemic standards, none can do better, in the name of self-improvement, than to persevere in applying the standards internal to itself.

particularly philosophical."[12] This verdict is, of course, the only one possible for a self-avowed quietist. For the quietist attitude requires us to distinguish between ("first-order") enquiry into the merits or demerits of some particular norm, and (properly philosophical) enquiry into the nature of normativity or of the demands of reason in general—between thinking that is integrated with practice (including the practice of ordinary theoretical disciplines such as history or mathematics), and thinking that "leaves everything as it is."[13] Yet one effect of his or her approach which the quietist can be expected to endorse, and indeed to welcome, is an increase in clarity about the nature and intellectual location of different kinds of question. Consider for example the observation that it is characteristic of our species to supplement its "first" nature with a "second" one, the substance of which admits of a certain amount of historical variation; and that this second nature comprises a certain habit of normative judgement, or a sense of "what is a reason for what." Having issued these "reminders," a quietist philosophy has to stop: it cannot tell us what judgement (if any) to pass on the second nature with which, when we come to reflect, we find ourselves provided. But this does not mean that it cannot help to sharpen our sense of some of the questions waiting to be asked when we move *outside* the bounds of philosophy. And the idea that it is "in our nature" to be, from one point of view, products or expressions of a historically specific

12. McDowell, *Mind and World*, p. 95.

13. See Wittgenstein, *Philosophical Investigations* §124. It is tempting to say that a good deal of our knowledge of the intellectual personality of Wittgenstein is based on remarks that are "not particularly philosophical" in the sense employed here. On the other hand, perhaps "philosophy" in this sense must be taken to embrace at least one kind of cultural fault-finding, namely, the kind aimed at that very mental pathology which it—that is, philosophy itself—seeks to cure. But then again, do we have any reason to think that there is just one such pathology? For a passage that suggests but, so far as I can see, does not resolve these questions, see Ludwig Wittgenstein, *Remarks on the Foundations of Mathematics*, ed. G. H. von Wright, R. Rhees, and G. E. M. Anscombe, trans. G. E. M. Anscombe (Oxford: Basil Blackwell, 1978), II, §23: "The sickness of a time is cured by an alteration in the mode of life of human beings, and it was possible for the sickness of philosophical problems to get cured only through a changed mode of thought and of life, not through a medicine invented by an individual. Think of the use of the motor-car producing or encouraging certain sicknesses, and mankind being plagued by such sickness until, from some cause or other, as the result of some development or other, it abandons the habit of driving."

form of life might well be thought to open up new ground for critical (even if "not particularly philosophical") enquiry.

Perhaps, then, it would be disingenuous to claim that the questions thrown up by this kind of enquiry are entirely innocent of any debt to philosophy. For philosophy (still in the quietist sense) does seem to be able to generate an abstract, speculative awareness of the diverse forces that act upon us in the name of family life, language and education, law and government, work and pleasure—forces that make human beings into something determinate by securing their participation in rule-governed systems of behaviour. However, our interest in the operation of these forces is not guaranteed to remain abstract and speculative—nor, consequently, philosophical, as the term is being used here. It may, on the contrary, take a practical turn of the kind illustrated by Foucault's own proposal for a "historical" or "critical ontology of ourselves"[14]—an "investigation into the events that have led us to constitute ourselves and to recognize ourselves as subjects of what we are doing, thinking, saying."[15] Such an investigation, as Foucault pictures it, will be inspired by the wish to wrest from established authority new areas of control over our own existence—that is, by an "impatience for liberty"[16] which links the political culture of the present day

14. Michel Foucault, "What is Enlightenment?" in Paul Rabinow, ed., *The Foucault Reader* (Harmondsworth: Penguin, 1986), pp. 32–50; quotations from pp. 45, 46, 50.

15. Ibid., p. 46. It is interesting to find Foucault, as a first-order practitioner of this kind of study, seemingly so unworried by the problem that exercises Barbara Herman ("Making Room for Character," in Stephen Engstrom and Jennifer Whiting, eds, *Aristotle, Kant, and the Stoics: Rethinking Happiness and Duty* [Cambridge: Cambridge University Press, 1996], pp. 36–60): "Much moral work can be done by a sensitivity that is both world-regarding and motivationally set. Agents are able to determine what is to be done through an appreciation or reading of what is morally salient in their circumstances . . . What seems to me a matter for concern is the apparent absence, in such a conception of character, of a way to criticize the sensitivity itself—for it to take itself as the object of its own critical regard" (quotation from pp. 54–55).

16. Foucault, "What is Enlightenment?," p. 50. For Foucault the modern critical project—whether or not it can be correctly located under the heading of "Enlightenment"—will neither seek to identify the universal structures of knowledge and action, nor lend itself to any political programme that claims to be "global or radical"; it will however "separate out, from the contingency that has made us what we are, the possibility of no longer being, doing or thinking what we are, do or think" (p. 46). Hence the point of critical thinking for us (in contrast to Kant, whose own essay "What is Enlightenment?" provides Foucault's starting point) is "to transform the critique conducted in the form of necessary limitation [of what

with that of the Enlightenment. Although we may agree that any thought-ful modern successor to the impulse of "Enlightenment" will be marked by a posthumanist modesty about the nature of our "creative role" as subjects of political action, the project of a *critical* "ontology of ourselves" clearly presupposes both that it is possible, and that we might find it worthwhile, to resist the workings of those purposive processes whereby we and our contemporaries are discursively constituted as subjects.

2

The idea of a "critical ontology of ourselves" suggests the possibility of a change of attitude to some of the phenomena highlighted in our account of formation. On that account, initiation into a form of life is essential to the development of proper receptivity to the demands of reason—essential as an adjunct to the necessarily finite stock of examples, exercises, verbal explanations, and the like which are available for use in communicating a rule or "form" of thought. Those engaged in the business of upbringing must therefore take advantage of the mimetic impulse that prompts us to identify ourselves—either through primitive sociability, or in play or exis-tential experiment—with the people around us; they must seek to harness this impulse to a creative social purpose, and must condemn as *recalcitrant* any behaviour that defies or subverts that purpose. Such recalcitrant ten-dencies bear witness to the enduring presence of an *apeiron*, or formless principle, in human nature. That, anyway, is how matters stand according to the practical reason view.

We have seen that although the "critical ontology of ourselves" is a theo-retical exercise, it is motivated by a practical interest in becoming some-thing other than our socialization has made of us up to now. And this is an interest that is liable to set us at variance with the agencies of upbringing. For anyone who shares it may have occasion to contemplate a withdrawal of cooperation from those agencies, and an alliance or *rapprochement* with the "recalcitrant": I mean, with some of the tendencies which attract that label.

Is this oppositional attitude already licensed, in principle, by the admis-sion that beliefs about the layout of the "space of reasons" are subject to a

we can know] into a practical critique that takes the form of a possible transgression" (p. 45).

process of reflective modification? That will depend on the nature of the opposition that it expresses.

There seems to be one kind of critique of ethical formation—we can call it the "determinate critique"—which is internal to the search for a satisfying articulation of the rationalist character ideal (Chapter 1, §2), or equivalently for a specification of the "good life." The determinate critique assumes that the regime of formation actually operating within a given community—and hence the array of beliefs, attitudes, habits of inference, and other psychological attributes which that community calls "rational"—may at any time be in need of reconstruction in order to make it *more* rational, or (in Platonist terms) to turn it into a more adequate realization of its "idea." Such a critique is perfectly capable of supporting gestures, or longer-term projects, of resistance to ethical formation, but it will do so on the basis of an alternative view of how formation ought to proceed—a view that can claim (possibly in some quite limited respect, but possibly also on a grander scale) to offer an improvement on the *content* of the dominant one. The way in which the content of the formative process can be seen as open to improvement will be determined by the nature of the defects thought to be present at any given moment in existing social institutions. So, for example, socialists may be prepared to take the side of the ethically recalcitrant insofar as it seems to express refusal to acquiesce in a class position that places one on the receiving end of economic exploitation, or refusal to cooperate fully with the physical and mental disciplines associated with that class position. Likewise, feminists will be disposed to side with the recalcitrant insofar as it seems to express refusal of a subordinate gender position.

By way of illustration, we can see the makings of a determinate critique of formation in Terry Eagleton's argument that whereas deconstructionist writing on ethics is strongly influenced by the Kantian divorce of practical reason from nature, Marxist thought is in a position to heal this rift and to benefit from a reappropriation of the discourse of virtue.[17] Invoking the idea that economic life needs to be "transformed into an arena of freedom, autonomy, equality and democratic rule by the socialization of industry,"[18] Eagleton represents the ethical basis of this programme as a synthesis of

17. Terry Eagleton, "Deconstruction and Human Rights," in Barbara Johnson, ed., *Freedom and Interpretation: The Oxford Amnesty Lectures 1992* (New York: Basic Books, 1993), pp. 122–145.
18. Ibid., p. 137.

classical "civic humanism" with the "commercial humanism" that emerged in the early modern period. Classical humanism is valuable for a conception of the "virtuous man" as one of a community of free, equal, economically independent citizens with a shared devotion to the public good; it is valuable too for the implicitly materialist recognition that this ideal can be realized only on the basis of sufficient wealth to free the individual from menial work. Commercial humanism, while retaining the conception of moral personality as requiring a foundation in property, corresponds to a more advanced stage of development of the forces of production and thus "views the unfolding and enrichment of the human subject in social and economic, rather than narrowly political, terms";[19] but against this, it tends to lose sight of the political altogether by promoting commercial, or property-centred, relationships to a position of dominance over those based on a common civic identity. In order to repair that defect without disowning the increased ethical sophistication of the bourgeois era, Marxism can argue that "the economy must itself become a field for the flourishing of public virtue, not just a private occasion or opportunity for it [that is, for virtue *tout court*], and virtue and commerce thus cease to be antithetical";[20] and that this project implies the "historical possibility of the practice of virtue being brought within the reach of all men and women."[21] (The wish to make socioeconomic life accountable to a more than merely technical rationality reveals, incidentally, a latent point of agreement between Marxist humanism and the more academic complaint that "modern moral philosophy" leaves ethics devoid of substance, so that anything whatsoever can in principle count as a "moral position,"[22] while at the same time no object of pursuit seems to make a sufficiently categorical claim on us to overcome our quasi-consumerist "choice fatigue."[23] In view of this agreement, one can see a kind of logic in the "odd alliance" noted by Samuel Scheffler between "a refined English Aristotelianism and a moral orientation with roots in the American counterculture of the late 60s"!)[24]

19. Ibid., p. 136.

20. Ibid., p. 137.

21. Ibid., p. 140.

22. See G. E. M. Anscombe, "Modern Moral Philosophy," in her *Collected Philosophical Papers*, vol. 3 (Oxford: Basil Blackwell, 1981), pp. 26–42.

23. See David Wiggins, "Truth, Invention, and the Meaning of Life," in his *Needs, Values, Truth* (Oxford: Clarendon Press, 1998), pp. 87–137.

24. Samuel Scheffler, *Human Morality* (Oxford: Oxford University Press, 1992), p. 14.

3

Eagleton, then, envisages the possibility of a Marxist virtue ethics, and hence (by implication) of a mode of upbringing suited to the variety of practical reasons arising within a democratized form of economic life. In doing so, he encourages us to look again at some of those phenomena which, within our mainstream ethical tradition, would often be put down to "recalcitrance"—in particular, at behaviour prompted by the will to resist exploitation and related abuses. Eagleton's reasoning suggests that such behaviour may be better understood as issuing not from disdain for the question of the relative merits of this or that form of social organization (the question of the "common good," as an Aristotelian might call it), but from a *different* way of answering that question.[25] But how typical is this case? To what extent can we treat those episodes that would interest a Marxist as representative instances of the breach of moral expectations, and quarry them for insight into the nature of the "recalcitrant" as such?

The point does not seem to be one that we can settle immediately by reference to the "phenomenology of dissent." True, there is a familiar kind of pleasure to be had from situations in which the recalcitrant, meaning what has evaded the established process of ethical formation, suddenly asserts itself. Often the concept of the "anarchic" seems to capture the source of this pleasure. Yet if we consider the satisfaction one may take—say, as the occupant of a subordinate social role—in the breach of some aspect of social discipline, it will not always be clear how far such feelings are inspired by "anarchism" in an absolute sense: that is, by an abstract or totalizing rejection of social order. For as so far described, they are consistent not only with this attitude but also with a more discriminating enjoyment of the

25. Platonists will recognize here a version of the device available to "logocentric" philosophy (or "logos philosophy": see Chapter 1, note 24) of reinterpreting *that which is not* (here, not included within the ethical) as *that which is—but differently* (see Plato, *Sophist* 257b, 258ab). (There is, of course, something ideologically odd in portraying the opponents of Marxism—for whom much of the social action it inspires would represent the merely *un-* *ethical*—as party to the rationalist programme of enquiry into the nature of the good life, since anti-Marxists may well be disposed, for their own theoretical reasons, to reject the objectivist presuppositions of that enquiry and hence to deny its intelligibility. Our excuse must be that these people do hold in common certain substantive social values dictated by their philosophical position, and hence do in fact subscribe to a certain answer to the traditional rationalist question, even though they believe the question to be senseless.)

discomfiture of authorities that we perceive as illegitimate or as somehow unworthy of respect.

The idea of "legitimate authority" is often—perhaps typically—approached by a negative route. Our most primitive reactions of dissent or opposition (as manifested in infantile rage and the like) have no more content than could be interpreted by an onlooker as: "At any rate, not *this*." But as we acquire greater intentional control over our behaviour and move into the phase of acting for the sake of ends that we represent to ourselves conceptually,[26] the reaction "not this" assumes a form in which it will be accompanied, much of the time, by an ability to say *why* not: to give a reason for our nonacquiescence. And this development seems to be connected with the one discussed in Chapter 4, §4, where the process of upbringing was said to direct us towards the acceptance of *universal accountability* as a constraint upon assertion—that is, of "the principle that only what is epistemically good enough for anyone is good enough for one's present audience." For to give a reason is to try to represent one's behaviour in a light in which it could also be seen, and appreciated, by others. As we gain in experience and sophistication, the reasons we offer can be expected to show an increasing sensitivity to the demand for accountability: they will be calculated with increasing care to win spontaneous (uncoerced) recognition from "any reasonable person" (whatever concrete meaning we may attach to this phrase). And where our negative reaction is directed towards an existing "morality" with its associated practice of upbringing, the wish to get this reaction endorsed by a community of "reasonable" others will express that concern with legitimacy—that desire to live under legitimate as opposed to arbitrary forms of authority—which is the distinguishing mark of the determinate critique. The correction or amendment required by existing "morality" may be taken, as by a humanist Marxism, to consist essentially in the promotion of values that would call for a more equal distribution of divisible goods; alternatively, the critic may invoke other recognizably ethical concerns such as the need for better maintenance of the social or natural "fabric,"[27] or the claims of liberal or libertarian values such as toleration, diversity, creativity, and hedonism.

26. For McDowell, this is the development by which we come to qualify as *agents* at all. Thus *Mind and World*, p. 89: "Movements of limbs without concepts are mere happenings, not expressions of agency." See also Chapter 1, note 12 and accompanying text.

27. See Onora O'Neill, *Towards Justice and Virtue: A Constructive Account of Practical Rea-*

I suggested in §2 above that the determinate critique of ethical formation represents a particular kind of oppositional attitude which, from the standpoint of a practical reason view of ethics, is at one with the social order it opposes in its commitment to (some variant of) the rationalist character ideal. This commitment has certain consequences which it may be useful to spell out in order to see more clearly what appearance it presents to those who do not share it, and who have a different conception of moral dissent.

Since the grounds for dissatisfaction with a programme of "reflective modification" of morality will be found to turn upon the idea of *difference* (see Chapter 8), we should acknowledge at the outset that the determinate critique inherits from traditional virtue ethics a structure of thought that is, in a certain sense, hostile to this idea. For it incorporates a disposition to judge people by the *quality of their response to the practical reasons that there are.* And once we consent to speak of the "reasons that there are" for doing or believing something, we effectively accept that anyone *perfectly* attuned to the presence of these items—even if that state of attunement is incapable of full verbalization—will agree, in their perception of the (practical or theoretical) reasons that obtain in any given context, with anyone else who is perfectly so attuned.[28] In other words, we assume that insofar as it is possible to realize the ideal of perfect responsiveness to reasons, the judgement of those who have done so will exhibit "sameness"; while "difference," in this connection at least, will bear a negative value since it will constitute a deviation from correctness.

"Recalcitrant" or oppositional social action, where it envisages the replacement of an established order with something better, is already implicated in this positive evaluation of "sameness" (in the sense of *conformity to a standard* of correct judgement). This is because to call one thing "better" than another means that, in one way or another, there is reason to prefer it. Hence it is to appeal to a strand of sensibility in our audience, a

---

soning (Cambridge: Cambridge University Press, 1996), p. 163; and compare Nicola Lacey, *State Punishment: Political Principles and Community Values* (London: Routledge, 1988), chap. 8.

28. Compare Plato, *Republic* 349b–350d. (We can see this—even if Plato did not—as leaving room for the occurrence of cases where the point on which our exemplary judges agree is that the available reasons are less than conclusive. Indeed, such a view seems to be forced on us by the idea of rational capacities as grounded in a historically constituted "second nature": see Chapter 9, §5.)

bit of "second nature" created by some putative local process of formation that unites them with ourselves, which will disclose to them that this reason exists. Like the traditional ethical rationalist, then, adherents of any programme of collective "recalcitrance" (assuming that the latter still invokes *judgements* of value, and is not pictured simply as the symbolic manifestation of a certain clash of social forces)[29] will have a stake in the success of ethical formation, and so in the persistence of whatever "institutions" or configurations of power are needed to keep it going. For them too—despite their dissent from specific features of an existing social order—the ethically recalcitrant will be a potentially hostile principle, since it may work against the uptake of rational considerations that happen to be integral to their own project.

It has long been a popular pastime to sneer at political movements of the Left for continuing to build on the Enlightenment postulate of a link between the *rational* and the *universal*—for example, by adopting the abolition of capitalist class divisions as their favoured means of constructing a "rational" (or maybe just a less demented) society. Such attacks may equally well come from a liberal or from a Nietzschean direction; from critics concerned with the evils of the bureaucratic state or with those of the "authoritarian personality."[30] Yet the only way to clear oneself definitively of any suspicion of having a stake in enduring "institutions," or in the intellectual authority they exert, would be to abandon once and for all the hope of commending any proposed course of action to others on the

29. This model of political conflict has been defended by Richard Rorty. For references and critical discussion, see my "Feminism and Pragmatism: A Reply to Richard Rorty," in *New Left Review* 193 (May/June 1992), pp. 56–74.

30. Thus Isaiah Berlin, "Two Concepts of Liberty," in his *Four Essays on Liberty* (Oxford: Oxford University Press, 1969), p. 144: "[A] rule does not oppress me or enslave me if I impose it on myself consciously, or accept it freely, having understood it, whether it was invented by me or others, provided that it is rational, that is to say, conforms to the necessities of things . . . This is the positive doctrine of liberation by reason. Socialized forms of it . . . are at the heart of many of the nationalist, communist, authoritarian and totalitarian creeds of our day"; or Gilles Deleuze, *Nietzsche and Philosophy,* trans. Hugh Tomlinson (London: Athlone Press, 1983), pp. 92–93: "Understanding and reason have a long history: they are instances which still make us obey when we no longer want to obey anyone. When we stop obeying God, the State, our parents, reason appears and persuades us to continue being docile because it says to us: it is you who are giving the orders. Reason represents our slavery and our subjection as something superior which make us reasonable beings." (For some further remarks about Berlin, see Chapter 9.)

basis of "the reasons that there are"—in other words, to abstain altogether from the attempt to *discuss* anything (as opposed, perhaps, to the attempt to make oneself into some other kind of causally dynamic social presence). So when we undertake, from political motives, to defend the ethically "recalcitrant" against the agencies of ethical formation, it would seem that insofar as these motives are expressible in terms of *reasons why the result aimed at would be preferable to the status quo,* our defence of the recalcitrant will exhibit a paradoxical dependence on the very "forces of law and order" which we (also) oppose. We oppose these forces to the extent that they uphold a mode of formation, and hence of (so-called) rational receptivity, which we—for reasons of our own—do not accept as the real thing (since in our view it is a less than adequate guide to the overall layout of the "space of reasons"). But we also depend on them to the extent that, in addressing others, we want these others to feel the rational cogency of what we have to say, and so have to rely on their previous exposure to an upbringing which, with any luck, will have prepared them to do that.

There is a corresponding point to be made in the psychological domain, and hence in connection with the "critical ontology of ourselves" (§§1–2 above). It is that, subject to the same proviso about openness to the exchange of reasons, any defence of the recalcitrant will demand our continuing submission to the ideal of full authorship that I claimed (in Chapter 5) to discern within the practical reason view of ethics. The basis for this demand becomes apparent when we notice the conceptual link between *being prepared to offer reasons* and *being prepared to account for oneself to others*—that is, to take responsibility for one's beliefs and decisions; and when we recall that in order to be able to do the latter, we need to be able to identify ourselves—not just fleetingly but in the way appropriate to an "animal with the right to make promises" (Chapter 4, §2)—with those mental tendencies that favour assent to the beliefs and decisions in question.

It is worth noticing that just as the "noumenal self" in Kant's ethics is not a theoretical, but only a practical postulate (compare Chapter 6, §3), so there is nothing in the picture just invoked—that is, in the idea of ourselves as beings equipped to respond to objective reasons and to refine that response through communication—that need prevent us from concurring theoretically with the view that subjectivity is an effect of language (or, in general, of "sign systems"). Indeed, I argued in Chapter 5 that an ancestor of this view is presupposed by the Aristotelian account of ethical formation. What is at issue here is not the empirically determinable nature of the "self," or of individual participation in a common language, but the *practical* consequences of making it our aim to do or believe only that which comes up to the appropriate standard of rational acceptability.[31] Now these consequences include not only the commitment to distinguish between reasons of better and worse quality, but also—and regardless of any pessimistic psychological considerations about the concept of authorship—a commitment to the activity of *internal* discrimination by which a "rational self" (meaning something designed to discharge our obligations as reason-sensitive beings) is made to detach itself from the background noise, the *apeiron*, of our inner life. And because the work of discrimination between better and worse reasons is performed in the service of a universal—that is, because it expresses a will on our part to instantiate as perfectly as we can a certain objective "mindedness"—it follows that this other, reflexive work of discrimination, the one that we practise upon our own mental contents, will minister (though at a further remove) to the same universal. For its purpose is to establish a stable identification with the psychological "form" (or in our terms, the array of sensibilities) in virtue of which one qualifies as a reasoner.

4

This chapter has been intended to promote self-consciousness about what we are doing, and about the implicit loyalties we display, when we mount a defence of the ethically "recalcitrant" in terms of *better* and *worse* forms of social order between which a choice can be made. The argument has been that in appealing to a capacity for evaluative judgement which we presume to be common to ourselves and our audience, we already signify our submission in principle to the demands of the "universal": "submission in principle," because although we may be prepared to defy the (supposed) claims of moral rationality in certain more or less clearly delimited contexts, this attitude of defiance will be based not on any "particularly philo-

31. "Practical" here means "pertaining to activity," including intellectual activity. As for the "appropriate standard of rational acceptability," I am not implying that human experience is, or ought to be, dominated in its entirety by the compulsion to kit ourselves out with reasons—merely reflecting on what it is like to engage in the kind of activity to which this aim actually relates. (Knowing what does and does not fall under this heading is itself a matter of "culture" in a broad sense: compare Aristotle, *Nicomachean Ethics* 1094b22–27.)

sophical" considerations, but on (what we regard as) substantive reasons for dissatisfaction with an existing social practice. Thus to the extent that it remains indebted to a common appreciation of "the reasons that there are," the critique of ethical formation must preserve within itself something of that conservationist impulse—that will to continue a specific tradition of substantive rationality—which was said in §1 above to be integral to formation in general. Advocacy of the different, in short, requires a grounding in the "same."

However, we must not lose sight of the conditional nature of this thought. We must remember that all it purports to do is to tell us something about the intellectual commitments of a particular kind of moral dissident—one who is willing to entrust her dissent to an at least notionally existing sphere of dialogue about the common good, or about the nature of the rationalist character ideal. But let us now make the acquaintance of another kind of critic of ethical formation. This different critic will agree that if moral dissent remains dependent on a discourse of objective reasons or of objective value, it must likewise remain answerable to the "mindedness" embodied in those people whom we accept as exemplars of how to think. But she will not yet be convinced that this Neurathian procedure represents the most that we can do when we undertake to call the claims of "reason" into question. For to her it looks like a bad sign that as practitioners of determinate critique, we still entertain the hope of getting our own thinking endorsed from a "universal standpoint." This desire may strike her as regressive, or morbid, or just plain comical. Think for a moment, she says: are we so sure that Kant's ambition to substitute an autonomous for a heteronomous "reason" has accomplished anything more than a subtle consolidation of the essentially external and manipulative forces that govern our lives?[32] Or should we, on the contrary, agree with Richard Rorty that the desire to equip our beliefs with "rational coerciveness" is in fact "a symptom of power-worship—of the conviction that unless something large and powerful is on one's side, one shouldn't bother trying"?[33] Or with the feminist philosopher Rosi Braidotti, who holds that it is one more by-product of the "*paranoid* order of a rationality in search of self-legitimation"?[34] Or, again, with Paul Feyerabend when he claims that

32. See note 30 and accompanying text.

33. Richard Rorty, "Feminism and Pragmatism," *Michigan Quarterly Review,* 30 (1991), pp. 231–258; quotation from p. 254, note 21.

34. Rosi Braidotti, *Patterns of Dissonance: A Study of Women in Contemporary Philosophy,*

"[m]ost of the misery in our world, wars, destruction of minds and bodies, endless butcheries are caused not by evil individuals but by people who have objectivised their personal wishes and inclinations and thus have made them inhuman"?[35]

Behind this protest lies a determination to break out of the target zone of the dialectical argument constructed just now (§3) on behalf of the practical reason view of ethics—the argument that any critic who proposes to exchange the *status quo* for something recognizable as objectively *better* continues, by virtue of this way of framing her intention, to adhere to the norm of rational receptivity. The protest is meant to exemplify a kind of intervention *not* already allowed for (compare §2 above) by the idea of a continual "reflective modification" of our mapping of the space of reasons. It expresses the suspicion that a critique of reason which still consents to let itself be regulated by the very thing it purports to criticize must harbour tendencies that are not merely "conservationist" but also *conservative.* Isn't there something a little tame about the Neurathian picture, asks the protester? Should we not at least make the experiment of distancing ourselves from the Pythagorean-Platonic identification of unitary form as a "good" principle and of anarchic plurality as a "bad" one? And what about the (so-called) ethically "recalcitrant"? Might there not be something here that ought to command respect in its own right—not just for the energy it can contribute to this or that rationally motivated project of social improvement? The "reflective modification" of existing cognitive traditions is a worthy, but still essentially reformist undertaking. By contrast, the discovery of an "ethical and teleological discourse of consciousness"—and of the organizing role of this discourse within the practical reason view—suggests the possibility of some more radical development which could be realized only by a *counter-teleological* mode of thought.

trans. Elizabeth Guild (Cambridge: Polity Press, 1991), p. 53 (emphasis added), with reference to the history of post-Cartesian philosophy; and compare pp. 215–216, "What women denounce in the dualist opposition of masculine to feminine are precisely the power struggles it involves: a masculine-dominated economy, and exercise of power, are inherent in the use of reason and necessary to the establishment of rational order. In other words, theoretical reason imposes itself through a logic of exclusion and domination, which posits the ideal of rationality as the norm. The violent character of the exercise of reason is thus reasserted, in a way that can be compared to Foucault's and Derrida's assertion of the rationalist aggression at work in philosophy."

35. Paul Feyerabend, *Farewell to Reason* (London: Verso, 1987), p. 311.

So far, we do not know whether this protest even makes sense. For as soon as we try to pursue it beyond the stage of character assassination (as in the charges of power worship, paranoia, and so forth), and to name a specific ground of dissatisfaction with the project of determinate critique, difficulties crowd in. What basis can there be for the suggestion that the ethically recalcitrant "ought" to be the object of any particular attitude, if that suggestion issues from a place where the commitment to giving reasons is itself in doubt? What incentive can there be for someone who accepts the authority of "the reasons that there are" to submit to criticism by someone who apparently finds this authority problematic?[36] Perhaps the objector is simply confused. Rather than jump to that conclusion, however, I want to try in the next chapter to develop a better understanding of the challenge to teleological thinking.

36. One writer who has explored this problem to good effect is Alasdair MacIntyre: see his *Three Rival Versions of Moral Enquiry* (London: Duckworth, 1990), esp. chap. 9. I agree in principle with MacIntyre's conclusion that where no common standard of correctness exists, the only strategy by which one party can establish a position of superiority is by showing that it understands the opposition better than the latter understands itself. However, I think he is also right to say that "in the tripartite hostilities between the heirs of encyclopaedia [that is, of nineteenth-century positivism], post-Nietzschean genealogy, and Thomistic tradition neither argument nor conflict is yet terminated" (p. 215), and the remainder of my discussion is offered in that spirit.

EIGHT

The Violence of Reason?

1

In the last chapter we embarked on a new line of discussion by calling into question, essentially for the first time, the idea of "morality" as something to which our proper relationship is one of uncomplicated loyalty and aspiration. We noted the existence of a certain tradition of social criticism—that of "determinate critique"—for which a place is already prepared within the ethics of practical reason. (McDowell in fact speaks of a "standing obligation," itself inherited from previous generations, to engage in critical reflection on one's cultural inheritance.)[1] The label "*determinate critique*" was chosen in order to mark the fact that such reflection is governed by the actual state of receptivity to reasons—in this case, reasons for making some change to an existing social practice, or alternatively for leaving it as it is—which we happen to have arrived at by learning what our own society has been able to teach us about the ethical; and to record that because of this dependence on our pre-existing grasp of what counts as a (practical) reason, the resulting criticism of inherited "morality" will proceed by pointing to certain *specific* flaws, identifiable on the basis of a common evaluative sensibility.

We also saw that the practitioner of determinate critique is herself exposed to censure from another, putatively more radical kind of oppositional thinker—one to whom the determinate critic appears to be in the grip of a psychologically questionable (and ultimately sinister) desire for moral safety. By the lights of the "counter-teleological" thinking that was beginning to take shape in Chapter 7, §4, this is what lies behind the wish

---

1. John McDowell, *Mind and World* (Cambridge: Harvard University Press, 1994), p. 126.

to portray oneself as not *really,* but only ostensibly and superficially, opposed to the claims of the ethical "universal," and so to secure legitimacy
for what might otherwise have looked like merely transgressive behaviour.
However, apart from registering a certain unfriendly atmosphere, we cannot really claim as yet to have understood that thinking; for we are not yet
in a position to explain how it might hook up with any preexisting "mindedness" by virtue of which the *questionable* or the *sinister*—or indeed any
other critical category—could acquire a clear argumentative role. So let us
now see if we can make good this deficiency and give some content to the
idea of a counter-teleological mode of resistance to ethical formation.

In using the term "counter-teleological," I am thinking of a family of
considerations originating mainly in French philosophy of the 1960s and
1970s, but influential since then in the English-speaking world on account
of the interest they have held for "alternative" disciplines such as feminist
theory, gender studies, and critical social theory insofar as this has survived
the eclipse of Marxism. These considerations issue, of course, from the
work of a variety of thinkers with their own very diverse preoccupations
and areas of expertise; so any attempt to bring them together under a single rubric will inevitably pay the penalty of overemphasizing similarities at
the expense of differences, and will thus fall foul of just those values to
which, as we shall see, the thinkers in question hope to sensitize us. Still,
given the cultural distance that separates this bit of late-twentieth-century
philosophy from the discussions of practical reason that have occupied us
so far, there may be some justification for proceeding—however hazard-
ously—at a high level of generality.

The counter-teleological attitude[2] to ethical formation, then, will draw

---

2. I am not sure that I have been completely consistent in avoiding mention of a counter-
teleological *critique* (of ethics or ethical formation), and in view of the precedent furnished
by Foucault's "critical ontology of ourselves" (see Chapter 7), it is probably not worth taking
a rigorous line about this point of usage. We should remember, though, that the word "critique" comes fraught with rationalist connotations. As Vincent Descombes has written, "The
definition of philosophy as *critique* belongs to the pre-1789 'Enlightenment'. By denouncing
the impostor-priest whose lies support the despot, philosophy aims to open the innocent
eyes of the people, to restore to them their ancient virtues" (*Modern French Philosophy,* trans.
L. Scott-Fox and J. M. Harding [Cambridge: Cambridge University Press, 1980], p. 183). It is
this venerable form of radicalism that provides a target for Jean-François Lyotard when he
says in a text dating from 1974: "We laugh at critique, since it is to maintain oneself in the
field of the criticized thing and in the dogmatic, indeed paranoiac, relation of knowledge"
(*Libidinal Economy,* trans. Iain Hamilton Grant [London: Athlone Press, 1993], p. 95)—a

on ideas worked out—in the words of Peter Dews—in the service of an attack on "the political and philosophical positions of the Hegelianized Marxism which was a powerful influence on French intellectual life throughout the 1950s and into the 1960s."[3] It is because of the universalist motif inherited from Greek rationalism both by these positions and by our own "practical reason" view that the widespread revolt against the former in the post-1960s period ought, I believe, to be a cause of concern to the latter also.

The central theme of counter-teleological thinking appears to be that of the *violence of reason*. This idea may strike one as paradoxical, if not down-right perverse. For we are led by the main current of Western thought, and by the Kantian tradition in particular, to expect that "reason" in the language of philosophy will denote our capacity—such as it is—for resolving conflicts of individual will or opinion *without* violence. (According to Onora O'Neill, for example, "'reason' is just the name we give to whatever may be most authoritative for orienting thought and action,"[4] or to the source of principles that can be followed by all those whose thought and action is to be coordinated.) The attempt to get one's interlocutor to produce *out of his or her own mouth,* and to take responsibility for, a judgement agreeing with one's own has after all been a defining feature of "rational" argument ever since its Socratic beginnings,[5] and the importance of succeeding in this might naturally be supposed to lie in the very fact that it releases us from the temptation to promote our own views by force.

How might one come to break with this tradition and to accuse reason itself of being implicated in violence? Here I would like to return to the notion of universality, and to the thought that upbringing—the process that confers rationality on successive generations—consists in the imposition of a certain (universal) form on the indeterminate psychological "matter"

statement expressive of Lyotard's "determination to break with the language of legitimation which is inherent in critique" (Kimberly Hutchings, *Kant, Critique and Politics* [London: Routledge, 1996], p. 127).

3. Peter Dews, *Logics of Disintegration: Poststructuralist Thought and the Claims of Critical Theory* (London: Verso, 1987), p. 202 (with reference to the thought of Foucault and Lyotard).

4. Onora O'Neill, *Towards Justice and Virtue: A Constructive Account of Practical Reasoning* (Cambridge: Cambridge University Press, 1996), p. 60.

5. Compare Gregory Vlastos, "*Anamnêsis* in the *Meno,*" *Dialogue,* 4 (1965), pp. 143–167; see esp. pp. 158–159.

encountered in the learner. I suggested in Chapter 3 that the ancient idea of a gradual realization of "form" in the individual *psuchê* anticipates the modern one of "immersion in a culture"—a process which, so far as it succeeds, enables us to remedy the inbuilt limitations of explicit symbolism by taking the words or gestures of others in the way they are *meant* ("objectively," or "as any reasonable person would know") to be taken. It was due to the *de facto* normality of a successful (or "good enough") outcome to this process of immersion that the uncodifiability of ethics (and other rational structures) did not condemn us to skepticism about the attribute of "practical wisdom," nor, therefore, about the existence of ethical knowledge. However, we have also seen that if the individual mind is pictured, within our inherited metaphorical scheme, as potentially receptive to cultural "form," it must likewise be recognized as potentially resistant to such form, or as "recalcitrant" from the point of view of the educator. Now the idea of the violence of reason can be understood as issuing, precisely, not from that point of view but from one that as it were tries to sympathize with the *apeiron* in its potential recalcitrance. And whereas in the determinate critique of ethical formation such sympathy comes already prepared to explain itself by pointing to some specifiable defect in existing institutions, the counter-teleological attitude revolves around the pathos of formation as such—that is, of *any* operation designed to assimilate to the established forms of a culture some "matter" that lies outside them. We might say, echoing Derrida, that the particular kind of violence that exercises it lies in "the necessity that the other not appear as what it is, that it not be respected except in, for, and by the same."[6]

The worry just outlined still looks "metaphysical" in a bad sense. (We know what it means to side with the object of a recognizably unjust or abusive process of formation, in contrast to one that would be free from these faults: we do not know what it would mean for our sympathy to be enlisted in a cause where no such contrast is at issue.) And yet there is abundant evidence of its power to shape experience. This is especially apparent in the new climate of opinion that emerges after 1968 about the forms of organization appropriate to oppositional politics, a climate marked by "special sensitivity for complex injuries and subtle violations,"[7]

6. Jacques Derrida, "Violence and Metaphysics," in his *Writing and Difference*, trans. Alan Bass (London: Routledge and Kegan Paul, 1978), pp. 79–153; quotation from p. 133. The essay consists of a detailed exposition of the thought of Emmanuel Levinas, to which Derrida alludes in the words quoted here.

7. Jürgen Habermas, *The Philosophical Discourse of Modernity*, trans. Frederick Lawrence

and hostile in particular to the theme of *authoritative guidance*. One of the main objects of this hostility has been the idea of a type of person with the special function of *representing*, to the maximum degree of explicitness achievable at any given moment, the collective consciousness of some larger unit—perhaps in the first instance a local or partial one in whose interests such a person is supposed to act (trade unionists, women, the working class . . .), but more remotely—at any rate insofar as these interests qualify as "progressive"—a unit consisting of the whole of humanity.

If we consider this idea in its application to the individual, it will probably conjure up a figure like that of Aristotle's *phronimos*, who sets the standard of practical intelligence for the community to which he belongs (Chapter 3, §2). Collect a few such persons together, however, and the dominant association may rather be with Plato's image of a rational society as a hierarchically ordered organism, within which one element—small in size but preeminent in value—"deliberates on behalf of the whole" (Chapter 4, §1). Well into the twentieth century, that image could be invoked without irony in an account of the nature and status of philosophy: thus Husserl argues in his "Vienna Lecture" of 1935 that "[w]ithin European civilization, philosophy has constantly to exercise its function as one which is archontic for the civilization as a whole," a function it discharges by striving to perfect its own self-consciousness and so "putting itself, and thereby a genuine humanity, on the road [to realization]."[8] Foucault, by contrast, denounces this way of thinking as a mechanism of social control. "For a long period," he writes,

> the "left" intellectual spoke and was acknowledged the right of speaking in the capacity of master of truth and justice. He was heard, or purported to make himself heard, as the spokesman of the universal. To be an intellectual meant something like being the consciousness/conscience of us all. I think we have here an idea transposed from Marxism, from a faded Marxism indeed. Just as the proletariat, by the necessity of its historical

(Cambridge: MIT Press, 1987), p. 337. These words are used by Habermas in relation to what he calls "a critique of reason with reckless disregard for its own foundations" (ibid.).

8. Edmund Husserl, *The Crisis of European Sciences and Transcendental Phenomenology: An Introduction to Phenomenological Philosophy,* trans. David Carr (Evanston: Northwestern University Press, 1970), pp. 289, 291. The words in square brackets are inserted by the translator. (Husserl's reference to "European civilization" is integral to his argument, since he also holds that in order to understand the current "crisis of European existence" it is necessary to "work out the *concept of Europe as the historical teleology of the infinite goals of reason*" (ibid., p. 299; emphasis in original).)

situation, is the bearer of the universal (but its immediate, unreflected bearer, barely conscious of itself as such), so the intellectual, through his moral, theoretical and political choice, aspires to be the bearer of this universality in its conscious, elaborated form. The intellectual is thus taken as the clear, individual figure of a universality whose obscure, collective form is embodied in the proletariat.[9]

This passage reveals the substructure of an illustrious "ethical and teleological discourse" of *political* consciousness—"teleological" because, in this picture, the intellectual's thought is supposed actually to be what that of the masses is "trying" to become (just as reason, the preserve of Husserl's philosopher, "is precisely that which man *qua* man, in his innermost being, is aiming for").[10] Moreover, it brings out a possible ground of objection to that discourse—one that did not occur to us in relation to the teleological conception of *individual* consciousness and of the "authorship" of one's own utterances. For the words I have quoted seem to convey a clear enough message to the naïvely "ethical" reader—namely, that the delegation of theoretical and representative functions to a specialist minority is disrespectful to those represented and is detrimental to their interests. It is detrimental because the authority and status accruing to the "intellectuals" from the supposed fact of their being further along the relevant teleological pathway is a standing incitement to these people to consolidate their own position at the expense of the "masses," and to the extent that such authority confers power, to exercise that power cynically and oppressively. (If some other person is the conscious and articulate bearer of a concept of the political which is also present, but in a more obscure and implicit way, in me, then any mismatch between my own political consciousness and theirs can be attributed to something in me that has so far eluded or resisted the relevant process of formation—in this case, presumably, a process of political education or enlightenment.)

What seems to be demanded here is a new conception of the function of the (politicized) intellectual that would dissociate him (or her) from the presumptuousness of his quasi-Platonic role as a "hero of consciousness." And in a dialogue recorded in 1972[11] we find Foucault and Gilles Deleuze

9. Michel Foucault, "Truth and Power," in Paul Rabinow, ed., *The Foucault Reader* (Harmondsworth: Penguin, 1986), pp. 51–75; quotation from pp. 67–68.

10. Husserl, *The Crisis of European Sciences*, p. 341. For the metaphor of "trying" in connection with teleological or idealist thinking, see Chapter 3, note 11 and accompanying text.

11. "Intellectuals and Power," in Michel Foucault, *Language, Counter-Memory, Practice:*

trying to spell out such a conception. Deleuze says: "A theorizing intellectual, for us, is no longer a subject, a representing or representative consciousness. Those who act and struggle are no longer represented, either by a group or a union that appropriates the right to stand as their conscience. Who speaks and acts? It is always a multiplicity, even within the person who speaks and acts. All of us are 'groupuscules.' Representation no longer exists; there's only action—theoretical and practical action which serve as relays and form networks."[12] Addressing Foucault, he later declares: "In my opinion, you were the first—in your books and in the practical sphere—to teach us something absolutely fundamental: the indignity of speaking for others."[13] Foucault meanwhile states that "[t]he intellectual's role is no longer to place himself 'somewhat ahead and to the side' in order to express the stifled truth of the collectivity; rather, it is to struggle against the forms of power that transform him into its object and instrument [?the instrument of "power" in the abstract] in the sphere of 'knowledge', 'truth', 'consciousness' and 'discourse'."[14]

With hindsight, these ideas can be seen to have had a major impact on the political culture of the "new movements" then emerging—not least on feminism, which never held the figure of the representative "intellectual" in particularly high esteem, but for which the importance (or otherwise) of locating women's oppression within a comprehensive social theory remained a point of contention into the 1980s.[15] Within the post-Marxist

Selected Essays and Interviews, ed. Donald Bouchard, trans. Donald Bouchard and Sherry Simon (Oxford: Basil Blackwell, 1977), pp. 205–217.

12. Ibid., pp. 206–207.

13. Ibid., p. 209.

14. Ibid., pp. 207–208.

15. For an intervention on the "antitheory" side of this debate, see Liz Stanley and Sue Wise, *Breaking Out: Feminist Consciousness and Feminist Research* (London: Routledge and Kegan Paul, 1983), pp. 83, 84: "[T]here is no 'going beyond' the personal, that chimera of contemporary feminist theory . . . Feminism's alternative to conventional theorizing must reject collecting experiences merely in order to generalize them out of all recognition. Instead it should be concerned with going back into 'the subjective' in order to explicate, in order to examine in detail what this experience is." As is well known, the drive towards abstraction associated with the pursuit of "grand theory" also created an opening for accusations of "essentialism" from groups who saw the political essence of "woman," or of "female" subordination, as having been usurped by a privileged minority—white, middle-class, educated, heterosexual . . .—at the expense of assorted "others." For commentary on this development, see Nancy Fraser and Linda J. Nicholson, "Social Criticism without Philosophy: An Encounter between Feminism and Postmodernism," in Linda J. Nicholson, ed., *Feminism/Postmodernism* (London: Routledge, 1990), pp. 19–38. By the late 1980s there was already a gen-

model of political activism inaugurated by the language of "relays and net-works," one is no longer expected to look to any total theory into which a given locally useful fragment of critical discourse is destined to develop or to be incorporated,[16] and so there is no longer any demand for the "univer-sal" theorist who would facilitate these processes.

The thesis of the "indignity of speaking for others" sounds like some-thing that could be duly honoured in practice by creating conditions in which *everyone speaks for herself* and in which "those who act and struggle" conduct their common business on a basis of direct democracy. And where that business involves talking or deliberating, this may well be part of Deleuze's vision in the lines just quoted.[17] But it cannot be the whole story, because he also says that that which speaks and acts is "always a multiplic-ity, even *within* the person." This indicates that it is not just the claim to represent another that is being treated as problematic, but also, and more remarkably, the claim to represent *oneself*. The thought seems to be, not that there is no such procedure as purporting to speak on behalf of a col-lective, but rather that we should recognize the artificiality of this proce-dure—all the elaborate work of suppression and omission that goes into selecting anything in particular for utterance—and should develop a prac-tice which, so far as possible, reflects our skepticism about it.[18] And a corol-lary of this thought will be that the same artificiality attaches to the proce-dure of speaking or acting—as an ostensibly unified subject—on behalf of

erational variant of the basic complaint: see Shelagh Young, "Feminism and the Politics of Power: Whose Gaze is it Anyway?" in Lorraine Gamman and Margaret Marchment, eds., *The Female Gaze: Women as Viewers of Popular Culture* (London: The Women's Press, 1988).

16. Compare Michel Foucault, "Revolutionary Action: 'Until Now,'" in *Language, Coun-ter-Memory, Practice*, pp. 218–233: "[The] need for theory is still part of the system we reject . . . 'The whole of society' is precisely that which should not be considered except as some-thing to be destroyed" (quotations from pp. 231, 233).

17. The contentious nature of this vision can be brought out by a reading of Alasdair MacIntyre, *Dependent Rational Animals: Why Human Beings Need the Virtues* (London: Duckworth, 1999), which argues for recognition of the virtues of "acknowledged depen-dence" alongside those of the "independent practical reasoner." See esp. p. 150 and context for a reminder that any of us may, at one time or another, have to rely on others to speak for us, and consequently that it is also important to learn how to act, when called on, as a proxy for others.

18. I realize it is unlikely to be an accident that Deleuze's words do not contain the "should" that I have introduced in paraphrasing them. However, no one is perfect: let us not forget that these words were *published,* and so placed at the disposal of anyone who might wish to use them—as I am doing now—as representative instances of a tendency.

the "multiplicity," or "groupuscule," that one is. If the image of unity created by this procedure (or technique) is rightly regarded as a cultural artefact, then the statement that "representation no longer exists" can be read as a menacing gesture in the direction of this artefact, as if it were, say, a vase that one was minded to smash.

An attack on the "indignity" of representation, to the extent that it hits its target, can hardly leave the project of ethical formation untouched. For the goal of formation, as envisaged in the practical reason view, is precisely to bring about a psychological condition in which (self-)representation is possible—a condition characterized by the "serious" (not merely opportunistic) deployment of any available forms of moral expression, and so by the ability to represent, or answer for, ourselves authoritatively to others. We know that this is the educational ideal held out by classical virtue ethics. Is it, however, an ideal that we accept at the price of a kind of violence towards the *rest* of what we are—towards something in ourselves that would correspond to those silenced "others" on whose behalf the "universal" theorist unworthily presumed to speak? On the other hand, if the answer is yes, we find ourselves thrown back upon the question: where or what is the normative basis for indignation at this unfamiliar species of indignity?[19]

2

The idea of an "ethical and teleological discourse of consciousness" has just incurred some explicitly political criticism. That criticism took the form of a protest against the unequal status such a discourse assigns, on one hand, to the representative and authoritative element, and on the other to the inarticulate, imperfectly "conscious" remainder which has to be represented. Let us now turn to another kind of hierarchical thinking, no less marked by "ethical and teleological" influences, which has been claimed to affect our traditional picture of the *unfolding of events in time*. The object of interest here is a disposition to see particular historical moments or events as fitting into a developmental narrative, within which some culturally significant (and valued) form emerges from obscure beginnings into

19. Critics have likewise wondered how Foucault's intellectual programme relates to the traditional normative foundations of radical politics. See Dews, *Logics of Disintegration*, chap. 7; Nancy Fraser, *Unruly Practices: Power, Discourse and Gender in Contemporary Social Theory* (Cambridge: Polity Press, 1989), chap. 1; and compare note 2 above.

full actuality. Because such narratives are supposed to display the working of an impersonal "reason," they can be accused of indulging us in the wishful belief that the present state of things rests, to quote Foucault again, upon "profound intentions and immutable necessities."[20] The true historical sense, however, "confirms our existence among countless lost events, without a landmark or a point of reference";[21] if we find this vision repugnant, our feelings can be attributed to the influence of "[a]n entire historical tradition (theological or rationalistic) [which] aims at dissolving the singular event into an ideal continuity—as a teleological movement or a natural process."[22] In Foucault's picture the disruptive "singular event," which is suppressed by the regimenting tendency of rationalist historiography, evidently plays a structurally similar role to the "singular" point of political resistance, as contrasted with the consoling—but specious—universality of a mass movement.

This hostile account of the teleological view of history is echoed by the (now famous) suggestion of Jean-François Lyotard, later in the 1970s, that we are living through a period marked by the eclipse of "grand narratives" or "metanarratives"—images of collective human experience as a unified and meaningful (because purposive) process. Examples of such metanarratives, which come down to us as part of the Enlightenment legacy, include the one associated with liberalism and with socialism, both of which have sought to interpret specific political events in terms of their (positive or negative) relevance to the supposed central theme of world history (the struggle for individual rights and freedoms, or for a classless society—in a word, "the story of [humanity's] emancipation from everything that prevents it from governing itself"); and the one enshrined in the Hegelian "dialectics of spirit" whereby humanity, through its speculative vanguard in the universities, advances towards the achievement of absolute knowledge.[23] The "modern" mentality can then be defined in terms of its reliance

20. Michel Foucault, "Nietzsche, Genealogy, History," in *The Foucault Reader*, pp. 76–100; quotation from p. 89. This essay was first published in 1971.

21. Ibid.

22. Ibid., p. 88.

23. Jean-François Lyotard, *The Postmodern Condition: A Report on Knowledge*, trans. Geoff Bennington and Brian Massumi (Manchester: Manchester University Press, 1984), p. xxiii; pp. 31–37; quotation from p. 35. My reference here to "examples" may, admittedly, be misleading. Perry Anderson points out in *The Origins of Postmodernity* (London: Verso, 1998) that "[i]n the vicissitudes of Lyotard's political trajectory, there had always been one constant. *Socialisme ou Barbarie* [a far-left group in which Lyotard was active in the 1950s

on ideas of this kind to ground or legitimate a particular body of theory, whereas the "postmodern" is marked by an "*incredulity* toward meta-narratives"[24] and by a rejection of the attempt to "totalize . . . into a real unity" the array of phenomena that Lyotard, following Wittgenstein, calls "language-games."[25] Just as the postmodern work of art has the character of a (singular) *event* rather than of an attempt to apply "familar catego-ries,"[26] so the postmodern historical agent will renounce the terroristic fan-tasy of "seizing reality" (through a totalizing metadiscourse that would make sense of the whole of experience at a stroke), and will seek to "acti-vate the differences" (between particular language-games) which make such a discourse unattainable.[27]

Although the idea of a metanarrative relates in the first instance to social rather than individual existence, it could readily be drawn into the service of a critique of ethical formation. Any philosophy that gives a benign or positive role to formation, it might be argued, proposes a metanarrative within which we could (in principle) situate all the particular narrative data about any given person. The subject matter of this metanarrative would be the success or failure of the formative process whose aim is to initiate the person in question into a certain preexisting "mindedness," and so to make her properly receptive to the demands of reason. The detail of the person's unfolding life would derive significance from the metanar-rative of formation in a way analogous to that in which historical events can derive significance, for better or worse, from an overarching teleologi-cal scheme.[28]

and 1960s] was vehemently anti-communist from the first, and whatever his other changes of mood or conviction, this remained an ineradicable element in his outlook . . . It was [in debates preceding the French elections of 1978] that he first formulated the idea of meta-narratives that was to figure so prominently in *The Postmodern Condition,* and made its real target crystal-clear. Just one 'master narrative' lay at the origin of the term: Marxism" (quo-tation from p. 29).

24. Lyotard, *The Postmodern Condition,* p. xxiv (emphasis added).

25. Ibid., p. 81.

26. Ibid.

27. Ibid., p. 82. The same theme is pursued in Jean-François Lyotard and Jean-Loup Thébaud, *Just Gaming,* trans. Wlad Godzich (Manchester: Manchester University Press, 1985), in which Lyotard returns to the theme of "terror," outlining a conception of *justice* as that which "[preserves] the purity of each game" and opposes the ambition of one game to "regulate" others (pp. 96, 99).

28. This particular metanarrative is in evidence in a certain genre of *literary* narrative, the "novel of formation," which has been seen by some as the characteristic symbolic form of

Conversely, if we accept the suggestion—or reminder—that iterability is the background condition of all (conventional) meaning (Chapter 5, §6), we can begin to see how our conception of our own subjectivity might lose its "ethical and teleological" character by parting company with the meta-narrative of formation. The idea conveyed by the term "iterability" was that all utterances—including those internal "utterances" which we can imagine acts of judgement to be[29]—display in some degree the aspect of a momentary appropriation or "grafting." It is for this reason that, as Aristotle puts it, the values communicated to us through upbringing "have to become part of our nature" over a period of time[30]—a remark that seems to acknowledge the *impurity* of the relation of authorship obtaining, initially at least, between ourselves and (what passes for) "our" moral thinking. Yet this impure form of authorship is traditionally understood as an approximation towards the pure form that is destined to replace it in the life of the successfully brought-up person. So as a token of faith in this projected outcome, and also as a means of promoting it, the symbolic materials borrowed and recycled by the moral learner may be received by others (when the learner gets things sufficiently right) as expressions of a "nature" assumed, for practical purposes, to be already determinate—received, therefore, as if they were the products of *pure* or fully realized authorship (see Chapter 6, §3 above). There is a compromise here between the actual incompleteness of formation, which may be freely admitted at the theoretical level, and the demands of social intercourse; and it is out of respect for these demands that we fall in with the convention of designating as our "real" self the (hypothetical) pure point of origin of the value judgements we take over in the course of our upbringing.[31]

modernity—the period in which formation as understood, say, in the moral philosophy of Aristotle ceases to be something that one can take for granted as a feature of the human scene, and hence becomes interesting as never before. For "when status society starts to collapse, the countryside is abandoned for the city, and the world of work changes at an incredible and incessant pace, the colourless and uneventful socialization of 'old' youth becomes increasingly implausible: it becomes a *problem,* one that makes youth itself problematic" (Franco Moretti, *The Way of the World: The Bildungsroman in European Culture,* trans. Albert Sbragia (London: Verso, 1987), p. 4).

29. See Plato, *Sophist* 263e3–5: "Isn't it the case that thought (*dianoia*) and discourse (*logos*) are the same thing—except that we have given just this name, 'thought', to the inward dialogue (*dialogos*) of the mind with itself, occurring without speech (*phônê*)?"

30. Aristotle, *Nicomachean Ethics* 1147a22; and compare Chapter 5, §5.

31. It may be worth stressing once more (compare Chapters 5, §1 and 7, §1) that in set-

But if the metanarrative of formation ceases to carry conviction—if it becomes an object of "incredulity," as Lyotard might say—then the "sideways on" standpoint will come to dominate our view of the formative process, and attention will settle upon the actual emptiness of the place reserved for the "real self" in the traditional (teleological) story. No special ontological privilege will any longer accrue to that "self" which we construct, under the organizational pressures of upbringing, for the purpose of representing ourselves to others; the item so constructed could be singled out as the effect of a particular "signifying practice"[32] (or in the language of §1 above, as a distinctive "cultural artefact"), but without the traditional disavowal of whatever resists inclusion in it or threatens its coherence.[33] For the expectation of coherence stands or falls with the "postulate of authorship"—the policy of assuming that in the absence of some special context, an action or judgement issuing from me must be one in which I am fully present in my capacity as a (self-representing) subject. If this postulate is abandoned, and if (what would traditionally have counted as) "my" thoughts and actions are attributed instead to a "multiplicity" that speaks and acts in me,[34] then my failure to achieve internal agreement should no longer occasion any special intellectual discomfort. We shall continue, no doubt, to see instances of conflict—or, as the case may be, harmony—between a person's actions and her words (or thoughts); but the further we lean towards a nonteleological (that is, a purely descriptive)[35] conception of the relation between author and utterance, the less the

ting out the practical reason view of ethics I did not suggest on my own behalf that this convention rests on a mistake, or that the demands to which it answers are illusory.

32. Compare Judith Butler, *Gender Trouble: Feminism and the Subversion of Identity* (London: Routledge, 1990), pp. 144–145: "The substantive 'I' only appears as such through a signifying practice that seeks to conceal its own workings and to naturalize its effects . . . [T]o understand identity as a [signifying] practice . . . is to understand culturally intelligible subjects as the resulting effects of a rule-bound discourse that inserts itself in the pervasive and mundane signifying acts of linguistic life." (See also, however, note 57 below.)

33. Recall, for example, the Platonic view that such elements are merely superficial accretions (*Republic* 611bd; and compare Chapter 4, §4).

34. See note 12 and accompanying text.

35. By a "purely descriptive" conception of this relation I mean one for which it would consist simply in a certain person's having performed a certain linguistic or "locutionary" act on a certain occasion. Of course, such a conception (in its "purity") is not much like the one with which we normally operate—a point that is reflected in the ease with which we accept Austin's contrast between "ordinary" contexts of utterance and non-"ordinary" ones such as acting or quoting (Chapter 4, §2).

case of conflict will give us to explain, and the less need we shall have of devices such as our ideal conception of "judging" (Chapter 5, §4) in order to make sense of it.

3

Finally, the idea of the violence of reason can exert an influence on attitudes to language. In this instance the worry will be that just as the subjects of a nation-state (or the adherents of a movement) may find their particularity betrayed by those "universal" structures that purport to bring them together and to represent them in the public space of political action, so particular realities may somehow be betrayed or "wronged" by those universals that purport to bring them together through a scheme of classification, or to group them as possessing in common certain objective characteristics. To be made the grammatical subject of a predicate is to be determined as instantiating the relevant concept, and hence to be identified as *pro tanto* the *same* as other instances of that concept. Yet if one imagines the subject as having its own unique character, which will be distorted or coarsened by the act of marshalling it under a universal, then one may be tempted to say that something "different" persists in it, something that is recalcitrant with respect to predication—which can thus be seen as "the first [that is, the original] violence."[36]

This genre of imagery is by no means a new arrival on the philosophical scene. It is scarcely even a new arrival on the scene of the present discussion, since we have already come across it in the guise of that preconceptual "bare presence" McDowell calls the "Given."[37] But the debates that give rise to McDowell's terminology have a much longer history. We may think

36. Derrida, "Violence and Metaphysics," p. 147—again with reference to the thought of Levinas, for whom, Derrida writes, "nonviolent language would be a language which would do without the verb *to be*, that is, without predication . . . Since the verb *to be* and the predicative act are implied in every other verb, and in every common noun, nonviolent language, in the last analysis, would be a language of pure invocation, pure adoration, proffering only proper nouns in order to call to the other from afar." For a helpful discussion of the possible application to political practice of this idea of invocation or "greeting," see Iris Marion Young, "Public Address as a Sign of Political Inclusion," in Claudia Card, ed., *On Feminist Ethics and Politics* (Lawrence, Kansas: University Press of Kansas, 1999), pp. 103–115.

37. See Chapter 1, note 58 and accompanying text. For McDowell, as we know, this "Given" is a myth (see *Mind and World*, p. 8 and context). I return in Chapter 9 to the nature of our imaginative involvement with the suspect notion.

for example of Plato's *Theaetetus,* where the decisive point alleged against the radically empiricist thesis that "knowledge is perception" is that it would make predication impossible and so render the content of experience completely indeterminate *(apeiron).*[38] Or, drawing nearer to the present, we may remember Nietzsche's preoccupation with the theme of "commonness":[39] his idea that the biological mechanisms which work to elicit a communicable content from the stuff of experience will always tend to ensure that conceptual thought is eluded by whatever is original or atypical in individual consciousness. For the moment, though, our concern is with the attempt to register a kind of protest against the universality of concepts: one that would mirror the gesture of affirmation of "those who act and struggle" against the claims of others to represent them, or to speak in their name.

The latter gesture, charged as it was with a sense of the "indignity of speaking for others," gave a strong impression of being ethically motivated. But it did not content itself (as it might have done, had it proceeded under the banner of determinate critique) with a complaint to the effect that some group of people currently being represented by others for the purpose of political action were being *badly* or *falsely* represented, and to that extent deserved better. Instead, we met with the claim (or slogan): "Representation *no longer exists*"—which appeared to be a way of denouncing it as flawed or objectionable in principle.

Some related thoughts on linguistic, as distinct from political, repre-

38. Plato, *Theaetetus* 183ab. That Plato is capable of entering into the view here criticized is, however, apparent from his sympathetic presentation of it earlier in the dialogue—especially around 166b where it is said to entail that, insofar as experience varies in content from moment to moment, the subject of experience should be regarded not as unitary but as an "indefinite multiplicity." Plato too can *take seriously* "the profundity of the empiricist intention" and "the dream of a purely heterological thought at its source" (Derrida, "Violence and Metaphysics," p. 151).

39. See for example Friedrich Nietzsche, *Beyond Good and Evil,* trans. R. J. Hollingdale (Harmondsworth: Penguin, 1973), §268: "The more similar, more ordinary human beings have had and still have the advantage, the more select, subtle, rare and harder to understand are liable to remain alone, succumb to accidents in their isolation and seldom propagate themselves. Tremendous counter-forces have to be called upon to cross this natural, all too natural *progressus in simile,* the continuing development of mankind into the similar, ordinary, average, herdlike—into the *common!*" Nietzsche returns to this theme in *The Gay Science* (trans. Walter Kaufmann [New York: Random House, 1974]), §354, which falls within the new material added in the second edition of 1887.

sentation are to be found in the work of the feminist legal philosopher Drucilla Cornell. In her book *The Philosophy of the Limit*[40]—a study of deconstructionism in which she aligns this movement with Theodor Adorno's critique of the "totalitarian" tendency of Hegelian dialectic— Cornell insists on "the failure of idealism to capture the real," and (most interestingly for us) on the "ethical aspiration" which underlies the deconstructionist account of that failure.[41] Here too, it would seem, the aspiration is an "ethical" one not by virtue of being directed at any historically specific set of linguistic institutions, but because we are being shown a responsibility to defend the "different" against the "violence of *language's* classifying power":[42] that is, against assimilation into a structure which purports to represent it (and so to allow it to "speak" or achieve expression), but which suffers from an inevitable or predestined failure to do so. For Cornell, accordingly, "[t]he ethical relation . . . focusses [not on any system of explicit behavioural norms, but] instead on the kind of person one must become in order to develop a nonviolative relationship to the Other."[43]

40. Drucilla Cornell, *The Philosophy of the Limit* (London: Routledge, 1992).

41. Ibid., pp. 1–2. This account, as reconstructed by Cornell, is based on the Derridian notion of *différance*—"the trace of what differs from representational systems and defers indefinitely the achievement of totality" (ibid., p. 69). "Idealism" here denotes the kind of philosophical position that equates *reality* with *that which can be known or truly said,* and hence renders it fully accessible to language or to (conceptual) thought; by contrast, Cornell situates herself within a tradition (also, she notes, embracing the American pragmatist C. S. Peirce) which insists on "the materiality that persists *beyond* any attempt to conceptualize it" (ibid., p. 1). To repeat: the question of how all this connects with the "unboundedness of the conceptual"—a corollary of the "quietist" approach introduced in Chapter 1, §4—is considered in Chapter 9.

42. Ibid., p. 51 (emphasis added); and compare p. 80, "[Derrida's] strategies are a promise to the thing, to the remains, to otherness, he knows he can't fulfil—the promise to let the thing speak." The acknowledgement that this is in principle an *unfulfillable* "promise" should be borne in mind as an antidote to the simplistic effect of an idiom of struggle, defence, resistance, and the like. See also Derrida, "Form and Meaning: A Note on the Phenomenology of Language," in *Margins of Philosophy,* trans. Alan Bass (Hemel Hempstead: Harvester Wheatsheaf, 1982), pp. 155–173—a discussion of Husserl, again dating from the 1960s and treating of logical universality. Derrida argues here that for Husserl "[t]he *telos* of scientific discourse bears within itself, *as such* [in virtue of the "impoverishment" effected by predicative form], a renunciation of completeness" (p. 168). Yet he disavows the intention to apply the discovery of "complicity" (p. 171) between Being and thought to the production of a "critique of language on the basis of the ineffable riches of [prelinguistic] sense" (p. 172).

43. Cornell, *The Philosophy of the Limit*, p. 13.

Taken in isolation, these words might appear to echo the language of mainstream virtue ethics, with its characteristic emphasis on the evaluation of agents rather than of acts. In fact, however, they point towards a character ideal that stands at a long remove from the one held out by the practical reason view. For whereas that view remains within the tradition for which "[r]ationality . . . consists in the thorough-going unity of the universal and the single,"[44] Cornell maintains that "[t]he oppressed thing—the object itself, the suffering, physical individual—bears witness to the failure of history to realize itself in the unity of subject and object"; and that, contrary to any hopes held out by the "relaxed naturalism" adopted in this book, "[t]he disruption of the circle of immanence [by the failure or refusal of reality to let itself be fully assimilated by thought] *does not allow* history the pretense that it is 'second nature.'"[45] The point is driven home by Simon Critchley, who tells us that whereas "[t]he very activity of thinking is . . . the reduction of plurality to unity and alterity to sameness," deconstruction undertakes to "affirm and say 'Yes' to the unnameable, a moment of unconditional affirmation that is addressed to an alterity that can neither be excluded from *nor included within* logocentric conceptuality."[46]

4

Here, then, we have the elements of what might be regarded as an ideology of solidarity with the "singular" or "recalcitrant"—a tendency to which I have attached the label "counter-teleological." This tendency, as we have seen, is at least as much political as it is (narrowly) ethical in its motivation. Yet it does nevertheless seem to stand in a discernibly negative relation to (our version of) the practical reason view of ethics, since it asks us to reconsider a commitment which that view expects us, as reflective or

44. G. W. F. Hegel, *Philosophy of Right,* trans. T. M. Knox (Oxford: Clarendon Press, 1952), §258Z.

45. Cornell, *The Philosophy of the Limit,* pp. 25–26 (emphasis added). (The remarks quoted form part of an exposition of Adorno's "negative dialectics," an internal critique of the Hegelian system which seeks to disrupt the movement envisaged in that system towards an "absolute identification of object and Concept" (ibid.) However, they also contribute to the development of Cornell's own position.)

46. Simon Critchley, *The Ethics of Deconstruction: Derrida and Levinas* (Oxford: Blackwell, 1992), pp. 29, 41 (emphasis added).

conscientious beings, to undertake—namely, the commitment to accommodate ourselves to an existing norm of moral rationality.

Against the background of this counter-teleological climate of thought, some philosophers have spoken of a comprehensive "*crisis* of reason,"[47] and before proceeding further it may be worth pausing to look at a potential area of misunderstanding for the epistemic naturalist. This centres on the suggestion that "reason" as a whole might be thrown into crisis by our growing awareness of the *materiality of the socializing process*—that is, of the various influences that seek to prevail against our physical "difference" from one another and to draw us into a common understanding of "what is a reason for what." By "materiality" I mean the fact that this process operates on the body and demands submission to disciplines and conventions governing bodily self-expression. For example, Rosi Braidotti introduces the book from which I have already quoted (Chapter 7, §4) by *defining* "philosophical modernity" as "the discourse of the crisis of the rational subject,"[48] a crisis whose resolution would require among other things that we acknowledge the "dispersal of [that] subject into a multiplicity of 'discursive practices'";[49] while for another feminist philosopher, Elizabeth Grosz, "[the] crisis of reason is a consequence of the historical privileging of the purely conceptual or mental over the corporeal . . . it is a consequence of the inability of Western knowledges to conceive their own

47. This is an idea known to me—doubtless for contingent, autobiographical reasons—primarily from the literature of feminist theory.

48. Rosi Braidotti, *Patterns of Dissonance: A Study of Women in Contemporary Philosophy,* trans. Elizabeth Guild (Cambridge: Polity Press, 1991), p. 1.

49. Ibid., p. 252 (from a passage expounding Luce Irigaray, of whom Braidotti says that "[l]ike all modern philosophy, she takes as her point of departure" this dispersal of the classical subject [ibid.]). More specifically, Braidotti thinks we need to learn how to do without the traditional "identification between human subjectivity and rational consciousness" (p. 18) and to "make philosophy coexist with psychoanalysis" (p. 84). I should stress that the attribution to Braidotti and to Elizabeth Grosz (see note 50) of an abstract doctrine of epistemic materialism, expressed without reference to the fact of *sexual* difference—although (I believe) correct so far as it goes—gives a very incomplete picture of the interests of either writer in the texts cited, which centre on the contrasting relations of female and male embodied subjects to the institutions of "knowledge"-construction. I discuss these writings in more detail in my "Feminism and the 'Crisis of Rationality'," in *New Left Review* 207 (Sept./Oct. 1994), pp. 72–86. It would be wrong, though, to leave this topic without noting that some feminists—especially those influenced by the work of Irigaray—have been willing to defy the sexism of traditional philosophy and to embrace the symbolic association derived from Platonism between the female sexual principle and the *apeiron* or "formless."

processes of (material) production, processes that simultaneously rely on and disavow the role of the body."[50] It is the state of affairs described here by Grosz whose relatively sudden reversal—summed up for example in Foucault's thesis that "truth is a thing of this world . . . produced only by virtue of multiple forms of constraint"[51]—is supposed to have brought about a "desublimation" of reason,[52] and to have demonstrated the complicity of the rationalist tradition with assorted agencies of (violent or repressive) social control.

But here again we should note that to affirm the involvement of the body in socialization (or upbringing) is not yet to pose a self-evident threat to the practical reason view of ethics. In order to bring such a threat unequivocally into play, one would need to specify the nature of the "crisis" in a way that could not be accused, from the standpoint of the practical reason view itself, of the fault of *ignoratio elenchi* or irrelevance—manifested, here, in a failure to advance beyond the frame of enquiry of "ordinary" (constructive) modern philosophy.[53] And this is something that considerations about the "worldly" character of truth (as well as of other epistemological notions such as knowledge, justification, validity, and evidence) do not in themselves accomplish. (That is, they do not specify the nature of the alleged crisis in a way that genuinely threatens the practical reason view.) In particular, the thesis that *there are* "techniques of the self"[54] whose purpose is to adjust our bodily existence to the demands of a moral code is one that can unite the classical virtue theorist and the posthumanist social critic; witness for example the emphasis already laid upon the material side of moral upbringing by Plato, who is firmly convinced of

50. Elizabeth Grosz, "Bodies and Knowledges: Feminism and the Crisis of Reason," in Linda Alcoff and Elizabeth Potter, eds., *Feminist Epistemologies* (London: Routledge, 1993), pp. 187–215; quotation from p. 187.

51. Foucault, "Truth and Power," in *The Foucault Reader,* pp. 51–75; quotation from pp. 72–73.

52. See Kenneth Baynes, James Bohman, and Thomas McCarthy, eds., *After Philosophy: End or Transformation?* (Cambridge: MIT Press, 1987), p. 4: "[In contemporary philosophy] the epistemological and moral subject has been definitively decentred and the conception of reason linked to it irrevocably desublimated. Subjectivity and intentionality are not prior to but a function of forms of life and systems of language; they do not 'constitute' the world but are themselves elements of a linguistically disclosed world."

53. See again McDowell, *Mind and World,* p. 95.

54. This idea is associated particularly with the later work of Foucault. For references and discussion see Lois McNay, *Foucault and Feminism* (Cambridge: Polity Press, 1992), chap. 2.

the potentially lasting effect on character of seemingly trivial mannerisms of speech and gesture.[55] The point may look at first glance like a rather banal, moralistic one about the unwisdom of acquiring bad habits. However, it can also be read as a tacit recognition of the insights about uncodifiability, or rather about the limits to codifiability, which we drew from Wittgenstein's discussion of rule-following (Chapter 3, §1)—a recognition that, from the outset, it is a totality of *behaviour* that equips us for the intellectual achievement of grasping "universal" structures such as semantic rules.

Adherents of a naturalized conception of practical reason can accept that ethical formation involves imposing on the learner not just a worldview or belief-set but a physical way of being—something as fine-grained in its specificity as it needs to be to support and express the relevant beliefs. So they need feel no special reluctance to concede the existence, within their own communities, of "techniques" brought to bear on the embodied person in order to convert him or her into a "subject" both of certain choices and attitudes, and also (in a different, but not utterly unrelated sense)[56] of certain authorities or configurations of power. Only in the context of an attempt to fashion these materialist observations about upbringing into a bit of "sideways on" epistemology, they can argue, might the concession induce a sense of crisis.

Beyond the reach of these quietist admonitions, though, lies the kind of intellectual development envisaged in Chapter 7, §1—a development for which we said that philosophy might find itself playing the unofficial role of facilitator. The idea was that in pointing to the historicity of the process whereby one habit of normative judgement rather than another becomes "second nature" to us, philosophy could make us aware of new possibilities for critical reflection. The characteristic outcome of this kind of reflection was said to be a heightened consciousness of the techniques of socialization employed within one's own society: a consciousness that is apt to generate new forms of moral skepticism, in themselves "not particularly philosophical" (since they will belong to the social or political domain rather than to our very idea of what it is to be a subject of thought), but no less existentially significant on that account—nor, therefore, any less condu-

55. Plato, *Republic* 395d1–3; see also 401b1–402a4.

56. Compare Ludwig Wittgenstein, *On Certainty,* ed. G. E. M. Anscombe and G. H. von Wright, trans. Denis Paul and G. E. M. Anscombe (Oxford: Basil Blackwell, 1969), §493: "So is this it: I must recognize certain authorities in order to make judgements at all?"

cive to an atmosphere of "crisis." Just as philosophy "proper" does not actively engage in, but only prepares the way for, a "critical ontology of ourselves," so it has nothing to say that could prevent the latter exercise from destabilizing our relationship with existing forms of moral or intellectual authority; for any crisis brought about in this sort of way will have to be understood as a political one, provoked by new insights into the constitution of socially dominant and subordinate identities.[57]

The general point here is that wide-ranging resistance to inherited canons of normativity is a readily intelligible response to a certain kind of historical conjuncture—one in which people have learned not only to regard their own rational capacities as products of a specific mode of upbringing, but also (and this is the crucial extra condition) to take a negative view of the particular upbringing they have received and of the institutions that regulate it. That is to say: such a development is intelligible in general, human, not-particularly-philosophical terms. It is a response not to the mere disclosure to consciousness of the materiality of upbringing, but to the specific material character (as we now perceive this) of the upbringing visited on *us*.[58]

57. Jacques Derrida argues in his 1968 essay "The Ends of Man" (in *Margins of Philosophy*, pp. 109–136; quotation from p. 134) that the "total trembling" currently affecting French thought "derives no more than any other [radical 'trembling'] from some spontaneous decision or philosophical thought after some internal maturation of its history"; instead, it is "played out in the violent relationship of the whole of the West to its other, whether a 'linguistic' relationship . . . , or ethnological, economic, political, military, relationships, etc." For a more recent assertion of the political motive that propels enquiry into the social or discursive constitution of the subject, see Judith Butler, "Contingent Foundations," in Seyla Benhabib, Judith Butler, Drucilla Cornell, and Nancy Fraser, *Feminist Contentions: A Philosophical Exchange* (London: Routledge, 1995), pp. 35–57, who holds that to engage in such enquiry "is not to do away with the subject or pronounce its death, but merely to claim that certain versions of the subject are politically insidious," or that they "[serve] in the consolidation or concealment of authority" (quotations from pp. 47, 49). (To the extent that "enfranchisement and democratization" count for Butler as proper goals of political struggle, while "domination" and "oppressive power" are evils to be resisted [pp. 48, 51], her work on the gendered subject seems to remain within the enterprise of "determinate critique.")

58. McDowell plausibly suggests that for the Protestant-individualist contemporaries of Kant, the main subjective difficulty in relation to upbringing was a "*loss or devaluation* of the idea that immersion in a tradition might be a respectable mode of access to the real" (*Mind and World*, p. 98; emphasis added). While this problem has not been resolved, it has perhaps undergone mutation within the experience of people alive today, to whom tradition may present itself less as "ossified or hidebound" (ibid.) than as *commodified*. See Anderson (*The*

There is no good reason, therefore, to resist the idea that a "crisis of reason" might result from the attempt to reintegrate reason and nature under (contingently) unfavourable historical conditions. Indeed, the concession should be a painless one for the practical reason view of ethics, since to make it is not yet to acknowledge this "crisis" as amounting to anything more than a particularly energetic round of internal, or "determinate," critique of moral rationality—and as we saw in Chapter 7, the practical reason view is more than willing in principle to accommodate such a critique.

So it is as if supporters of that view were to reach out to anyone coming forward with news of a "crisis of reason," and were to say to them: "By all means join us; the business you have undertaken is something that we have already acknowledged as a 'standing obligation,' namely, the application of the Neurathian procedure of immanent criticism to our existing standards of rationality. It is impossible to say in advance how far we may agree in our substantive views as to what is wrong with these standards—that is something that will have to be established through further, 'not particularly philosophical' dialogue—but it would be a pity if that dialogue were to be stalled at the outset because of a false impression that our own negative thoughts about 'reason' as currently constituted have nothing in common with yours."

Origins of Postmodernity, p. 55), who writes of the "postmodern" phase of capitalist development—following Fredric Jameson—as one in which social and economic modernization is "all but complete, obliterating the last vestiges not only of pre-capitalist social forms, but every intact natural hinterland, of space or experience, that had sustained or survived them." In such a world, he continues, "culture has necessarily expanded to the point where it has become virtually coextensive with the economy itself, not merely as the symptomatic basis of some of the largest industries in the world—tourism now exceeding all other branches of global employment—but much more deeply, as every material object and immaterial service becomes inseparably tractable sign and vendible commodity." Compare also Lyotard's claim (in *The Inhuman,* trans. Geoffrey Bennington and Rachel Bowlby [Cambridge: Polity Press, 1991], p. 6) that "'development' is the ideology of the present time" ("development" here meaning, apparently, economic growth, globalization, and the like). Lyotard's brief introduction to this book opposes to one another a cultural principle analogous to the "instrumental reason" of Frankfurt School Marxism in the 1930s and 1940s; and on the other hand a principle that is not so much cultural as *pre*cultural—something reminiscent of what Lyotard romantically describes as the "obscure savageness of childhood" (ibid., p. 4), and to which, under various names, he says he has always tried to offer intellectual support. One designation he chooses for it here—the "unharmonizable" (ibid.)—is worth thinking about in connection with some of our less articulate impulses to befriend the ethically "recalcitrant" (see Chapter 9).

How might someone influenced by the counter-teleological considerations of §§1–3 above respond to these overtures? Since this question is
concerned with the reasoning not of an identifiable person but of a somewhat precarious ideal construct, we had better not treat it with more solemnity than it can bear. But I think we can already make an informed
guess that, on occasion at least, the friendly overtures will meet with a re-
buff. "No, you don't understand: we are not just another bunch of critical
theorists. We *laugh* at critique, since it is to maintain oneself in the field of
the criticized thing.[59] We cannot settle for a way of thinking that refuses to
let the *other* appear as what it is."[60]

Our unfinished business in this discussion, then, is to reach a considered
view of the various discursive moves by which philosophers have tried to
carry the critique of reason beyond the limits envisaged for it in the practical reason view of ethics. These discursive phenomena are, in their own
way, familiar features of our social landscape; their rise to prominence
seems to be linked with a long-term process of fragmentation or diversi-
fication of the forms of expression available to "our impatience for liberty."
But to recognize them as instances of a kind of thing that people are disposed to *say* is not yet to reach a position from which one could arbitrate
(or mediate) *philosophically* between the practical reason view and its
counter-teleological critics. And it is on that basis—I mean, philosophically—that we need to investigate how the abstract injunction to "care for
difference"[61] might impinge on a moral philosophy that turns on our willingness to entrust ourselves to *universal* structures of thought and action.

59. See note 2 above.

60. See note 6 above and accompanying text.

61. Cornell, *The Philosophy of the Limit*, p. 57: "[T]he conventions of a community cannot be shown to be a closed totality. The ethical message in both Derrida and Adorno reminds us to care for difference, the difference we can only glimpse as beyond contradiction
and appropriation . . . The danger of certainty is that it turns against the generous impulse to
open oneself up to the Other, and to truly listen, to risk the chance that we might be wrong."

NINE

Reason and Unreason:
A Problematic Distinction

1

To "care for difference": this formula seems to capture better than any other the moral and political programme (so far as one can speak of such a thing) of the kind of thinking I have labeled "counter-teleological." However, the responsibility to which it directs us may be felt to be fundamentally at odds with the view of ethics developed in this book; for it seems to call into question the methodological "quietism" on which that view has depended almost from the outset. The principle of quietism has suggested a view of experience that equates *openness to the layout of reality* with the *ability to find one's way around within a space of reasons* (which is also a space of concepts). But at the same time, we have seen that philosophical pleas on behalf of the "other" sometimes involve a warning against the imperial ambitions of language itself (Chapter 8, §3), or against the propensity of the "same"—as embodied in the thinking subject who deploys concepts on the basis of rules for their correct application—to "comprehend and englobe all possible reality."[1] Should such warnings cause us to reconsider our acceptance of the neo-Hegelian claim that although thought can be distanced from the world by being false, still "there is no distance from the world implicit in the very idea of thought"?[2] (Has the idea of

1. Thus Simon Critchley, *The Ethics of Deconstruction: Derrida and Levinas* (Oxford: Blackwell, 1992), p. 6: "For Levinas, the Same is *par excellence* the knowing ego . . . The ego comprehends and englobes all possible reality; nothing is hidden, no otherness refuses to give itself up . . . Non-ontological philosophy . . . would consist in the resistance of the other to the Same. It is this resistance, this point of exteriority to the philosophical *logos*, that Levinas seeks to describe in his work." See also Chapter 4, notes 5–6 and accompanying text.

2. John McDowell, *Mind and World* (Cambridge: Harvard University Press, 1994), p. 27.

the *unboundedness* of the conceptual been discredited by the arguments of those other post-Hegelian thinkers who have insisted on the "non-identity between concept and object"—for example, on the "'more-than-this' [which] serves as a corrective to realist and conventionalist ethics"?)³ The idea that the conceptual is "unbounded" was put forward in the attempt to show that a nonreductive understanding of discourses concerned with something other than "mere" nature—"nature as the realm of law"—is achievable without any departure from the ("relaxed") naturalist worldview. Indeed, McDowell might be said to bring a materialist commitment of his own into play when he condemns the postulate of a world external to the space of concepts precisely on the ground that it "*slight[s] the independence* of the reality to which our senses give us access."⁴ Yet apparently it can also be claimed, from a position dialectically subsequent to the assimilation of absolute idealism, that materialist thinkers recognize a "constitutive outside"⁵ to thought and that they "[honour] the pledge to otherness which idealism renounces."⁶

When we first encountered the "other" of negative dialectics or of deconstruction—the imagined source of a mute reproach to the whole business of predication—it was inevitable that we should recall the empiricist idea of an experiential "Given" as discussed (and condemned) by McDowell. On closer inspection, however, the match may no longer appear so striking. For the mythical "Given," while itself excluded from the sphere of the conceptual, was supposed to constitute a *rational basis* for the mind's operations within that sphere. The foundationalist who is the target of McDowell's criticism holds that the real exceeds or transcends the conceptual for reasons which might be expressed by saying that "all we can put into words is what *follows from* our sense-impressions—not the sense-impressions themselves."⁷ Deconstructionism by contrast, at any rate in the

---

3. Drucilla Cornell, *The Philosophy of the Limit* (London: Routledge, 1992), pp. 19, 17.

4. McDowell, *Mind and World*, p. 44 (emphasis added).

5. Cornell, *The Philosophy of the Limit*, pp. 56: "Derrida and Adorno, in their recognition of the constitutive outside, are materialists. *Geist* [spirit, mind] cannot encircle itself, protecting us from that reality of finitude."

6. Ibid., p. 29. Cornell also says (ibid., p. 1) that Derrida "continually points to the failure of idealism to capture the real."

7. Compare Ludwig Wittgenstein, *Philosophical Investigations* (trans. G. E. M. Anscombe (Oxford: Basil Blackwell, 1967), §486: "Does it *follow* from the sense-impressions which I get that there is a chair over there?—How can a *proposition* follow from sense-impressions?"

hands of some of its interpreters, seems to posit a kind of limitation to which language (or thought) will remain subject even when released from its supposed logical dependence on how things stand outside the "think-able":[8] a limitation that must somehow be kept in view even after we have acknowledged, for all the world like traditional idealists, that the reality to which our minds are opened in (veridical) experience is one endowed with the same structural characteristics as experience itself. (Derrida does after all say that "[w]hat is valid for intentions, always differing, deferring and without plenitude, is also valid, correlatively, for the object (qua signified or referent) thus aimed at.")[9] The problem now is to see what this limita-tion could be. Isn't it the case that thought and reality, in this picture too, are made for each other?

I take it the reply must be that what we are being asked to acknowledge is a new element of elusiveness in the idea of reality itself, which now has to evolve in a direction dictated by the critique of the "metaphysics of pres-ence." We can still, if we wish, think of the "real world" as that which dis-closes itself to a subject who represents, in good quietist fashion, an exem-plary standard of receptivity to normative requirements (Chapter 3, §2). But we must remember that this subject—for all his or her cognitive mer-its—nevertheless exists *in time,* and is thus (at best) an exemplary par-ticipant in signifying practices marked by that *repetition-with-a-difference* which, according to the thesis of iterability (Chapter 5, §6), is the destined mode of use of conventional signs. Meanings, thought contents, and the reality to which we open ourselves in (veridical) thought—all alike are touched by the necessary incompleteness of the historically unfolding to-tality of "speech acts" (or the like) that gives meaning to symbolism of any description.

But does this kind of commentary upon the quietist picture really de-liver the idea of a "reality" or "materiality that persists beyond any attempt to conceptualize it"[10]—the origin of our supposed obligation to "care for

8. Compare McDowell, *Mind and World,* p. 28: "'Thought' can mean the *act* of thinking; but it can also mean the *content* of a piece of thinking: what someone thinks. Now if we are to give due acknowledgement to the independence of reality, what we need is a constraint from outside *thinking* and *judging,* our exercises of spontaneity. The constraint does not need to be from outside *thinkable contents.*"

9. Jacques Derrida, *Limited Inc* (Evanston: Northwestern University Press, 1988), p. 58. The passage continues: "However, this limit, I repeat (*"without"* plenitude), is also the posi-tive condition of possibility of what is thus limited."

10. Cornell, *The Philosophy of the Limit,* p. 1.

difference"? (Aren't "reality" and "materiality" themselves *words,* after all? And why should just these words have the power to direct our thoughts to something beyond the bounds of the conceptual?)[11] We may think here of Wittgenstein's remarks on the pathological state of mind whereby we are led in philosophy to "imagine that we have to describe extreme subtleties, which in turn we are after all quite unable to describe with the means at our disposal," and to "feel as if we had to repair a torn spider's web with our fingers."[12] Wouldn't anxiety about the imperialism of the "same" point to just the kind of condition that the method of the *Philosophical Investigations* is intended to correct?

In response to this question, let us dwell for a moment longer on the "thing," the particular, which (some feel) cannot "speak"—or cannot do so without compromising itself—because the only medium available to it is *language* in its unavoidable generality. It is true, I believe, that the feeling just mentioned is in effect a variant on the one discredited by Wittgenstein's famous observation about the "beetle" in the box—the symbol of what is incommunicable in subjective experience—that "[t]he thing in the box has no place in the language-game at all; not even as a *something:* for the box might even be empty."[13] Yet among the symptoms of our urge to run up against the limits of language,[14] this discredited motif stubbornly continues to appear. "The very fact that we should so much like to say: '*This* is the important thing'—while we point privately to the sensation—is enough to show how much we are inclined to say something which gives no information."[15] And it seems to me that having accepted the idea of language as "part of our natural history,"[16] and of orientation within the "space of reasons" as something accomplished through upbringing, we may be well placed to enter into the distinctive values or concerns encoded—however obscurely—in the advocacy of the dialogically redundant "this."

11. Compare Judith Butler, *Bodies That Matter: On the Discursive Limits of "Sex"* (London: Routledge, 1993), Introduction.

12. Wittgenstein, *Philosophical Investigations* §106.

13. Ibid., §293.

14. Ibid., §119.

15. Ibid., §298—a passage which illustrates A. W. Moore's comment (*The Infinite* [London: Routledge, 1990], p. 196) that Wittgenstein in both his earlier and his later phase treats what he is officially committed to regarding as "nonsense" with "a distinctive combination of antagonism and respect."

16. Wittgenstein, *Philosophical Investigations* §25.

We can start by reminding ourselves that just as upbringing is a temporally extended process, it is also a temporally (and culturally) *limited* one: that is, the experience that each of us has of being initiated into the ways of the world occupies a finite time (even if we assume, with becoming modesty, that that experience continues throughout a person's life), and has a unique content determined by the circumstances of our own individual existence. Focussing on the case of two contemporary speakers of a single language, we can say that if these two are to communicate successfully, they must be able to rely on one another to project the current rules of usage into new contexts—to "go on"—in what each can acknowledge as "the same way"; and that insofar as communication between them does not break down, this shows that their common culture is continuing to be reproduced with sufficient accuracy to meet that requirement. However, even where the convergence between two speakers' dispositions with respect, say, to a particular word is such as to justify the claim that they attach the same meaning to it, it follows from the *physical separateness* of persons in general that the dispositions of person *A* in this respect (or if we prefer, the tacit understanding they represent) will not coincide with those of person *B* in the way that *A*'s dispositions coincide, as it were, with *themselves*—that is, by possessing the same history and entailing the same behavioural output in *any conceivable future circumstance*. (Wittgenstein's "1004, 1008 . . ." scenario at *Philosophical Investigations* §185 is designed to draw attention to the unfathomable implications of this separateness even for the case in which we have no determinate reason to doubt that we are communicating successfully with another person.) So although *A* and *B* may "understand one another perfectly" according to the practical criteria that govern the concept of mutual understanding "within the language-game"—a setting in which it gets its point by contrast with understanding one another poorly or not at all—their separate physical existence will still entail a permanent possibility of mismatch in what they take to constitute *following the rule* for the use of this or that expression, and so will give rise to what we should like (albeit waywardly or "nonsensically") to call an element of difference between them in regard to it: "not a *something,* but not a *nothing* either!"[17] Perhaps, then, the recognition of this nonsensical (yet

17. Ibid., §304: "'But you will surely admit that there is a difference between pain-behaviour accompanied by pain and pain-behaviour without any pain?'—Admit it? What greater difference could there be?—'And yet you again and again reach the conclusion that the sensation itself is a *nothing*.'—Not at all. It is not a *something,* but not a *nothing* either! The con-

also nonarbitrary) impulse can teach us how to create a place in our considerations for an ethical claim attributable to the "other" of (universal) reason: not by canceling our assent to the "unboundedness of the conceptual" (the idea that judgement, and hence the concepts employed in it, reach all the way out to reality), but rather by setting this idea against the background of the impulse just described.

2

Any historical account of the abstract, or counter-teleological, defence of "difference" would have to note its indebtedness to the anti-egalitarian polemics of Nietzsche on which we touched for a moment in Chapter 8, §3. In Nietzsche, the attitude of *solidarity with the unassimilated* issues from an "aristocratic radicalism"[18] dedicated to protecting the spiritually superior against the banality of modern life. A constant theme of his last works is the systematic awfulness of Enlightenment universalism: in conscious opposition to the Kantian categorical imperative in its formal guise as a "principle of universalizability" ("Act only on that maxim . . ."), Nietzsche considers it a mark of nobility "never to think of degrading our duties into duties for everyone; not to want to relinquish or share our own responsibilities."[19] This view is of course in conflict with the characteristic political ideals of modernity—the vision of a social order in which participation will be extended to the whole of "rational nature," and in which only what is permitted to all will be permitted to any particular one.[20] Yet as the subsequent history of philosophy confirms, opposition to the claims of the universal can also be mounted from within the political mainstream; and

clusion was only that a nothing would serve just as well as a something about which nothing could be said."

18. See Keith Ansell-Pearson, *An Introduction to Nietzsche as Political Thinker: The Perfect Nihilist* (Cambridge: Cambridge University Press, 1994), chap. 4, note 5. Nietzsche apparently accepted this description of his philosophy by a contemporary critic as "the shrewdest comment on me I have so far read."

19. Friedrich Nietzsche, *Beyond Good and Evil*, trans. R. J. Hollingdale (Harmondsworth: Penguin, 1973), §272.

20. Georg Lukács goes so far as to say that "[t]he binding or systematic factor lies in the social content of [Nietzsche's] thinking, in the struggle against socialism" (*The Destruction of Reason*, trans. Peter Palmer [London: Merlin Press, 1980], p. 394; emphasis added). For a recent restatement of this unfashionable view, see Ishay Landa, "Nietzsche, the Chinese Worker's Friend," in *New Left Review*, 236 (July/August 1999), pp. 3–23.

with the emergence (in §1 above) of the familiar liberal motif of the separateness of persons, we gain some insight into the principle by which Nietzsche's anti-universalism has been able to detach itself from his substantive politics and to establish itself within the dominant Western ideology of the postwar period.

Consider, for instance, the case of Isaiah Berlin, commenting in 1958 on "the great clash of ideologies that dominates our world."[21] Berlin associates with one of these ideologies—that of Marxism, as the rest of the essay makes clear—the Platonic or Hegelian conception of a "dominant self . . . variously identified with reason, with my 'higher nature', with the self which calculates and aims at what will satisfy it in the long run, with my 'real', or 'ideal', or 'autonomous' self or with my self 'at its best'";[22] the same self that would figure in a rationalist model of ethical formation—or so I argued in Chapters 4 and 5—as the point of origin of those expressive acts of which one is, not just ostensibly but *really* or *fully*, the author. Though he speaks respectfully of the "severe individualism"[23] upheld by this idea in the ethics of Kant, Berlin regards it as the germ of a more or less repellent political doctrine subsequently favoured by "defenders of authority, from Victorian schoolmasters and colonial administrators to the latest nationalist or communist dictator," namely, that "no law, provided that it was such that I should, if I were asked, approve it as a rational being, could possibly deprive me of any portion of my rational freedom."[24] On this basis, he warns, "I am in a position to ignore the actual wishes of men or societies, to bully, oppress, torture them in the name, and on behalf, of their 'real' selves, in the secure knowledge that whatever is the true goal of man . . . must be identical with his freedom."[25]

The heroes of Berlin's account are those who, like Bentham, Mill, and

21. Isaiah Berlin, "Two Concepts of Liberty," in his *Four Essays on Liberty* (Oxford: Oxford University Press, 1969), p. 131.

22. Ibid., p. 132.

23. Ibid., p. 152.

24. Ibid. Berlin notes that Kant himself endorses this doctrine: his repudiation of rule by experts in the sphere of (personal) morality does not extend to the political.

25. Ibid., p. 133. As this sentence illustrates, "Two Concepts of Liberty" is a rich source for the kind of "man"-talk condemned by feminists from the 1970s onwards. It is certainly striking, in view of Berlin's broad terms of reference and generally cosmopolitan tone, that the essay contains no mention of women's emancipation—not even in Section VI, "The search for status," where it would have been particularly relevant. A present-day reader may feel that this was the dark hour before the dawn of ("second-wave") feminism.

Constant,[26] have refused to accept the argument that a democratic political authority—one that represents the ("real") will of every member of the community—cannot in principle act oppressively. The last of these thinkers provides Berlin with a particularly interesting formula. Despite Rousseau's claim that "by giving myself to all I give myself to none," Constant "could not see why, even though the sovereign is 'everybody', it should not oppress one of the 'members' of its indivisible self, if it so decided."[27] Accordingly, he held that the real threat to (individual) freedom lay not in the mislocation of power but in the accumulation of too much of it in any one place, and that often where government is felt to be oppressive "[i]t is not the arm that is unjust, but the weapon that is too heavy—some weights are too heavy for the human hand."[28]

We have here a contrast between the weight of the weapon (symbolizing the amount of force exerted in the name of political or social order) and the identity of the hand that wields it (the specific character of the order it serves to maintain). This contrast marks a distinction corresponding to the one drawn in Part III of this book between two forms of resistance to the claims of the moral "universal"—those forms which I have called, respectively, the "counter-teleological attitude" and the "determinate critique." It reminds us that in addition to misgivings about the content of the (putative) practical rationality governing socialization within any given community—the kind of misgiving that issues in the "reflective modification" of moral institutions—there is a further critical tradition that centres upon the very fact of our exposure, as (relatively) unformed subjects of thought and action, to the agencies charged with converting us into (more definitively) "rational" beings. The reading of Constant's maxim in terms of *socialization* depends, of course, on a transition from macrocosm to microcosm—from the government of nation-states to the Foucauldian "politics" of subjectivity. But if this transition is permissible, then we have the makings of a plausible liberal (or libertarian) discourse of resistance to ethical formation. The idea will now be that like the excessive accretion of power to the state, excessive zeal in relation to the emergence of a "real" self—one

26. Benjamin Constant (1767–1830) was leader of the liberal opposition in the French Chamber of Deputies under the post-Napoleonic Bourbon monarchy.

27. Berlin, "Two Concepts of Liberty," p. 164.

28. Quoted, ibid., p. 163. (Constant was an economic "libertarian" also, that is, a defender of private property and unregulated markets: see Anthony Arblaster, *The Rise and Decline of Western Liberalism* [Oxford: Basil Blackwell, 1984], pp. 233–234.)

that would be unswerving in its obedience to the demands of objective reason—is a pernicious social (or educational) tendency against which vigilance is always needed, whatever the particular ideological character of the
prevailing "regime." Such vigilance may be manifested in some degree of
general willingness to take a sympathetic or charitable attitude towards the
ethically recalcitrant—an attitude which can be seen as the *internal* (psychological) counterpart of the liberal commitment to make room for the
expression of dissent from current forms of *external* (political or social)
organization. In either context, the commitment will be an abstract one in
that it will not be conditional on the specific intention or content of the recalcitrant act. It will rest on a belief that the reason why we should not
hope for the complete success of formation, and why the capacity for active resistance to that process is valuable in its own right,[29] has to do not
just with local conditions (objectionable as these may sometimes be) but
with the nature of the rationalist programme as such.

3

In Chapter 8, having invoked the idea of a contemporary "crisis of reason,"
I explored the possibility of understanding this "crisis" as merely a super-
vigorous phase in the *determinate critique* of existing moral traditions—an
assessment from which it would follow that the "reflective modification" of
such traditions, if pursued with sufficient energy, could incorporate everything worth having in a critique of ethical formation. I did not, however,
claim to have shown conclusively that there was nothing in the counter-teleological attitude beyond what it retained, in a confused or rhetorically
pretentious form, from the tradition of critical theory, and in the present
chapter I have begun to introduce some considerations that point the
other way—considerations that look as if they might be capable of leaving
their mark upon the practical reason view. I would now like to try to ad-

---

29. As an antidote to the Socratic considerations of Chapter 5, Peter Railton made the apt
suggestion that the capacity mentioned here should be seen as "not a bug, but a feature" of
the human mentality, and pointed out that this view of it could reasonably be allowed to influence our attitude to acrasia. See also Robert Merrihew Adams, "Involuntary Sins," in
Philosophical Review 94 (1985), pp. 3–31, who argues that both for the state and for the individual, "[t]he ever present possibility of internal conflict is not only a vexation and a potential hindrance to resolute action: it is also a wellspring of vitality and sensitivity, and a check
against one-sidedness and fanaticism" (quotation from p. 11).

vance the discussion by staging an encounter between the supporter of
"morality"—the self-conscious, though not unquestioning, aspirant towards those virtues actually recognized in her social world—and a pro-
"difference" position based on the kind of liberal (or libertarian) notions
now at our disposal. I shall not engage in argument with the doctrine of
outright (Nietzschean) antimoralism, since although that position is open
to the familiar—and by rationalist standards, unassailable—objection that
to jettison morality is to leave the weak at the mercy of the strong, we also
know that this objection will carry weight only with the (morally) converted.[30] Instead, I shall be following a line of thought which perhaps runs
parallel to the one traced by Peter Dews when he says that through a growing appreciation of the ineliminable role of moral and political principles
in any consistent defence of pluralism, "the implicitly liberal themes of
post-structuralist discourse began [during the 1980s] to break out of their
ill-adapted Nietzschean modes of presentation."[31] Specifically, I shall suggest that insofar as it escapes capture within the format of determinate critique, the main function performed by counter-teleological thinking—albeit under the misleading banner of hostility to the universal as such—
may be to give expression to an unexceptionable sense of the *limits* marked
out for "reason" in the lives of embodied creatures.

Suppose, then, that we return to first principles in our attempt to reconstruct the "differentist" challenge (to the practitioner of determinate critique, or as I will now begin to call him or her, the "critical theorist"). We
might represent this challenge as arising not from a rejection of the common stock of ethical value concepts as empty, or as irrelevant to rational

30. Not that that need cause us too much concern, unless we remain committed to the at-
tempt to *argue* moral skeptics out of their skepticism. For criticism of this foundationalist
undertaking, see John McDowell, "Two Sorts of Naturalism," in Rosalind Hursthouse, Gavin
Lawrence and Warren Quinn, eds., *Virtues and Reasons: Philippa Foot and Moral Theory*
(Oxford: Oxford University Press, 1995), pp. 149–179; also his "Might There Be External
Reasons?," in J. E. J. Altham and Ross Harrison, eds., *World, Mind and Ethics: Essays on the
Ethical Philosophy of Bernard Williams* (Cambridge: Cambridge University Press, 1995),
pp. 68–85.

31. Peter Dews, *Logics of Disintegration: Poststructuralist Thought and the Claims of Critical Theory* (London: Verso, 1987), p. 218. For the reasons indicated in §2 above, I agree with
"ill-adapted," despite the element of truth in Alasdair MacIntyre's claim that "Nietzsche's
stance turns out not to be a mode of escape from or an alternative to the conceptual scheme
of liberal individualist modernity, but rather one more representative moment in its internal
unfolding" (*After Virtue: A Study in Moral Theory* [London: Duckworth, 1981], p. 241).

deliberation, but rather from skepticism about a certain assumption which the critical theorist makes. The assumption I have in mind concerns the conditions under which it is possible, with regard to any act of resistance to ethical formation, to refrain from seeing that act as simply hostile to the universal (and, *pro tanto,* as bad). Roughly speaking, what the critical theorist assumes is that if such an act is to have a claim to our sympathy then it must not express *mere* negativity but must, somehow or other, *have reason on its side.* But if we try to speak less roughly, this formula seems to reveal an indeterminacy of which the opposition can take advantage. To "have reason on one's side," in this context, must mean: to produce words or actions for which *there is* some reason, a reason that others could recognize as such and about which they could ask whether it should be taken to outweigh any countervailing reasons that may exist. (Even if this enquiry leads to the conclusion that the recalcitrant action is not in fact justified, our critical theorist will still expect disinterested onlookers to give some credit to an agent who seems to *appreciate the importance* of being able to justify oneself publicly, within the "space of reasons.") Perhaps it is too much to ask that the disputed action should have the backing of a conscious project of social reconstruction, a detailed account of what it would be like for the agencies of formation—those social forces which are currently provoking "recalcitrance"—to be purged of their present faults. But if recalcitrant behaviour is to have the support of reason, then it must at any rate admit of explanation in terms that would enable us, on further reflection, to connect it with that question—and thus to start working towards a picture of the recalcitrant agent as someone who, if things were otherwise,[32] could after all be identified as a friend of the (moral) "universal." (A friend of the universal, and hence—by implication—a potential bearer of authority, one capable of assuming unreservedly the *role* of author of any normative thought contents implicit in the work of formation.) Accepting the need for the concession just mentioned, our critical theorist may say: no, "recal-

---

32. See Chapter 7, note 25 and accompanying text. But note that there is a risk of confusion here: the Platonic, or "logocentric," solution to the problem of "not being" involves an account of negation in terms of the difference between *that predicate actually applied to a subject* (in the proposition to be negated) and *those that are true of it*—a difference, therefore, internal to the field of predication. By contrast, the maxim of "caring for difference" carried over from Chapter 8, and by extension the term "differentist" which I press into service in this section of the text, is meant to advert to something that eludes altogether our existing resources for predicative judgement.

citrant" phenomena do not need the backing of a fully articulate conception of the common good in order to earn our respect. But they do need to be able to say something in their own defence that would make it possible to see them *in the light of* our interest in that good. Or, failing this, someone else needs to be able to say something, to provide this defence: it can come from *elsewhere* (compare Chapter 2, §4), but it must be forthcoming from *somewhere*.

Now we can think of the defender of "difference" as saying: your concession is an important one, but the modified principle to which you remain committed is still too restrictive. You are still saying that "recalcitrant" phenomena have a claim on our sympathy or interest only to the extent that they point us, intellectually, in the direction of some imaginable alternative order, an order in which the reasons for (that kind of) recalcitrance will no longer exist. The effect of your concession is only to allow that the pointing may be at a considerable remove and may depend on the interpretative co-operation of others—invoking, perhaps, the possibility of assistance from someone like the *designated* "intellectual" whose place in Marxist theory was described in our passage from Foucault in Chapter 8, §1. (This image of cognitive dependency would be in keeping with your earlier views about the uncodifiability of what is known by the exemplary practical reasoner.) But what if neither the agent herself, nor any such intellectual ally or sponsor, can provide the kind of interpretation that would legitimize the disputed behaviour in your terms?[33] Or what if any sponsors who may come forward happen to be lacking in "credibility," that is, in the socially recognized markers of rational authority?[34]

33. Kate Chopin gives the following (apparently guileless) words to Edna Pontellier, the heroine of her novel *The Awakening* and a woman in the process of removing herself from the conventional married state: "One of these days . . . I'm going to pull myself together for a while and think—try to determine what character of a woman I am; for, candidly, I don't know. By all the codes which I am acquainted with, I am a devilishly wicked specimen of the sex. But some way I can't convince myself that I am. I must think about it" (Kate Chopin, *The Awakening and Selected Stories,* ed. Sandra Gilbert [Harmondsworth: Penguin, 1984], pp. 137–138). But Edna's thinking never issues in anything like a sexual politics on the basis of which she could represent herself as not really wicked. (Sandra Gilbert reports on the initial reception of this book in 1899: "The novel 'leaves one sick of human nature', complained one critic; 'it is not a healthy book', declared another; 'the purport of the story can hardly be described in language fit for publication', asserted a third" [ibid., p. 8].)

34. On the way in which the distribution of power in society can influence our perception of who is "credible" in this sense, see Miranda Fricker, "Rational Authority and Social Power:

Before replying to these questions, the critical theorist may seek some elucidation of the word "restrictive." Of course, if we allow our sympathy for the recalcitrant to extend no further than the ability of the latter to produce (or to attract to itself) a specifically moral justification, then we shall sometimes have to avert our thoughts from sources of value on which our response could otherwise have drawn; for example, aesthetic value or the value that consists in "fullness of life."[35] And that is an undeniable restriction. However, it is not obvious that this point is effective against someone who—like the critical theorist—does not herself profess to be a "postmoral" thinker, and who may therefore already accept that in exemplary practical reasoning, nonmoral value considerations will from time to time be "silenced" by moral ones, even though in other circumstances the nonmoral considerations would have weight and might legitimately move one to action.

What would be more striking would be a claim to the effect that the conditions our critical theorist attaches to her support for the recalcitrant are such as to reduce the scope for realizing value of just that kind towards which, in her own view, exemplary practical reasoning is orientated: that is, such as to thwart the realization of the "good life as a whole." This claim, if made out, would give rise to a retaliatory dialectical criticism balancing the one already presented by the critical theorist—I mean the argument by which the latter sought to implicate other objectors to traditional morality, including (perhaps) unwary "differentists," in a commitment to "sameness" (Chapter 7, §3). So let us now see whether the recalcitrant—simply as such—can be shown to be a resource for *critical* thought and practice: in particular, for thought and practice whose goal is to make the process of ethical formation less imperfect or objectionable. This would be an interesting conclusion, since it would entail that a certain narcissistic protectiveness towards the *apeiron* in ourselves—with all its potential for hostility to the moral universal—cannot be prohibited, even by those who would wish the reflective modification of our inherited normative culture to proceed under the guidance of democratic or "enlightened" values. It would constitute a warning against allowing the practical reason view to be too firmly subordinated to the "bourgeois contempt of instinct."[36]

Towards a Truly Social Epistemology," in *Proceedings of the Aristotelian Society,* New Series 98 (1997/8), pp. 159–177.

35. Nicolai Hartmann's *Fülle* (known to me through H. W. B. Joseph, *Essays in Ancient and Modern Philosophy* [Oxford: Clarendon Press, 1935], p. 159).

36. See Theodor Adorno, *Minima Moralia: Reflections from Damaged Life,* trans. E. F. N.

4

The more ambitious claim can perhaps be defended as follows. Recall, first, that anyone embarking on a critique of formation aims at nothing less than a reconstruction of (what currently passes for) *rationality*—the capacity for finding one's way around within a "space of reasons." On its practical side, this will be a capacity for deciding between alternative courses of action in the light of the *reasons that there are* for and against each. Conversely, any attempted reconstruction of practical rationality will demand of us a willingness to suspend judgement, as and when the occasion may arise, about the merits of the process of ethical formation currently in force: that is, about whether it does in fact instill a genuine sensitivity to the practical reasons that there are. It will ask us to entertain the possibility of a mismatch, with regard to ethical formation, between ideal and actuality.

Of course, there is nothing especially intimidating in principle about this situation, which we negotiate on a small scale all the time: a "mismatch between ideal and actuality" is, if one cares to put it that way, our cue for critical intervention of any kind. Just as babies are not slow to express negativity (Chapter 7, §3), children are vigorous, if not particularly influential, critics of the practice of upbringing. And by exploiting certain fixed points within a collective way of thinking—a "store of historically accumulated wisdom"[37] and stupidity—we can move on from these beginnings to interrogate other features of that way of thinking in a more disinterested spirit: if the hinges stay put, the door can turn.[38] However, as our questions

Jephcott (London: Verso, 1978), p. 60; and compare Nietzsche on "the lie of culture which poses as the sole reality." *The Birth of Tragedy,* trans. Douglas Smith (Oxford: Oxford University Press, 2000), p. 48.

37. McDowell, *Mind and World,* p. 126.

38. Ludwig Wittgenstein, *On Certainty,* ed. G. E. M. Anscombe and G. H. von Wright, trans. Denis Paul and G. E. M. Anscombe, §343: "But it isn't that the situation is like this: We just *can't* investigate everything, and for that reason we are forced to rest content with assumption. If I want the door to turn, the hinges must stay put." Bernard Williams is pursuing a thought experiment on the same lines when he writes (in J. J. C. Smart and Bernard Williams, *Utilitarianism: For and Against* [Cambridge: Cambridge University Press, 1973], p. 92): "One might have the idea that the *unthinkable* was itself a moral category . . . [A man might] find it unacceptable to consider what to do in certain conceivable situations. Logically, or indeed empirically conceivable they may be, but they are not to him morally conceivable, meaning by that that their occurrence as situations presenting him with a choice would represent not a special problem in his moral world, but something that lay be-

become more global (Should people be taught that the family is the cornerstone of society? Should one be willing to die for one's country? What view should we take of our economic responsibility to strangers?), the accumulated wisdom becomes increasingly indecisive. Questions like these seem to reveal a need for some more systematic or reflective scheme of values by reference to which our current practices of ethical formation (the practices that determine what *counts as* a normal or acceptable attitude to such matters) could be assessed; without such a scheme, we can hardly expect to find the necessary common ground on which to base the assessment. But since (by hypothesis) it is precisely the construction of our value-sensitive, or practical reason-evaluating, capacity that is under scrutiny, a map of the domain of value will be just what cannot be drawn with any authority in advance of our finding answers to the very questions with which it is meant to help us. This is because in order to bring determinacy to our map, we would have to be in a position, with regard to any arbitrary feature that might be included in it, to evaluate correctly the reasons for and against including that feature and to arrive at a correct "unitary" judgement about the relative weighting of these reasons.[39] And in an imperfect world we cannot think of ourselves as being in such a position because, however hard we may work towards coherence and comprehensiveness in our appreciation of value, we have no right to assume that our sensitivity to the relevant sorts of reason is in a sufficiently developed state to confer any ultimate reliability on the weighting we give to them.

It has been plausibly argued that deliberation with a view to the "good life as a whole"—the kind of deliberation at which the Aristotelian *phronimos* excels—involves an attempt to *specify* our end, or to determine what would count as realizing it, rather than to discover instrumental means to the realization of some state of affairs of which we already possess a "blueprint."[40] In the current discussion we are concerned with a par-

yond its limits . . . they are situations which so transcend in enormity the human business of moral deliberation that from a moral point of view it cannot matter any more what happens."

39. For "unitary," see Chapter 2, note 12 and accompanying text.

40. See for example J. L. Ackrill, "Aristotle on *Eudaimonia*," in his *Essays on Plato and Aristotle* (Oxford: Clarendon Press, 1997), pp. 179–200, esp. §III (also in A. O. Rorty, ed., *Essays on Aristotle's Ethics* [Berkeley: University of California Press, 1980], pp. 15–33, where the same section appears as §IV); David Wiggins, "Deliberation and Practical Reason," in his *Needs, Values, Truth: Essays in the Philosophy of Value* (Oxford: Clarendon Press, 1998),

ticular application of this thought, or rather with its bearing on the good life under one particular aspect—namely, as the agent of its own perpetuation (through upbringing). The point here is that if we lack a full specification of what is to be aimed at in the way of moral or social order, then *a fortiori* we lack a full specification of what agencies of upbringing would operate, or of how the constitution of the subject would proceed, under ideal social conditions. And this latter deficiency has, or should have, consequences for our attitude to the ethically recalcitrant. For it means that we will not always have the resources to say of any given "recalcitrant" act which of two possibilities it exemplifies: is it a case of individual failure to comply with the requirements of an essentially benign process of socialization? Or is it one in which a less than benign process of socialization is meeting the resistance that, in one way or another, it deserves? To the extent that we fall short of being able to answer this question, we have to remain open to the second as well as to the first possibility, and to remain so even in the absence of any "credible" discourse of dissent which we can claim that the recalcitrant behaviour is trying to express.

Under any social conditions that we take to be less than ideal, therefore, we must resign ourselves—assuming that "deliberation with a view to the good life" is indeed a search for constitutive, not instrumental means—to the incomplete decidability of a certain distinction: I mean the distinction between *mere* recalcitrance ("bad") and the recalcitrance that is potentially, even if not yet actually, articulate dissent ("good"—or, anyway, a possible candidate for "goodness"). These "good/bad" labels represent a contrast which the *critical* theorist, as such, would like to be able to draw in all cases. The present argument, however, aims to show that this cannot be done (for who can claim expert knowledge of the *potential,* or lack of it, for new "language games" to come into existence?),[41] and thus to move the

pp. 215–237, esp. at p. 225; John McDowell, "Deliberation and Moral Development in Aristotle's Ethics," in Stephen Engstrom and Jennifer Whiting, eds., *Aristotle, Kant, and the Stoics: Rethinking Happiness and Duty* (Cambridge: Cambridge University Press, 1996), pp. 19–35.

41. This unsurveyable potential seems to be connected with the Derridian idea (or conceit) of a "promise to otherness" (see Chapter 8, note 42 and accompanying text). Derrida has written of the need, in view of the dissolution of the Soviet Union and the "end of history" which some have taken this to signify, "not to renounce [historicity], but on the contrary to open up access to an affirmative thinking of the messianic and emancipatory promise as promise: as *promise* and not as onto-theological or teleo-eschatological program or

critical theorist towards acceptance of that element of anarchism contained in the counter-teleological attitude to ethical formation.[42] That is: it asks us to put up with not knowing exactly how much of our hostility (or maladjustment) to the ethical universal could, in the end, be represented as rationally motivated and how much is attributable to what we ourselves—in our capacity as friends of the "universal"—might condemn as our "false private self,"[43] the self that is the enemy of reason. Uncertainty about this question could be eliminated only if a fully determinate conception of the good life—and of the "true self" which, in the rationalist tradition, affirms that life without ambivalence—could be brought in to adjudicate it. But no such conception is within reach; its role in our thinking is only that of a "regulative idea."[44]

design. Not only must one not renounce the emancipatory desire, it is necessary to insist on it more than ever . . . This is the condition of a re-politicization, perhaps of another concept of the political" (Jacques Derrida, *Specters of Marx: The State of the Debt, the Work of Mourning, and the New International,* trans. Peggy Kamuf [London: Routledge, 1994], p. 75).

42. Here we may think of the liberal anti-Platonist thesis that good and bad are ontologically conjoined. See Friedrich Nietzsche, *On the Genealogy of Morals,* trans. Walter Kaufmann and R. J. Hollingdale (New York: Random House, 1969), Essay III, §9, "All good things were formerly bad things"; Paul Feyerabend, *Farewell to Reason* (London: Verso, 1987), p. 314: "I . . . would like to consider a different view where Evil is part of Life just as it was part of creation. One does not welcome it—but one is not content with infantile reactions either. One delimits it—but one lets it persist in its domain. For nobody can say how much good it still contains and to what extent even the most insignificant good thing is tied up with the most atrocious crimes"; John Gray, *Berlin* (London: HarperCollins, 1995), p. 35: "Berlin's value-pluralism may diverge from [Joseph] Raz's in holding that goods may depend upon, or presuppose, evils, and right actions contain, or entail, wrongs"; and contrast Plato, *Republic* 379bc. Admittedly, no argument emerging from a quietist philosophy can compel us to accept "anarchism," or indeed liberal toleration, as a substantive political principle. What it can do is to point to the epistemological indeterminacy mentioned in the text above and leave us to draw our own conclusions.

43. This phrase is taken from F. H. Bradley, "My Station and Its Duties," in his *Ethical Studies,* 2d ed. (Oxford: Clarendon Press, 1927), pp. 160–213, a text I used in my *Realism and Imagination in Ethics* (Oxford: Basil Blackwell, 1983; see esp. §§20, 39–41 and 43–45) to illustrate the (politically) conservative application of ethical holism or organicism. Bradley argues at p. 180 that "[the moral] universal on the inner side is the will of the whole, which is self-conscious in us, and wills itself in us against the actual or possible opposition of the false private self."

44. I am not arguing that a rational response to this state of affairs would be to refuse even to try to say anything concrete about the goals of social action. One example of such a response is deplored by Steven Lukes when he says that the dominant strain of normative

5

More than once in this discussion we have encountered claims which, while unproblematic in their ordinary use, seem unable to "tolerate a metaphysical emphasis." One example is the attribution (to oneself or others) of moral beliefs or commitments (Chapter 6, §1). A second is the claim to understand another person (§1 above). With regard to linguistic understanding, we often "know perfectly well what someone means" in the unreflective context of the relevant practice; yet when we reflect on that practice, a philosophy that remains within the "zone of mere significa-tion"[45] will bring us up against possibilities—like the one captured by Wittgenstein's "1004, 1008 . . ." scenario—which show that if we insist on passing beyond the normal (throwaway) context of the claim to "know perfectly well" what the other person means, we shall reach a place where that claim does not admit of justification at all (unless by "God himself": see Chapter 6, §1). For such a philosophy will remind us that the normal context for a claim of this kind is that of our lives as physically separate natural creatures—a context in which we have to (and do) proceed in the *faith* that our mutual understanding will not break down.

Our recent remarks about the position of the critical theorist are a variation on the same theme. For they too amount to a reminder of the limited natural context within which a certain "language game"—in this case, the practice of ethical formation—is normally set. In that context, it is not "presumptuous" for someone who has been (well enough) initiated into the moral spirit of their community to feel that they know (well enough) what does and what does not have practical reason on its side. But the sus-

thought within Marxism "inhibits the specification of its ultimate aim," while still "presuming to foresee the future, in which its [Marxism's] eventual realization is somehow guaranteed" (*Marxism and Morality* [Oxford: Clarendon Press, 1985], p. 146). (In the face of Marx's anti-utopian insistence that the working class "have no ideals to realize, but to set free elements of the new society with which old collapsing bourgeois society is pregnant" [quoted, ibid., p. 144], those who wish to represent Marxism as the source of a determinate critique of existing morality may be well advised to maintain, with Norman Geras and Terry Eagleton, that "Marx did, in fact, believe in morality, but he did not know that he did, because he identified moral discourse with the impoverished juridical notions of the bourgeois liberal tradition" [Eagleton, "Deconstruction and Human Rights," in Barbara Johnson, ed., *Freedom and Interpretation: The Oxford Amnesty Lectures 1992* (New York: Basic Books, 1993), pp. 122–145; quotation from p. 142].)

45. See Chapter 6, note 10.

pension of some substantial part of that context (either speculatively, or through one or another kind of real social breakdown) may create a situation in which it does indeed look presumptuous to persist in claiming that we know how to keep our judgement aligned with that of the "exemplary practical reasoner": to make such a claim might be to lay oneself open to the charge of thinking that "God himself can't say anything to us" about the meaning of the (finite) moral experience allotted to us so far.

An (intermittently) agnostic attitude towards the ethically "recalcitrant," as opposed to a policy of automatic mobilization against it, is something that the critical theorist should be prepared to attribute to the difficulty of identifying a context within which we can unproblematically claim to know anything about the ethical. She should be able to see that difficulty as arising, not from considerations of "moral relativism," but from the fact that the legitimacy of the existing context—its status as one in which properly *ethical* formation can occur—is continually being called into question by all those who recognize, as she does, a "standing obligation" to do so (Chapter 8, §1). As already noted, much must remain in place at any given moment, or criticism could not get a foothold; the critic is always also a participant, someone taking advantage of her prior initiation into "a tradition as it stands."[46] But the degree of potency of this principle of intellectual conservation cannot be exactly specified. Hence the incomplete decidability, as regards ethically "recalcitrant" phenomena, of the contrast between good and bad.

With the emergence of this element of incompleteness, the attempted reconciliation of nature and (practical) reason may suggest some thoughts which are reminiscent of more typically "modern" moral philosophies—existentialism, say, or prescriptivism—in point of the dignity conferred by these theories on the act of decision itself. For it brings into view the possibility that intentions which would be condemned as illicit from the standpoint of an inherited or socially dominant morality might nevertheless strike us as understandable or justifiable from that of a better "answer" to the question of the (collective) good life; and it gives this possibility a claim on our attention *despite the lack of any guarantee* that someone who adopts it as a basis for action will come out at a point from which they can see themselves retrospectively as justified in having done so.

The historical aspect of the concept of a "*second* nature" makes all the

---

46. McDowell, *Mind and World,* p. 126.

difference here. Without benefit of the thought that our access to ethical reasons might be through "immersion in a tradition," it would seem frivolous to suggest that the scope of deliberation—that is, the range of actions we can regard as morally possible—might be *enlarged* by an awareness of gaps or indeterminacies in our understanding. Thus for Kant "it is a basic moral principle, which requires no proof, that *one ought to hazard nothing that may be wrong* . . . [It is not] absolutely necessary to know, concerning all possible actions, whether they are right or wrong. But concerning the act which *I* propose to perform I must not only judge and form an opinion, but I must be *sure* that it is not wrong; and this requirement is a postulate of conscience, to which is opposed *probabilism,* i.e. the principle that the mere opinion that an action may well be right warrants its being performed."[47] If on the other hand we think of moral personality as the outcome of a process of appropriation of evaluative responses encountered, in the first instance, elsewhere than in one's own experience (compare Chapters 2, §4 and 5, §6), then it is hard to see why the distance traversed in securing this outcome should not stretch beyond that which separates us from the particular set of fellow humans who happen to be present in our immediate social environment. If formation exploits the iterability of signs and the mimetic capacity that enables a certain preexisting "mindedness" to become second nature to us, then it becomes possible to think of ourselves as obtaining some of our paradigms not just from local or "communitarian" sources but from others of a historical, fictional, or theoretical kind[48]—sources to which, despite their not being as consistently present to consciousness as our contingent local ties, we might still wish to give weight in our efforts to comply with the principle that "one ought to hazard nothing that may be wrong."

The idea of a future with its own evaluative point of view, and with standards of value more or less sharply distinct from those of the present, can of course be entertained in a cynical or antimoral spirit. Ethical naturalists of the "balder" variety can fantasize, with Plato's Thrasymachus, about achieving control over the entire ethical sign system and turning this control to their personal advantage.[49] Yet the same idea can also be experi-

47. Immanuel Kant, *Religion within the Limits of Reason Alone,* trans. Theodore Greene and Hoyt Hudson (New York: Harper and Row, 1960), pp. 173–174.

48. "Historical" here is intended to cover information about present as well as past states of the world.

49. Plato, *Republic* 344ac. The lines I have tried to paraphrase are those about the tyrant

enced as a source of demands which, like those of traditional morality, may call for "virtue" in the sense of an overcoming of inertia or of contrary inclinations. For once we come to see practical rationality in the way suggested by a "relaxed naturalism"—that is, as an attribute of natural beings whose form of life happens to include the use of signs and the exchange of reasons—we may conclude that the difference between traditional and future-directed conscientiousness is one of degree rather than of kind. The imaginative construction of a character ideal out of material presented to us through social experience (Chapter 3, §2)—through a succession of examples, hints, images, and formulae capable of more than one application—can produce results that tend more towards conservatism or more towards innovation,[50] but at any point on this spectrum it can issue in a way of seeing whereby certain courses of action stand out for us as required or forbidden.

Regardless of the actual merits or demerits of her practical reasoning, someone who tries to act in the way she takes to be required by a determinate critique of existing morality can still be seen as a "moral" agent in the formal sense of wishing to "hazard nothing that may be wrong." (It is the persistence of this wish—however unrealistic, if we take into account the kind of passive wrongdoing constituted by acquiescence in morally objectionable states of affairs—that creates an opening for Nietzschean gibes about "obedience" and "docility" (Chapter 7, §§3–4).) But the historical dimension of our present account of practical reason makes the wish for rectitude newly problematic. For example, where a conflict of values receives political expression, a conscientious person will—uncontroversially, I assume—accept the risk of being on the losing side, and so of having to forgo the recognition sometimes accorded, with hindsight, to "recalcitrant" elements as a result of changes in the relevant ethical culture. But

who, by the very completeness of his political success, induces people to suspend the moral condemnation they would mete out to pettier criminals and to "call him happy and blessed."

50. As Henry Staten observes, "According to Wittgenstein a rule, when there is a rule, a boundary, when there is a boundary, determines but need not itself be determinate . . . Because any social practice is carried on by different persons who will vary from each other in their sense of how to apply any given rule, any form of life is always transected by diverging lines of possible practice . . . This formulation is not an answer or an explanation or even a theory, but a way of putting a problem. The problem is how to live with other human beings under such circumstances" (*Wittgenstein and Derrida* [Oxford: Basil Blackwell, 1985], p. 134).

our undecidability considerations go further; for they seem to entail that even the most conscientious must sometimes bring to such conflicts a willingness, precisely, to "hazard" actions which may for all they know be wrong,[51] since whatever course they choose, they will be aware that their choice could be vindicated only through the elimination of some indeterminacy in our conception of practical reason and of the social forms needed to implement it.[52]

To the extent, therefore, that we believe good causes are furthered by a certain lack of fastidiousness—a readiness, sometimes, *simply* to express (or condone) recalcitrance without looking for guarantees that such and such a gesture is warranted, on balance, by "the reasons that there are"— we can say that the abstractly anti-authoritarian attitude of the defender of "difference" is a valuable enabling presence within such undertakings as the "reflective modification" of moral institutions. And to the extent that we believe such causes can be endangered by the *conviction of being in the right,* we can see in the kind of thinking which reminds us of the unfinished character of any putatively universal "mindedness" an equally valuable pointer in the direction of fallibilism.[53]

51. W. H. Auden, in the poem "Spain" (in Robin Skelton, ed., *Poetry of the Thirties* [Harmondsworth: Penguin, 1964], pp. 133–136), imagines a (Republican) combatant's *"conscious acceptance of guilt* in the *necessary* murder" (quotation from p. 136; emphasis added). This state of mind is projected on to someone with commitments both to the normal moral outlook (for which this murder, like any other, is wrong), and also to an outlook—to be consolidated in a possible (and desirable) future—which could condone it as necessary (even though contrary to morality) in order to bring that future about ("Tomorrow the bicycle races . . . But today the struggle": ibid.). Granted, one does not know that the struggle will be successful, but this does not necessarily mean that one can put oneself in the right by doing nothing ("History to the defeated/May say alas but cannot help *or pardon*": ibid., emphasis added). Perhaps some political situations are like the one pictured by Jonathan Dancy (*Moral Reasons* [Oxford: Blackwell, 1993], pp. 51–52), in which rational action demands that moral considerations *undergo* "silencing" by nonmoral ones. Or perhaps morality itself is just more ambiguous than we normally assume. See also, however, note 53.

52. This may suggest that the question on which such an agent must gamble can be formulated in consequentialist terms as that of "whether the end justifies the means." However, what our ethical risk-taker wants to know is whether her present line of action (or inaction) will appear justified from the point of view of some ethical outlook, or conception of the virtues, which she could find tenable in future. The terms of *this* question do not presuppose that it is possible to rank states of affairs in respect of their success in realizing some single value.

53. Compare Cornell, *The Philosophy of the Limit,* pp. 167–168, who argues, again follow-

But perhaps the idea of fallibilism is too purely epistemological to serve our purposes here. For what such thinking suggests is that at the point of undecidability, even the most sincere regard for the demands of reason cannot prevent us from lapsing, as it were, into the state of (mere) nature—into things without the power of moral self-determination. It suggests that our predicament at that point is like the one attributed by Wittgenstein to "the man who does not have an ethics," and who, in the aftermath of a moral crisis, may reflect on his actual decision and say "Thank God"—*or* just the opposite.[54]

Ethical naturalists can agree. But just as they did not conclude from the critique of an idealized notion of authorship that the goal of ethical formation was illusory, so they will not conclude from the fact that practical reason runs out at a certain point that it amounts to nothing at all.

ing Derrida, that "the justificatory language of *revolutionary* violence depends on what has yet to be established, and of course, as a result, might yet come into being . . . That separation of cognition and action by *time* means that no acts of violence can be truly justified at the time they take place, if by truly justified one means cognitive assurance of the rightness of action. I believe that this interpretation of Derrida's engagement with [Walter] Benjamin is the reading that does full justice to the seriousness with which both authors take the command 'thou shalt not kill.'"

54. See Ludwig Wittgenstein, "Wittgenstein's Lecture on Ethics," §II, "Notes on Talks with Wittgenstein," in *Philosophical Review*, 74, 1965, pp. 12–26; quotation from p. 23. Compare also Wittgenstein, *Philosophical Investigations* §211: "How can he *know* how he is to continue a pattern by himself—whatever instruction you give him?—Well, how do I know?—If that means 'Have I reasons?' the answer is: my reasons will soon give out. And then I shall act, without reasons."

INDEX

Index

Ackrill, J. L., 188n
Acrasia, 88–100, 109, 124n, 182n. *See also* Socratic thesis
Adams, R. M., 182n
Adorno, T., 166, 167n, 173n, 175n, 186n
Anarchism, 142, 149, 190
Anderson, P., 160–161, 171–172n
Annas, J., 52n, 63n
Anscombe, G. E. M., 6n, 16n, 141n
Ansell-Pearson, K., 179n
Apeiron. See Form/formlessness
Arblaster, A., 181n
Aristotle/Aristotelianism, 8n, 68, 70, 73, 78n, 82n, 87, 89n, 95, 124n, 131, 141, 142, 146, 147n, 155, 162, 188; and practical reason approach to ethics, 9–11, 14, 19n; on moral knowledge, 27–31, 34, 45; on form and formation, 43, 52–63; on Socratic thesis, 97–102; on praise and blame, 125–126
Auden, W. H., 195n
Austin, J. L., 74–75, 80–83, 85, 87, 103–106, 107n, 111, 163n
Authorship, 85, 87, 96, 98–102, 105–106, 108–109, 125, 134, 146–147, 156, 159, 162–163, 180, 184, 196
Ayer, A. J., 5n, 16n

Barthes, R., 134
Baynes, K., 169n
Benjamin, W., 196n
Bentham, J., 180
Berlin, I., 145n, 180–181, 190n
Blackburn, S., 5n, 17n

Bohman, J., 169n
Bok, S., 79
Bradley, F. H., 190n
Braidotti, R., 148, 148–149n, 168
Brandom, R., 78n, 81n
Burnyeat, M. F., 97
Butler, J., 163n, 171n, 177n

Candlish, S., 76
Caygill, H., 25n
Chopin, K., 185n
Community. *See* Culture
Conceptual, unboundedness of, 20, 108, 135, 166n, 175–177, 179
Consciousness, philosophy of, 102
Consequentialism, 14n, 28, 37n, 195n
Cornell, D., 166–167, 173n, 175n, 176n, 195–196n
Cornford, F. M., 55n
Constant, B., 181
Critchley, S., 167, 174n
"Critical ontology of ourselves," 138–139, 146, 152n, 171
Critique, 152n, 161, 173, 187, 192; determinate, 140–144, 148, 150, 151, 154, 165, 171n, 172, 181–183, 191, 194. *See also* Reflective modification
Cullity, G., 4n, 90n
Culture, 25, 29–33, 38, 42–43, 47, 59, 62, 108, 132–135, 139, 151, 154, 171n, 178, 192–193

Dancy, J., 10, 11–12n, 13n, 32n, 51, 91n, 195n